A Study of Dōgen

A Study of Dōgen

His Philosophy and Religion

Masao Abe

Edited by
Steven Heine

State University of New York Press

Published by
State University of New York Press, Albany

For information, address State University of New York
Press, State University Plaza, Albany, N.Y. 12246

Production by Dana Foote
Marketing by Dana E. Yanulavich

Library of Congress Cataloging-in-Publication Data

Abe, Masao, 1915–
    A study of Dōgen : his philosophy and religion / Masao Abe ;
edited by Steven Heine.
       p. cm.
    English and Japanese.
    Includes bibliographical references and index.
    ISBN 0–7914-0837–X (CH : alk. paper). — ISBN 0–7914-0838–8 (PB :
alk. paper)
    1. Dōgen, 1200–1253.   I. Heine, Steven, 1950–   . II. Title.
BQ9449.D657A625   1992
294.3'927'092—dc20
                                      90–93566
                                        CIP

10 9 8 7 6 5 4

Contents

Notes on Abbreviations

Citations from Dōgen's *Shōbōgenzō* [hereafter SG] are taken from volume 1 of the two-volume *Dōgen zenji zenshū* [hereafter DZZ], edited by Ōkubo Dōshū (Tokyo: Chikuma shobō, 1969 and 1970), unless otherwise noted.

Citations from some SG fascicles are from translations in *The Eastern Buddhist* [hereafter EB] by N. A. Waddell and Masao Abe, including:

SG "Bendōwa" EB 4 (1): 124–157;
SG "Busshō" (1) EB 8 (2): 94–112
             (2) EB 9 (1): 87–105
             (3) EB 9 (2): 71–87;
SG "Genjōkōan" EB 5 (2): 129–140
SG "Shōji" EB 5 (1): 70–80;
SG "Uji" (tr. Waddell) EB 12 (1): 114–129
SG "Zenki" EB 5 (1): 70–80.

Occasionally minor changes in terminology are made for the sake of consistency.

Additional EB translations:

Fukanzazengi (tr. Waddell and Abe) EB 6 (2): 115-28;
Hōkyōki (tr. Waddell) (1) EB 10 (2): 102-39
                     (2) 11 (1): 66-84.

Editor's Introduction

One testimony to the greatness of an original thinker is the greatness of his or her commentators. In recent Western thought, for example, Heidegger's two-volume reading of Nietzsche's notions of will to power and eternal recurrence (entitled *Nietzsche*) and Ricoeur's lectures on Freudian analysis from the standpoint of hermeneutics (*Freud and Philosophy: An Essay on Interpretation*) stand out as unique expositions that disclose as much about the views of the commentators as about the source material.[1] In twentieth-century Japan, Dōgen has proven to be one of the major sources or texts taken up for interpretation by leading Japanese philosophers and scholars. The value and significance of Dōgen's thought is evident in the important role it has played in generating discussion and analysis by such key modern figures as Watsuji Tetsurō, Tanabe Hajime, Nishitani Keiji, Ienaga Saburō, Karaki Junzō, and Tamaki Kōshirō in addition to Masao Abe, who for several decades has been helping to disseminate Dōgen's approach to Zen theory and practice in the West. The tremendous interest in Dōgen today has led the "way back" to the original thinker in a manner that will continue to influence the future of Asian and comparative thought. Yet this has been a surprising development, because for centuries after his death in 1253 Dōgen was generally known only as the founder of Sōtō Zen who required strict adherence to zazen practice in contrast to the Rinzai Zen emphasis on kōan exercises, and his works were unfamiliar to those outside the sect. Watsuji's crucial 1926 monograph, "Shamon Dōgen" (Monk Dōgen), part of a series on the foundations of Japanese spirituality, is credited with singlehandedly rescuing Dōgen from sectarian oblivion and appropriating his life and works for their universal relevance in a contemporary, comparative philosophical setting. Watsuji sought to discover the "truth" (*shinri*) of Dōgen as a "person" (*hito*) who is not just a cult figure but belongs to all humanity. For Watsuji, the true meaning of Dōgen is discovered by grasping the universalizable philosophical, religious, and moral implications of his major work, the *Shōbōgenzō*, rather than following the precepts of the sect founded in his name.

Since Watsuji's monumental initial commentary, Dōgen studies have progressed in two seemingly opposite but complementary directions: speculative, comparative examination by thinkers either in or, like Watsuji, associated with the Kyoto school of Japanese philosophy (also known as the Nishida-Tanabe philosophical tradition); and Tokyo-based scholarship focusing on textual and biographical issues. Nishida Kitarō, founder of the Kyoto school, cited Dōgen in his writings from time to time. Some of Nishida's philosophical notions, such as the "continuity of discontinuity" (*hirenzoku no renzoku*), seemed to be influenced by Dōgen's understanding of time expressed in the doctrine of the "abiding dharma-stage" (*jū-hōi*) encompassing the immediacy of "right-now" (*nikon*) and the continuity of "passageless-passage" (*kyōryaku*). Perhaps the most illuminating early philosophical study is the 1939 essay by Tanabe, Nishida's foremost follower (and critic), entitled *Shōbōgenzō no tetsugaku shikan* (My Philosophical View of Dōgen's *Shōbōgenzō*). Tanabe analyzed Dōgen's views on language, time, and history in terms of his own understanding of absolute reality, and he situated the original thinker as an important figure not only in Japanese intellectual history but at the forefront of international philosophy. A series of lectures on Dōgen ("*Shōbōgenzō kōwa*") by Nishitani, former "dean" (d. 1990) of the Kyoto school, was published in the journal *Kyōdai* over several years beginning in 1966, and in book form in 1988. Nishitani examined Dōgen's approach to metaphysics, mysticism, meditation, and morality in comparative light with Western thought from the pre-Socratics through medieval theology to existential phenomenology. Karaki's 1967 essay "Mujō no keijijōgaku—Dōgen" (Dōgen's Metaphysics of Impermanence), the concluding section of his monograph *Mujō* (Impermanence), evaluated the Zen master's radical affirmation of impermanence in relation to death and dying, and being and time, as the culminative point in the typically Japanese contemplative view of transient reality. Also, Ienaga's 1955 essay "Dōgen no shūkyō no rekishiteki seikaku" (The Historical Character of Dōgen's Religion) examined

Dōgen's approach to spirituality in terms of the ideological unfolding of medieval Japanese Buddhism.

Tokyo-based studies have been conducted primarily by scholars at Komazawa University, formerly the Sōtō-sect University and now a leading center of Buddhist studies in Japan. These include Etō Sokuō's commentaries on the *Shōbōgenzō* and interpretation of Dōgen as "founder of the sect" (*Shūso to shiteno Dōgen zenji*, 1944), and Kagamishima Genryū's analysis of Dōgen's citations of Mahayana Buddhist scriptures and Zen recorded sayings (*Dōgen zenji to in'yō kyōten-goroku no kenkyū*, 1965). To cite a couple of other prominent examples from amongst the dozens of outstanding works, Ōkubo Dōshū of Tohoku University has collected the definitive version of Dōgen's complete works (*Dōgen zenji zenshū*, 1970) that is cited throughout this volume, and Tamaki Kōshirō of Tokyo University published a challenging philosophical translation of selected portions of the *Shōbōgenzō* in modern Japanese (*Dōgen sho*, 1969).

Masao Abe's method of studying Dōgen is a combination of Kyoto-school speculation and Tokyo-based textual scholarship. In order to assess Abe's contribution to this field, we must take into account his considerable background and wide-ranging interests in Zen and Western thought. A close associate of Nishida, Tanabe, and Nishitani, Abe ranks as one of the leading representatives of the Kyoto school. Like his colleagues, his main philosophical concern is to construct a dynamic synthesis of Western philosophy and religion and the Mahayana tradition. Abe has also been strongly influenced by D. T. Suzuki and Hisamatsu Shin'ichi, and he shares their commitment to Zen as a form of religious praxis over and above philosophical theory. Abe was a visiting professor of Buddhism and Japanese philosophy for over twenty years at major American colleges and universities, and since Suzuki's death he has become the leader in interpreting Zen thought based on traditional sources in comparative light with the West. In addition, he is deeply involved in promoting Buddhist–Christian dialogue. Abe's award-winning first book, *Zen and Western Thought* (1985), a collection of his most important essays, deals with four main areas concerning the origins and contemporary relevance of Zen: a philosophical clarification of Zen awakening against charges of anti-intellectualism or intuitionism; an explication of the Zen approach to negation, nonbeing, and nothingness; a focus on Buddhism as a compassionate way of life; and the proposal of a Zen-oriented new cosmology, rather than humanism, as a means of establishing the spiritual foundation for the hoped-for unified world.

Abe's studies of Dōgen constitute a minor masterpiece within his overall scholarly production. His efforts have been two-fold: translation and interpretation. The first English-language translation of Dōgen was done by Masunaga Reihō of Komazawa University in 1958 (*The Sōtō Approach to Zen*). Since then many noteworthy translations have become available, including several complete versions of the *Shōbōgenzō*. However, the series of translations by Abe and Norman Waddell published in *The Eastern Buddhist* in the 1970s has set a remarkably high standard in Asian studies for precise and reliable yet readable renderings with detailed annotations. Covering most of the important *Shōbōgenzō* fascicles as well as numerous shorter writings, the overall excellence of the translations may never be matched. Coupled with Abe's 1971 essay in the same journal, "Dōgen on Buddha Nature" (chapter 2 below), these works helped stimulate and develop still-formative Western studies in the field.

This volume takes its place among English-language studies of Dōgen that have progressed dramatically since Abe's early essay and translations. Now there are numerous commentaries, comparative studies, and translations of Dōgen's major works. These include a systematic analysis of Dōgen's theory and practice (Hee-jin Kim, *Dōgen Kigen—Mystical Realist*) and several specialized studies, including one each on biography (Takeshi Jamese Kodera, *Dogen's Formative Years in China*), meditation (Carl Bielefeldt, *Dōgen's Manuals of Zen Meditation*), poetry (Steven Heine, *A Blade of Grass: Japanese Poetry and Aesthetics in Dōgen Zen*), and philosophy of time (Joan Stambaugh, *Impermanence is Buddha Nature: Dōgen's Understanding of Temporality*). There is also a collection of essays by leading scholars (William R. LaFleur, ed., *Dōgen Studies*), lengthy discussion in a history of Zen (Heinrich Dumoulin, *Zen Buddhism: A History*, volume II), and in a history of Japanese Buddhism (Daigan and Alicia Matsunaga, *Foundation of Japanese Buddhism*, volume 2). The comparative studies, focusing mainly on Western phenomenology, include T. P. Kasulis, *Zen Action/Zen Person*; David E. Shaner, *The Bodymind Experience in Japanese Buddhism: A Phenomenological Study of Kūkai and Dōgen*; and Heine, *Existential and Ontological Dimensions of Time in Heidegger and Dōgen*. In addition, there are two complete translations of the *Shōbōgenzō* (one by Nishiyama Kōsen and John Stevens, and the other by Yokoi Yūhō) and several translations of selected fascicles, including:

Tanahashi Kazuaki, *Moon in a Dewdrop: Writings of Zen Master Dōgen;* Francis Cook, *How to Raise an Ox* and *Sounds of Valley Streams: Enlightenment in Dōgen's Zen;* Thomas Cleary, *Shōbōgenzō: Zen Essays by Dōgen;* Kim, *Flowers of Emptiness: Selections from Dōgen's Shōbōgenzō;* and Yokoi, *Zen Master Dōgen: An Introduction with Selected Writings.* Finally, there are two versions of the *Shōbōgenzō Zuimonki* text—Masunaga Reihō, *A Primer of Sōtō Zen,* and Cleary, *Record of Things Heard*—as well as translations contained in some of the above works of Dōgen's shorter writings, such as *Hōkyōki, Fukanzazengi, Sanshōdōei,* and *Gakudōyōjinshū.*[2]

Abe's interpretations of Dōgen display the comparative philosophical bent of the Kyoto school combined with a mastery of textual scholarship. Throughout the essays in this volume, Abe's scholarly apparatus is sparse; he sticks to the text at hand, and he does not discuss Dōgen as the basis for his own philosophical system. What Abe does provide is a deftly probing analysis that penetrates to the core of Dōgen's philosophy and religion. Abe offers a consistent and coherent portrait of Dōgen's fundamental doctrines of the "oneness of practice and attainment" (*shushō-ittō*) as the resolution of his doubt concerning Tendai "original awakening thought" (*hongaku shisō*), the "casting off of body-mind" (*shinjin-datsuraku*) as the awakening he attained under the guidance of Chinese master Ju-ching, and "impermanence-Buddha-nature" (*mujō-busshō*) as the experience of the eternal now, or reconciliation of time and eternity. Based on an interpretation of the origin and solution of Dōgen's formative "doubt," Abe's essays explore the profundity of the Zen master's philosophy of time, death, Buddha-nature, enlightenment, and morality in comparison with Buddhist and Western thinkers such as Hui-neng, Shinran, Spinoza, Kant, Hegel, Kierkegaard, and Heidegger. Abe shows how the doctrine of *shushō-ittō* is the crux of Dōgen's unique approach to the Buddhist middle way of nonduality in his handling and overcoming of the conventionally presumed polarities of life and death, space and time, self and world, beings and Buddha-nature, and illusion and realization. Reading Abe on Dōgen, to cite a traditional Mahayana metaphor, is like entering a great ocean with waves rippling in multiple directions. For Abe, a Dōgen quotation concerning death becomes an opportunity for comparison with Shinran, which in turn leads to reflection on the different conceptions of life and afterlife in Christianity and Buddhism. His comparative analysis of Dōgen and Heidegger is thoroughly grounded in an understanding of both thinkers and always retains its critical edge, so that the broader similarities and finer contrasts come into focus in an appropriate and compelling manner.

The articles in this volume were written on major topics in Dōgen's thought on different occasions spanning over twenty years. Thus there is some inevitable repetition, much of which has been edited out—though not entirely, so as not to sacrifice the integrity of the original writings or the sense of the seasoning of the author's perspective. I have tried to be sensitive to Abe's style, which is a kind of meditative approach, "leaping into" key issues and building arguments in a spiral-like fashion that is well suited to the material under discussion. That is, despite some overlap in these essays, the overall effect of the collection is to create a kind of symphony in which various tones and themes in Dōgen's thought resurface and resound upon one another.

The importance of the doctrine of the oneness of practice and attainment highlighted by Abe must be seen in the context of Dōgen's criticism of Tendai original awakening thought, which played a dominant role in the late Heian/early Kamakura era of Japanese religion. The notion of original awakening was initially found in *The Awakening of Faith in Mahayana Buddhism,* and it was refined in the Japanese Tendai school as an extension of Mahayana nonduality by accepting and affirming the concrete phenomenal world as coterminous with absolute reality. Abe shows that according to the traditional biographies, Dōgen deeply questioned during his early monkhood why it was necessary to practice meditation at all if awakening was already provided as an original endowment, as the Tendai doctrine suggests. After his awakening, Dōgen went on to severely criticize Tendai teaching of original awakening as tending toward an heretical or non-Buddhist position by at once hypostatizing an eternal, *a priori* mental nature in contrast to ephemeral phenomena and affirming the natural world in a way that obviated the need for a sustained commitment to religious training.

Yet Dōgen's relation to Tendai is rather ambivalent and complex, for several reasons.[3] First, Dōgen, like other leading thinkers of his day, was greatly influenced by Tendai thought. Although he avoided the notion of *hongaku,* he used similar terms—*honshō,* or "original realization," and *honrai no memmoku,* or "original face"—in the "Bendōwa" fascicle. He also praised Chih-i, founder of the sect in China, and cited the central Tendai scripture, the *Lotus Sutra,* over fifty times in his writings, endorsing many of its main tenets, such as *shohō-jissō* (all dharmas are true form). On the other hand, Dōgen was certainly not alone in his criticisms, but was joined by other reformers of the "new" Kamakura Buddhism, including Hōnen, Shinran, and Nichiren. Nor was Dōgen the first to raise the issue of practice. An earlier Tendai monk, Shōshin, criticized the *hongaku* mainstream along much the same lines and tended to stress the notion of *genjō* (spontaneous manifestation), which was a central topic in Dōgen's writing. Abe makes it clear that fundamentally Dōgen affirms the notion of original awakening by giving a new interpretation on the basis of his realization of the oneness of practice and attainnment as expressed in the "Bendōwa" fascicle: "In the Buddha Dharma practice and attainment are identical. Because one's present practice is practice in attainment, one's initial negotiation of the Way in itself is the whole of original attainment."[4] To Dōgen, "practicing Buddha [*gyōbutsu*] is...neither *shikaku* [acquired awakening] nor *hongaku*"[5] in the usual sense but is based on original awakening in the above or *genjō*-oriented sense. That is, Dōgen did not try to maneuver from original awakening as one extreme to the opposite extreme of acquired awakening (*shikaku*), which is equally problematic. Rather, while uncompromisingly embracing nonduality, he also thoroughly stressed the differences and distinctiveness of each and every phenomenon that can only be fully realized at each and every moment through continuous, unceasing practice.

As Abe explains in chapter 1, "The Oneness of Practice and Attainment," and chapter 3, "Dōgen's View of Time and Space," the key to Dōgen's breaking through his spiritual impasse concerning original awakening is a clarification of the meaning of time, death, and Buddha-nature. Dōgen realized that the true nature of time is beyond the polarities of now and then, before and after, means and end, potentiality and actuality, and reversibility and irreversibility. Therefore, enlightenment cannot be considered to occur either prior to practice, as an innate potentiality from the past awaiting actualization, or at the conclusion of practice, as a teleological goal to be reached in the future. Dōgen overcame any subtle inclination to hypostatize or conceptualize either practice or attainment as a static occurrence rather than to realize their dynamic unity as a ceaselessly unfolding event fully integrated with all aspects of temporality.

True time encompasses the simultaneity and particularity of past, present, and future as well as the spontaneity of the moment and the fullness of continuity. From this standpoint, life at once contains death and yet is complete unto itself as a manifestation of absolute reality, and death at once contains life and yet is complete unto itself as a manifestation of absolute reality. Dōgen's self-power understanding of the identity-in-difference of life-and-death realized through meditation stands in contrast to Shinran's other-power, Pure Land view that there is no liberation from life and death without the transformative grace of Amida Buddha's compassionate vow. Thus, for Dōgen, "the Buddha-nature is not incorporated prior to attaining Buddhahood; it is incorporated upon the attainment of Buddhahood. The Buddha-nature is always manifested simultaneously with the attainment of Buddhahood."[6] However, at the conclusion of chapter 6, the second essay in the two-part study "The Problem of Death in Dōgen and Shinran," Abe makes a fascinating and important point concerning the relation between self-power (which Abe refers to as "true correspondence to the Dharma") and other-power ("inverse correspondence"). Since both views are encompassed by the Dharma itself, according to Mahayana holistic metaphysics, Abe shows that Dōgen and Shinran must ideologically confront and engage each other as necessary philosophical opposites, and that this encounter allows for the completion of their respective doctrinal standpoints. This section raises some fascinating and crucial questions not only concerning Dōgen, but about Mahayana Buddhist philosophy and religion as a whole.

In chapter 2, "Dōgen on Buddha-nature," Abe explains how Dōgen's understanding of the nondualities of practice and attainment, life and death, and beings and Buddha-nature fulfills the Buddhist deanthropocentric, nonsubstantive, and cosmological approach. Dōgen grasps the world of absolute nothingness unbound by humanly fabricated deceptions or presuppositions, but at the same time he is eminently concerned with the concrete, personal issue of authenticity or attainment. That is, the human dimension is only realized by transcending it, and vice versa. Furthermore, Abe shows that Dōgen's philosophical vantage point of being and nothingness, based on the religious experience of the casting off of body-mind, is the basis of the underlying differences between the Zen master and Martin Heidegger, who is the focal point for comparative examinations in chapter 4, "The Problem of Time in Heidegger and

Dōgen," and elsewhere. Among Western thinkers Heidegger appears closest to Dōgen in stressing temporality as the key to unlocking the question of Being. Like Dōgen, Heidegger penetrates to the inseparability of life and death and the three tenses of ecstatic temporality from a nonsubstantive philosophical perspective. Yet even though Heidegger's insights are revolutionary in Western thought, he remains bound to an anthropocentrism that values thinking over nonthinking, beings over nothingness, or the future over the eternal now, and therefore Heidegger never fully resolves the religious quest for self-awakening.

ACKNOWLEDGMENTS

This volume contains articles recently translated from Japanese and revised versions of articles previously published in English. Masao Abe and I thank the respective publishers for the permission they have kindly granted to reprint with some revisions for the sake of consistency and continuity the following articles: "The Oneness of Practice and Attainment: Implications for the Relation between Means and Ends," ed. by William R. LaFleur, in *Dōgen Studies* (Honolulu: University of Hawaii Press, 1985): 99–111; "Dōgen on Buddha-nature," originally published as "Dōgen on Buddha Nature" in *The Eastern Buddhist* 4 (1): 28–71, and reprinted with revisions as "Dōgen on Buddha-Nature" in *Zen and Western Thought,* ed. by William R. LaFleur (London and Basingstoke: Macmillan, 1985): 25–68; "Dōgen's View of Time and Space," tr. by Steven Heine, in *The Eastern Buddhist* 21 (2): 1–35, originally published in *Kōza Dōgen,* vol. 4, ed. by Kagamishima Genryū and Tamaki Kōshirō (Tokyo: Shunjūsha, 1980): 164–90; and "The Problem of Time in Heidegger and Dōgen," in *Being and Truth: Essays in Honour of John Macquarrie,* ed. by Alistair Kee and Eugene T. Long (London: SCM Press, 1986): 200–244. In addition, my translations of the following articles from Japanese appear by permission of M. Abe: "The Problem of Death in Dōgen and Shinran, Part 1" (Dōgen to Shinran ni okeru shi no jikaku) in *Risō,* no. 366 (1963): 75–87; and "The Unborn and Rebirth: The Problem of Death in Dōgen and Shinran, Part 2" (Fushō to Ōjō: Dōgen to Shinran ni okeru shi no jikaku) in *Zen no honshitsu to ningen no shinri,* ed. by Hisamatsu Shin'ichi and Nishitani Keiji (Tokyo, 1969): 643-693. Also, we are using Dōgen's calligraphy of "Fukanzazengi" for the book cover through the courtesy of Eiheiji Temple, for which we are deeply grateful. We are also thankful to Prof. Yasuaki Nara and Rev. Kakuzen Suzuki for their help in this regard.

I express my greatest admiration and deepest appreciation to Masao Abe. Helping to prepare this book with his guidance and support has been a singularly illuminating and enjoyable task both personally and professionally. I began working with Abe in 1985 when he was the Margaret Gest Visiting Professor of Philosophy at Haverford College. Prior to that, I had long been an admirer of his writings, which were a main source of inspiration in my studies of Zen and Japanese thought, as they have been for so many others. For two years Abe conducted biweekly symposia on Japanese philosophy at Haverford that were organized by Ashok Gangadean and attended by a host of engaging scholars in Asian and comparative thought. The substance of the material we discussed was always compelling and challenging, but I was especially struck by Abe's unassuming manner, which attracted a diverse and fascinating group of people who gathered to discuss and debate ideas East and West. Abe's personal and philosophical approach to ongoing dialogue is best characterized by William R. LaFleur in his introduction to *Zen and Western Thought:* "[Abe's] concern to do this was always without discrimination; it included notable philosophers as well as curious undergraduates. He has always been eager to carry on this kind of inter-religious and inter-philosophical dialogue not only with his professional peers but also with the next generation which will themselves take it up and continue it in new ways in the years to come."[7] I was delighted when Masao Abe asked me to assist him with this book, and I hope that my efforts can help in some small way to highlight his invaluable and enduring contributions to the field of Dōgen studies.

Author's Introduction

Dōgen Kigen (1200–1253) has been credited traditionally as being the founder of the Japanese Sōtō Zen sect. However, his importance goes well beyond that historical aspect, for at least the following three reasons. First, Dōgen is a unique figure in the long history of Zen in China and Japan, in that he combined the experience of a profound religious realization with keen philosophical and speculative skills that surpassed his predecessors and followers. Second, on the basis of his penetrating awakening he interpreted Mahayana Buddhism in a radical way that brought its doctrinal standpoint to its culmination. Third, Dōgen's understanding of Buddha-nature, being, time, death, and morality has a philosophical significance that is at once consonant with and yet challenging to some of the key contemporary philosophers and issues. In this book, I seek to elucidate Dōgen's philosophy and religion, keeping these three points in mind.

The terms *philosophy* and *religion* in the subtitle of the book are, however, not used in their strict Western senses. In the West, philosophy and religion are generally understood as two different entities: the former is a human enterprise for understanding humans and the universe based on intelligence or reason, whereas the latter is faith in divine revelation. The intellectual history of the West may be regarded as a history of opposition, conflict, and in some cases synthesis of philosophy and religion. In the East, especially in Buddhism, philosophy and religion are not two different entities. Since Buddhism is originally not a religion of faith in a transcendent deity but a religion of awakening to the true nature of self and others, *praxis* and *theoria,* to use Western terms, are interfused and undifferentiated. In the Mahayana tradition, Hua-yen (J.

Kegon) and T'ien-t'ai (Tendai) Buddhism are particularly strong in terms of doctrinal construction, yet their doctrines are not "philosophy" as distinguishable from "religion," but the self-realization of practice. Perhaps more emphatically than other forms of Buddhism, Zen stresses the priority of direct awakening through concentrated practice, as expressed in the saying "Not relying on words or letters, [Zen is] an independent self-transmitting apart from any doctrinal teaching."

Dōgen, however, is unique even in the Zen tradition, for as already stated, he combined profound religious realization with speculative reflection in a way that exceeded his predecessors and followers. In this book, I refer to Dōgen's speculative aspect as "philosophy" and his practical or soteriological aspect as "religion." However, his speculation is not based on "thinking" in the conventional sense. Rather, it is based on "thinking of nonthinking," which is realized only through the complete negation of ordinary thinking. It is the thinking realized in and though practice ("religion"), which is for Dōgen nothing but "the casting off of body-mind." (See chapter 4 below.) In short, the terms *philosophy* and *religion* in the subtitle of the book indicate the thinking of nonthinking, which is provisionally bifurcated but primordially nondifferentiable, based on Dōgen's enlightenment experience.

This volume has not been written systematically by undertaking a comprehensive plan of research. Rather, it is a collection of my essays on Dōgen written over nearly thirty years on various occasions. The first article, "The Oneness of Practice and Attainment," is relatively recent, written in 1981 and presented at the First International Dōgen Conference held at Tassajara Springs, California, in October of the same year. It was later published along with other papers presented at the conference in *Dōgen Studies,* edited by William R. LaFleur, in 1985. (For more detailed information on this book and the other publications from which these articles are taken, see the Editor's Introduction.) In this essay I interpret the doubt young Dōgen encountered at Mt. Hiei concerning the Tendai doctrine of "original awakening"—that is, the question of why practice is necessary if all beings are originally enlightened—which led him to sail to China to study Zen with an authentic teacher, Ju-ching. The doctrine of *shushō-ittō,* the oneness of practice and attainment, is the solution of the doubt that he attained during his study in China, which became the foundation on which he developed his philosophy and religion after returning to Japan.

It is also perhaps the central idea of Dōgen's that can be applied to contemporary individual and social issues. With this under-standing, I have placed the essay at the beginning of the book.

The second essay, "Dōgen on Buddha-nature," was written in 1971 for the 50th Anniversary Special Edition of *The Eastern Buddhist* while at the same time I began a series of translations of Dōgen's *Shōbōgenzō* and other writings with Norman Wad-dell (the translation of the "Bendōwa" fascicle appeared in the same issue). Since Dōgen's unique and penetrating understand-ing of Mahayana Buddhism is most clearly seen in his notion of Buddha-nature (*busshō*), in this essay I examine Dōgen's view by analyzing the "Busshō" fascicle in terms of three main issues: "whole-being is Buddha-nature" (*shitsuu-busshō*), "no-Buddha-nature" (*mu-busshō*), and "impermanence-Buddha-nature" (*mujō-busshō*). I clarify Dōgen's approach by contrast-ing it with the conventional Mahayana understanding of Bud-dha-nature, and also by comparing his philosophy of religion to the Christian notion of God as well as to the thought of Spinoza, Hegel, and Heidegger.

The third essay, "Dōgen's View of Time and Space," was originally written in Japanese in 1980 and published in *Kōza Dōgen*, volume 4, in the same year. It was translated by Steven Heine and appeared in *The Eastern Buddhist* (21 (2), 1988). Here, I emphasize that Dōgen's view of time and space cannot be understood properly apart from his standpoints of Buddha-nature and continuous practice (*gyōji*). His view of the identity of being-time (*uji*) does not represent an unmediated unity but an identity realized in and through the Buddha-nature and the self-liberating self, or "the self prior to the universe sprouting any sign of itself." Thus, being-time is not based on philosophi-cal reflection but expresses a deeply religious concern with human liberation.

The fourth essay, "The Problem of Time in Heidegger and Dōgen," was written in 1985 and published in *Being and Truth: Essays in Honour of John Macquarrie* in the following year. The intention of this essay is to clarify the affinities and differences in the views of time and temporality of Martin Heidegger and Dōgen. Paying particular attention to the *Kehre*, or "turn," from Heidegger's early period to the later one, I compare Dōgen to the two stages of Heidegger's thought. I conclude that while Heidegger is closer to Dōgen in his later period than in his early period, the thinkers are still quite different. For instance, for Heidegger being and time do not completely "belong together," and time is not understood as completely reversible. All of the differences emerge in the final analysis from the lack, on Heidegger's part, of a thoroughgoing realization of "absolute nothingness" (*zettai mu*), which is beyond the duality of being and nothingness and yet includes both.

The fifth and sixth essays, "The Problem of Death in Dōgen and Shinran, Part 1" and "The Unborn and Rebirth: The Problem of Death in Dōgen and Shinran, Part 2," were written in Japanese in 1963 and 1964 successively and were recently translated for this book by Steven Heine. They are the earliest essays I wrote on Dōgen included here. Both articles compare Dōgen and Shinran, two outstanding Buddhist thinkers of Kamakura Japan representing, respectively, the "self-power" (*jiriki*) path of Zen and the "other-power" (*tariki*) path of Pure Land. Here I try to clarify their parallels and differences in terms of the problems of death, sin, faith, practice, and naturalness. I interpret Dōgen's standpoint as the true correspondence of the Dharma, and Shinran's as the inverse correspondence of the Dharma. In the concluding sections of "The Unborn and Rebirth," somewhat rewritten in preparing this volume, I explore the possible overcoming of the fundamental differences between these dimensions in Buddhism and suggest the need for an awakening to the most authentic Dharma, which is beyond the opposition between Buddha and Mara (demon).

As I previously stated, this book has not been written with a systematic, comprehensive plan, and it consists of a collection of essays, three in English and three in Japanese, written for various occasions. With the help of the editorship of Steven Heine, I have arranged the essays as systematically as possible. You see the result here before you.

This book could not have been published without the help and advice of many people. My great and sincere appreciation is extended to Steven Heine, who not only translated three essays—"Dōgen's View of Time and Space," "The Problem of Death in Dōgen and Shinran, Part 1," and "The Unborn and Rebirth: The Problem of Death in Dōgen and Shinran, Part 2"— but also carefully and appropriately did the editorial work throughout the entire process of preparing the volume. Although I revised his translations considerably, his understanding and translation skill in Japanese philosophical/Buddhist writings is truly admirable. Steve gave me valuable suggestions to improve the essays, and he reconstructed some paragraphs to avoid the repetition inevitable in a collection of articles written at different times. He also compiled the glossary of Sino-Japanese terms and the index.

I also express my gratitude to William R. LaFleur, Norman Waddell, and Joan Stambaugh, who gave me valuable suggestions at the final stages of writing "The Oneness of Practice and Attainment," "Dōgen on Buddha-nature," and "The Problem of Time in Heidegger and Dōgen," respectively. Dennis Hirota and Eishō Nasu were especially helpful in translating and referencing Shinran's works. We are using Dōgen's calligraphy of "Fukanzazengi" on the book cover through the courtesy of Eiheiji temple, for which we are extremely grateful. We thank Prof. Yasuaki Nara and Rev. Kakuzen Suzuki for their help in this regard. Thanks also go to the San Francisco Zen Center for supporting me as a scholar-in-residence for the academic year 1989–90. I am also grateful for Dr. Muriel Pollia's financial aid, which supported my teaching position at the Pacific School of Religion for the academic year 1990–91. Last but not least, I am deeply indebted to Shin'ichi Hisamatsu-*sensei* and Keiji Nishitani-*sensei* for my understanding of Dōgen and Western philosophy.

I sincerely hope that this small work on Dōgen will contribute to the ongoing Eastern and Western philosophical and religious encounter.

I

The Oneness of
Practice and Attainment

Implications for the Relation between Means and Ends

YOUNG DŌGEN'S DOUBT

Dōgen is one of the most outstanding and unique Buddhists in the history of Japanese Buddhism. He is unique in at least the following three senses.

First, rejecting all existing forms of Buddhism in Japan as inauthentic, he attempted to introduce and establish what he believed to be genuine Buddhism, based on his own realization that he attained in Sung China under the guidance of Zen master Ju-ching (Nyojō, 1163–1228). He called it "the Buddha Dharma directly transmitted from the buddhas and patriarchs." He emphasized zazen (seated meditation) as "the right entrance to the Buddha Dharma," in the tradition of the Zen schools in China since Bodhidharma, originating from Śākyamuni Buddha. Yet he strictly refused to speak of a "Zen sect," to say nothing of a "Sōtō sect," which he was later credited with founding. For Dōgen was concerned solely with the "right Dharma," and regarded zazen as its "right entrance." "Who has used the name 'Zen sect?'" he asks rhetorically. "No buddha or patriarch ever spoke of a 'Zen sect.' Those who pronounce a devil's appellation must be confederates of the devil, not children of the Buddha."[1] He called himself "the Dharma transmitter Shamon

(Monk) Dōgen who went to China" and returned "empty-handed" but with the strong conviction that he had attained the authentic Dharma that is directly transmitted from buddha to buddha and should transplant it to Japanese soil. Thus he rejected the idea of *mappō* (final or degenerate Dharma), an idea that had gained wide acceptance in the Japanese Buddhism of his day. It may not be too much to say of Dōgen that just as Bodhidharma transmitted the Buddha Dharma to China, he intended to transmit it to Japan.

Secondly, though Dōgen came to a realization of the right Dharma under the guidance of a Chinese Zen master whom he continued to revere throughout his life, the understanding of the right Dharma is unique to Dōgen. Based on his religious awakening and penetrating insight, Dōgen grasped the Buddha Dharma in its deepest and most authentic sense. In doing so, he dared to reinterpret the words of former patriarchs, and even the sūtras themselves. As a result, his idea of the right Dharma represents one of the purest forms of Mahayana Buddhism, in which the Dharma that was realized in the Buddha's enlightenment reveals itself most profoundly. All of this, it is noteworthy, is rooted in Dōgen's own existential realization, which he attained through long and intense seeking. Based on this idea of the right Dharma, he not only rejected all existing forms of Buddhism in Japan, as stated above, but severely criticized certain forms of Indian and Chinese Buddhism, though he generally considered the practice of Buddhism in these two countries to be more authentic than it was in Japan.

The third reason Dōgen is unique in the history of Japanese Buddhism is because of his speculative and philosophical nature. He was a strict practitioner of zazen who earnestly emphasized *shikantaza* (just sitting). He spent his whole life in rigorous discipline as a monk. He encouraged his disciples to do the same. Yet he was endowed with a keen linguistic sensibility and philosophical mind. His main work, the *Shōbōgenzō* (A Treasury of the Right Dharma Eye), perhaps unsurpassable in its philosophical speculation, is a monumental document in Japanese intellectual history. In Dōgen, we find a rare combination of religious insight and philosophical ability. In this respect, he may well be compared with Thomas Aquinas, born twenty-five years after him.

Dōgen wrote his main work, the *Shōbōgenzō,* in Japanese, in spite of the fact that leading Japanese Buddhists until then had usually written their major works in Chinese. Dōgen made penetrating speculations and tried to express the world of the Buddha Dharma in his mother tongue by mixing Chinese Buddhist and colloquial terms freely in his composition. The difficult and distinctive style of his Japanese writing is derived from the fact that, in expressing his own awakening, he never used conventional terminology, but employed a vivid, personal style grounded in his subjective speculations. Even when he used traditional Buddhist phrases, passages, etc., he interpreted them in unusual ways in order to express the Truth as he understood it. In Dōgen, the process of the search for and realization of the Buddha Dharma, as well as the speculation on and expression of that process, are uniquely combined.[2]

The aim of this essay is to analyze and clarify one of the fundamental doctrines in Dōgen's thought that opens up his whole approach to philosophy and religion: the "oneness of practice and attainment" (*shushō-ittō*). Dōgen's views on this topic were developed because of a basic doubt or question he encountered in studying Tendai Buddhism during his early years of monastic training. He overcame this doubt through his personal liberation experience, attained under Ju-ching, of "the casting off of body-mind" (*shinjin-datsuraku*). The standpoint Dōgen set forth after his return to Japan was based on this enlightenment experience. In particular, his notion of the oneness of practice and attainment is a key to clarifying the uniqueness of his understanding of such crucial issues in Buddhism as the relation between illusion and enlightenment, beings and Buddha-nature, temporality and continuity, and life and death.

How did Dōgen come to realize the standpoint of the oneness of practice and attainment? To clarify this point, we must first examine the doubt that Dōgen faced on Mt. Hiei that led him to travel to Sung China to seek a resolution. According to such traditional biographical accounts of Dōgen's life as *Sansogyōgōki* and *Kenzeiki*,[3] Dōgen in his younger days encountered a serious question in his study of Tendai Buddhism on Mt. Hiei. It was expressed as follows:

> Both exoteric and esoteric Buddhism teach the primal Buddha-nature [or Dharma-nature] and the original self-awakening of all sentient beings. If this is the case, why have the buddhas of all ages had to awaken the longing for and seek enlightenment by engaging in ascetic practice?[4]

This question concerns the Tendai idea of "original awakening" (*hongaku*) as opposed to "acquired awakening" (*shikaku*).

Tendai Buddhism emphasizes original awakening, the doctrine that everyone is originally awakened or enlightened. It rejects acquired awakening as inauthentic, because that doctrine indicates that awakening can be acquired only as a result of sustained practice. Dōgen came to doubt this fundamental standpoint of Tendai Buddhism, and asked, "Why should people engage in religious practice to overcome delusion if they are originally enlightened?"

This was the most crucial question for the young truthseeker, and it finally compelled him to travel to China. The solution realized during that journey provided the foundation for Dōgen's later religion and philosophy.

Dōgen's initial question may be restated as follows: If, as Tendai Buddhism expounds, all sentient beings are originally endowed with the Buddha-nature and are inherently awakened to their true nature, why is it necessary for so many Buddhist practitioners in the past, present, and future to set upon a religious quest and practice various forms of Buddhist discipline to attain enlightenment? Are not that resolve and practice unnecessary?

This question is unavoidable for Tendai Buddhism in its expounding of original awakening. When young Dōgen came across this question, however, he apparently took the Dharma-nature, or innate self-nature, to be Reality as it exists immediately without the mediation of practice. He apparently grasped original awakening simply as a reality arising directly beyond time and space, something with a real existence independent of all practice. It must be said that in such an understanding there lurks a kind of idealization and conceptualization of original awakening. Strictly speaking, not only the Dharma-nature and original awakening, but also religious resolution and practice, are conceptualized in that understanding. But as Chih-i, the founder of Tendai Buddhism, had said: "Where can there be an innate Maitreya and a naturally enlightened Śākyamuni Buddha?"[5] The Dharma-nature, or original awakening, does not exist immediately without the mediation of practice in time and space. Rather, it discloses itself only through our own resolution and practice in time and space. Resolution and practice are therefore indispensable factors in the disclosure of the Dharma-nature.

In contrast to the question encountered by Dōgen concerning the standpoint of original awakening, there is another question that could arise from a totally opposite direction. That is, if our own resolution and practice are indispensable, we cannot legitimately say that we are originally endowed with the Dharma-nature or that all sentient beings are originally enlightened. Why then does Tendai Buddhism expound the primal Dharma-nature and the original awakening of all sentient beings?

This question is posed from the standpoint of acquired awakening. In that standpoint, the Dharma-nature and one's true nature, seen as not originally endowed, are taken as something to be realized only as a result of resolution and practice and are not understood as existing directly without the mediation of practice in time and space. It must be said, however, that here again there lurks a kind of idealization and conceptualization. Although it is from a direction totally opposite that of the previous case, Dharma-nature is now equally idealized as the goal to be reached, and resolution and practice are conceptualized as the means to reach it. And so, by taking our own resolution and practice in time and space as indispensable, we misconceive them as the indispensable *basis* for attaining Dharma-nature, or awakening to one's true nature.

The unavoidable question that tormented young Dōgen was, Why are resolve and practice considered necessary if the original Dharma-nature is an endowment? In contrast to that, this other doubt wonders how the Dharma-nature is said to be originally endowed, if resolve and practice are indispensable. Both of the above questions are nothing but the idealization, conceptualization, and objectification from opposite directions of the matter of awakening in Mahayana Buddhism—also referred to as "Buddha-nature," "self-nature," "Mind," "Dharma," or "Thusness." Both of these doubts abstract equally in taking as an object the Reality of the Buddha-nature or awakening, which is fundamentally unobjectifiable and cannot be idealized.

To overcome this error of abstraction, we must clearly realize the distinction between that which must be the *ground* or *basis* and that which must be the *condition* or *occasion*. From the Mahayana Buddhist perspective, both the Buddha-nature and resolution-practice are indispensable and necessary for awakening. They are, however, indispensable in two different senses. Buddha-nature is indispensable as the *ground* or *basis* of awakening, whereas resolution-practice is necessary as the *condition* or *occasion* for awakening. The aforementioned errors of abstraction stem from the confusion of ground and occasion (or basis and condition); in this confusion, only one side is recognized, while the role and function of the other side is neglected. Or the errors derive from mistaking both sides for one another.

Put more concretely, in the case of young Dōgen, Dharma-nature, or one's true nature, is recognized as the Reality that is the ground of awakening for all sentient beings and beyond the limitations of time and space. But there is a doubt about the necessity of our own resolution-practice in time and space as the indispensable condition for realizing that ground as the ground. The Dharma-nature as ground is grasped abstractly by Dōgen as something existing immediately without the mediation of resolution-practice as a condition. The other standpoint, however, overemphasizes the necessity of our own resolution-practice in time and space and treats it as if it were the ground. This view thereby commits the abstraction of conceiving of the Dharma-nature as a direct extension of our own resolution-practice. In this case the Dharma-nature, which should originally be the ground, loses its reality and its character as the ground and is grasped merely as a sign to guide our resolution and practice; that is, it is grasped as nothing more than a condition or occasion. Even though the Dharma-nature is understood to be realized at the last extremity of time and space, it is not seen as beyond the limitations of time and space.

As we saw before, the question young Dōgen encountered was that of why resolution-practice is necessary if we are originally endowed with the Dharma-nature. To Dōgen it was an existential and subjective question. At least intellectually, however, Dōgen must have fully realized the existence of another question, that of how the primal Dharma-nature can be seen as fundamental if resolution-practice is indispensable. For these questions are the two sides of the same issue of Dharma-nature, or awakening, and they are essentially connected with one another. Among novices and monks at Mt. Hiei, where Dōgen was studying, there must have been many who encountered one or the other of these two questions, even though their doubts might not have been as clear and acute as Dōgen's.

At any rate, while studying Tendai Buddhism at Mt. Hiei, Dōgen unconsciously idealized the Dharma-nature and doubted the necessity of practice. And yet, precisely at that point, he could not help feeling restlessness and anxiety over his own existence, which was somewhat separated from the fundamental Reality. This may be why in the opening pages of *Hōkyōki*, a record of Dōgen's dialogues with his Chinese teacher Ju-ching,

Dōgen says:

> The mind that aspires to enlightenment arose in me at an early age. In my search for the Way I visited various religious teachers in my own land and gained some understanding of the causal nature of the world. Yet, the real end of the three treasures (Buddha, Dharma, and Sangha) was still unclear. I clung vainly to the banner of mere names and forms.[6]

By this Dōgen means that he was shackled by doctrinal concepts and formulations and, in his understanding, was unable to penetrate to Reality. It must have been this anxiety stemming from his feeling of separation from the fundamental Reality that motivated him to sail to China, even though this arduous journey was undertaken at the risk of his life.

THE SOLUTION: ONENESS OF PRACTICE AND ATTAINMENT

In China, Dōgen "visited many leading priests of Liang-che, and learned of the different characteristics of the five Gates."[7] Dōgen wrote: "Ultimately, I went to T'ai-pai peak and engaged in religious practice under the Zen master Ju-ching until I had resolved the one great matter of Zen practice for my entire life."[8] At this point Dōgen attained an awakening that overcame all the previous idealization, conceptualization, and objectification of the Dharma-nature. There was not even an inch of separation between the Dharma-nature and Dōgen's existence. Dōgen's statement "The practice of Zen is the casting off of body-mind"[9] implies that all possible idealization, conceptualization, and objectification engaged in concerning awakening and discipline, attainment and practice, since his study on Mt. Hiei are completely cast off through the body-mind of Dōgen himself. Then the "innate self" in its true sense is fully realized as the body-mind that has been cast off.

How was the problem of the relationship between resolution-practice and the Dharma-nature solved at the very moment of the "casting off of body-mind" (*shinjin-datsuraku*), which is simultaneously "body-mind that has been cast-off" (*datsuraku-shinjin*)? His solution is shown here and there in his writings:

> This Dharma is amply present in every person, but unless one practices, it is not manifested; unless there is realization, it is not attained.[10]

To think practice and realization are not one is a heretical view. In the Buddha Dharma, practice and realization are identical. Because one's present practice is practice in realization, one's initial negotiation of the Way in itself is the whole of original realization. Thus, even while one is directed to practice, he is told not to anticipate realization apart from practice, because practice points directly to original realization. As it is already realization in practice, realization is endless; as it is practice in realization, practice is beginningless.[11]

As for the truth of the Buddha-nature: the Buddha-nature is not incorporated prior to attaining Buddhahood; it is incorporated upon the attainment of Buddhahood. The Buddha-nature is always manifested simultaneously with the attainment of Buddhahood. This truth should be deeply, deeply penetrated in concentrated practice. There has to be twenty or even thirty years of diligent Zen practice.[12]

In the Great Way of buddhas and patriarchs there is always continuous practice which is supreme. It is the way which is circulating ceaselessly. There is not even the slightest gap between resolution, practice, enlightenment, and nirvāna. The way of continuous practice is ever circulating.[13]

These statements all show that awakening is not a subordinate to practice, attainment to discipline, Buddha-nature to becoming a buddha, or vice versa. Both sides of such contraries are indispensable and dynamically related to each other. Such expressions of Dōgen's as "the oneness of practice and attainment," "the simultaneous realization" of Buddha-nature and the attainment of Buddhahood, and "the unceasing circulation of continuous practice" clearly indicate this dynamic and indispensable relation. Unless one becomes a buddha, the Buddha-nature is not realized as the Buddha-nature, and yet at the same time one can become a buddha only because one is originally endowed with the Buddha-nature. It is at this point that the dynamic truth of the simultaneous realization of the Buddha-nature and its attainment can be seen.

As we see in Figure 1.1 below, the standpoint of acquired awakening may be illustrated by a horizontal line, for it presupposes a process of resolution and practice leading to attainment as its end. It indicates the dimension of time and space. On the other hand, the standpoint of original awakening may be illustrated by a vertical line, because by completely overcoming the notions of process and time and space implied by acquired awakening, it indicates the transspatial and transtemporal dimension, which is a matter not of process but of depth.

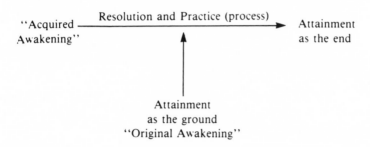

Figure 1.1

As already discussed, in Mahayana Buddhism, especially in Tendai Buddhism, both resolution and practice as the condition (occasion) and attainment as the ground (basis) are indispensable. Nevertheless, the standpoint of acquired awakening takes resolution and practice as the necessary ground for attainment, which is seen as the end. It takes only the horizontal dimension as the real and overlooks the vertical dimension, which is actually the indispensable ground for resolution and practice. On the other hand, the standpoint of original awakening as understood by the young Dōgen takes attainment as the one true reality and doubts the significance of resolution and practice. That view takes only the vertical dimension as the real and neglects the horizontal dimension, which is seen as something unncessary.

However, as Dōgen realized through his experience of the casting off of body-mind, practice and attainment are not two but one and constitute a dynamic whole in which the horizontal dimension (practice) and the vertical dimension (attainment) are inseparably united. Thus he emphasizes, "As it is already *realization in practice,* realization is endless; as it is *practice in realization,* practice is beginningless."[14] This dynamic relation of practice and realization (attainment) may be illustrated as in Figure 1.2.

The center of this dynamic whole is the intersection of the horizontal dimension and the vertical dimension. We are always living in, and living as, this intersection. Since the horizontal process of practice is beginningless and endless, *any point* of the process of practice is *equally* a point of intersection with the vertical line of attainment, which is infinitely deep. This means that attainment, as the ground, supports and embraces the whole process of practice, and that *any point* of practice points *directly* to original attainment.

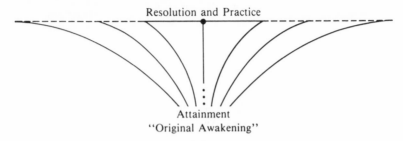

Resolution and Practice

Attainment
"Original Awakening"

Figure 1.2

In order to properly grasp this matter, however, it may be necessary to clarify the issue by dividing it into two aspects as follows:

1. Both attainment (awakening, or the Buddha-nature) and practice (discipline, or becoming a buddha) are indispensable; but the former is indispensable as the *ground*, or *basis*, whereas the latter is indispensable as the *condition*, or *occasion*. In this regard, their distinction, and especially the irreversible relationship between them, must be clearly realized; attainment (awakening) is more fundamental than practice, not the other way around.

The young Dōgen recognized the indispensability and the reality of attainment of the Buddha-nature. Precisely because he did so, however, the indispensability of practice in becoming a buddha was questioned. He clearly realized the transcendental reality of attainment (the Buddha-nature), which is beyond time and space, but could not help doubting the reality of resolution, practice, and becoming a buddha, which do not escape the limitations of time and space. This is because Dōgen was trying to understand the reality of the latter by only taking the reality of the former as the standard. In other words, at that point, without distinguishing between "that which must be the ground" and "that which must be the condition," Dōgen was trying to grasp both attainment and practice, the Buddha-nature and becoming a buddha, in one and the same dimension. It is, however, an abstraction to grasp both of them in that way, for the standpoint of attainment (or the Buddha-nature), which is beyond time and space, is clearly different in its dimension from the standpoint of practice (becoming a buddha), which is inseparable from the limitations of time and space. The former is "that which must be the ground" of human existence, whereas the latter is not. But even so, one should not immediately say that only the former has reality whereas the latter lacks it. If one were to understand the issue in that way, it would be yet another form of abstraction and conceptualization of the matter, and one would not arrive at the reality of the issue. The standpoint of resolution, practice, and becoming a buddha is an indispensable reality in a different sense than is Buddhahood. It is indispensable not as "that which must be the ground" but as "that which must be the condition" whereby one realizes the ground as ground. In that case it has an *indispensable reality as the condition* for Buddhahood. Further, "that which must be the ground" is more fundamental than "that which must be the condition," and thus there is an irreversible relationship between them. That is to say, attainment, or the Buddha-nature, is more fundamental than resolution and practice, and this relationship should not be reversed.

In short, although both attainment (the Buddha-nature) and practice (becoming a buddha) are equally real and equally indispensable to human existence, the former is so as the ground, whereas the latter is so as the condition or occasion. Attainment and practice—the Buddha-nature and becoming a buddha—are inseparable from one another, and yet the former has priority over the latter. In order not to abstract from the concreteness of the matter, however, one must not miss the distinction between "that which must be the ground" and "that which must be the occasion" as well as their irreversible relationship. This is precisely because, as quoted before, Dōgen says:

> This Dharma is amply present in every person, but unless one practices, it is not manifested; unless there is realization, it is not attained.

This is one of the things Dōgen awakened to at the point of the casting off of body-mind.

A question opposite to the one young Dōgen faced was the question of why the primal Dharma-nature is emphasized, if resolution and practice are indispensable. In this question, the questioner understands resolution, practice, and becoming a buddha as if they were the ground of the Buddha-nature, for the question overemphasizes their indispensability. Here again, there is a confusion between "that which must be the ground" and "that which must be the occasion." That this standpoint, too, has fallen into an abstraction distant from Reality must have been clearly recognized by Dōgen in his awakening realization of the casting off of body-mind.

2. As stated above, there is an irreversible relationship between attainment (the Buddha-nature), which is indispensable as the ground of one's awakening, and practice (becoming a buddha), which is indispensable as the condition of attainment. Attainment (the Buddha-nature), however, is not something substantial; in itself it is nonsubstantial and nonobjectifiable no-thingness. Accordingly, through a realization of the nonsubstantiality of its ground, practice as the condition is realized as something real in terms of the ground. Thus, in going beyond the irreversible relationship between attainment (the Buddha-nature) and practice (becoming a buddha), these two aspects come to be grasped in terms of a reversible identity.

As Dōgen says, "You say no (Buddha-nature) because Buddha-nature is emptiness."[15] Attainment (the Buddha-nature), indispensable as the ground of human existence, is not a being or something substantial, but is in itself empty and no-thing. Accordingly, even though the Buddha-nature is the ground that is realized only through practice as its condition, it is not a substantial ground or a ground that is some particular thing, but a ground as no-thing, that is, a nonsubstantial and nonobjectifiable ground. It is a ground that is different from ground in the ordinary sense as something simply distinguished from a condition. In this way, the distinction between ground and condition in the ordinary sense is overcome. Further, the irreversibility between them is also overcome. At that point, that which is conditional is directly realized as the ground. This is the reason Dōgen expounds "impermanence-Buddha-nature" (mujō-busshō) by saying, "Impermanence is in itself Buddha-nature."[16]

In other words, at that point impermanence itself, which is strictly limited by time and space, is realized in its suchness as the Buddha-nature that is beyond time and space. Accordingly, resolution, practice, and becoming a buddha not only are occasions or conditions for attaining the Buddha-nature, but also come to have the meaning of original attainment, which must be the ground. Conversely, original attainment, which must be the ground, cannot be attained apart from resolution, practice, and becoming a buddha, which are usually understood as conditions. Therefore, a reversible relationship between attainment and practice, the Buddha-nature and becoming a buddha, is realized. This is the reason Dōgen says:

> In the Buddha Dharma, practice and realization are identical. Because one's present practice is practice in realization, one's initial negotiation of the Way in itself is the whole of original realization.... As it is already realization in practice, realization is endless; as it is practice in realization, practice is beginningless.[17]

Again, it is for this reason that Dōgen says:

> There is not even the slightest gap between resolution, practice, enlightenment, and nirvāna. The way of continuous practice is ever circulating.[18]

Practice now is not mere practice but "practice in attainment" (*shōjō no shū*). Accordingly, it is realized as "wondrous practice" (*myōshū*) and is not different from "original attainment pointed to directly" (*jikishi no honshō*). In other words, the Buddha-nature is not merely "incorporated prior to attaining Buddha-hood." There is an aspect in which we must say, "It is incorporated *upon* the attainment of Buddhahod." And so, in the final analysis, as Dōgen said, "the Buddha-nature is always manifested simultaneously with the attainment of Buddhahood." This is what Dōgen calls "the truth of the Buddha-nature."[19]

In this, we see Dōgen's emphasis on the oneness of practice and attainment, Buddha-nature, and the ever-circulating way of continuous practice. This is precisely what Dōgen awakened to at the moment of the casting off of body-mind, and it was a complete solution to the question that arose in him on Mt. Hiei. This emphasis, however, does not indicate an immediate identity between practice and attainment—or the Buddha-nature and becoming a buddha—that exists apart from the mediation of any negation. One should not overlook the fact that Dōgen's realization of the "oneness of practice and attainment" includes a dynamism mediated by negation—it is a dynamic, nondualistic identity between practice and attainment that is mediated by the realization of impermanence-Buddha-nature. The realization includes, as stated before, (1) an aspect in which attainment (the Buddha-nature), as ground, and practice (becoming a buddha), as condition, are both indispensable and must be distinguished from one another, and (2) an aspect in which attainment is nothing but the attainment of impermanence-Buddha-nature. Attainment as ground, and practice as condition, are nondualistically identical in the realization of impermanence-Buddha-nature. In other words, Dōgen's view of the oneness of practice and attainment, that is, the ever-circulating way of continuous practice, does not indicate a mere reversible identity between attainment and practice, the Buddha-nature and becoming a buddha. Rather, it indicates a reversible identity, in which an absolute irreversibility between attainment and practice, the Buddha-nature and becoming a buddha, can be reversed by virtue of the nonsubstantiality of attainment and the emptiness of the Buddha-nature. This point must not be overlooked. What is involved here is a reversible identity that is always inseparably connected with the aspect of irreversibility. Dōgen's realization of the oneness of practice and attainment consciously includes within itself this sort of reversible identity.

This means that Dōgen, and all of us, are always standing at the intersection of the temporal-spatial horizontal dimension and the transtemporal-transspatial vertical dimension insofar as we awaken to the oneness of practice and attainment. We are also always standing at a dynamic intersection of irreversibility and reversibility, between practice as a means and attainment as a ground. Each and every moment of our life is such a dynamic intersection. We are living such moments from one to the next, realizing that impermanence is in itself Buddha-nature.

CONTEMPORARY IMPLICATIONS

What significance does Dōgen's idea of the oneness of practice and attainment have for us today? Needless to say, it has undeniable significance for our religious life. First of all, in zazen practice and religious life in the narrow sense, we must clearly realize the dynamic oneness of practice and attainment. Dōgen's idea of the oneness of practice and attainment, however, has rich implications that are applicable, in terms of the oneness of means and end, to a much wider domain of our human life than just religious life in the narrow sense. I would now like to discuss briefly two areas to which the idea of the oneness of means and end may be significantly applied. One area is the understanding of the present and future in our individual and social life; the other is the understanding of one's personality and its relationship to other persons and other things.

The Understanding of the Present and Future

In our individual and social lives we tend to set up an end or purpose in the future and think about how to live in the present in order to attain that end. This aim-seeking, or teleological, approach has been quite prevalent throughout history, but it is most evident in the modern West. In the West, the notion of "progress" has been strongly emphasized, and the progessionist view of history has been predominant. (Even Marxism may be regarded as a sort of progressionism.) In this view of history, and in the aim-seeking approach, the present is regarded simply as a step toward a future goal. This implies at least the following three points:

1. The present is not grasped as something meaningful in itself, but as something significant only as a means to arrive at the end projected in the future.
2   We are always "on the way" to the attainment of a goal and, though we may approach the projected goal, we cannot completely arrive at it. Thus we are not free from a basic restlessness.
3. This basic restlessness stems from the fact that in the aim-seeking approach we objectify or conceptualize not only the future but also the present, and thus we are separated from reality.

In contrast to the aim-seeking approach, the realization of the oneness of means and end implied in Dōgen's idea of the oneness of practice and attainment provides an entirely different view of the present and future. In the realization of the oneness of means and end, each and every step of the present is fully realized as the end itself, not as a means to reach the end. And yet, at the same time, each and every step of the present is totally realized as a means toward a future goal, because we are living at the dynamic intersection of the temporal-spatial dimension and the transtemporal-transspatial dimension. In this way, firmly grounding ourselves on reality, we can live our lives creatively and constructively toward the future.

To realize the oneness of means and end, and the dynamic intersection of the temporal-spatial and transtemporal-transspatial dimensions, we must turn over the aim-seeking progressionist approach from its base. Only when we clearly realize the unrealistic, illusory nature of the aim-seeking, progressionist view of life and history do we come to the realization of the dynamic oneness of means and end.

The Understanding of One's Personality

Unlike a thing, that is usually regarded as existence that is a means, a person is regarded as existence with the self as its own end. This is especially clear in Kantian ethics, which has given a philosophical foundation to the modern notions of personality, freedom, and responsibility. Kant distinguishes things and human personality, and insists that while things can only have value as existence that is a means, human personality has dignity and grace as existence with self-purpose. Although a human being can be used as a means, at the same time he or she must always be treated as an end. In the Kantian framework, this superiority of people over things, and end over means, should not be overcome. Thus Kant talks about the "Kingdom of ends" as the community of personality. Viewed in the light of Dōgen, this Kantian notion of personality not only is limited by anthropocentrism but also is not completely free from reification of the human self. In Dōgen, people are not essentially distinguished from other beings, but are grasped as a part of the realm of beings. People and other beings are equally subject to impermanence, or transiency. Although only people who have self-consciousness can realize the impermanency common to all beings *as* impermanency, they can overcome the problem of life and death only when they can overcome the transiency common to all beings. In Dōgen both suffering and emancipation from it are grasped on this transanthropocentric dimension. Hence Dōgen's emphasis on the simultaneous attainment of Buddha-nature for self and others, and for humans and nature. In this simultaneous attainment, each person becomes an occasion or means for the others' attainment just as each person realizes his or her own attainment. Here self-awakening and others' awakening take place at the same time. While maintaining one's individuality in terms of self-awakening, one serves as the means for the awakening of others. This dynamic mutuality takes place not only between the self and others, but also between humans and nature. This is the reason Dōgen emphasizes, in the "Bendōwa" fascicle, that

> trees and grasses, wall and fence, expound and exalt the Dharma for the sake of ordinary people, sages, and all living

beings. Ordinary people, sages, and all living beings in turn preach and exalt the Dharma for the sake of trees, grasses, wall, and fence. The dimension of self-enlightenment-qua-enlightening-others basically is fully replete with the characteristics of realization, and causes the principle of realization to function unceasingly.[20]

This mutual help for enlightenment between humans and nature, however, cannot take place insofar as humans take only themselves as the end. As Dōgen maintains:

> To practice and confirm all things by conveying one's self to them, is illusion; for all things to advance forward and practice and confirm the self, is enlightenment.[21]

The self must be emptied, for all things to advance and confirm the self. Accordingly, "to forget one's self" is crucial. To forget one's self is nothing other than body-mind casting off. And when body-mind are cast off, the world and history are also cast off. If body-mind are cast off without the world and history being cast off, it is not an authentic "body-mind casting off." Further, "body-mind casting off" is not something negative. It is immediately the cast-off body-mind, that is, the awakened body-mind that is freed from self-attachment and ready to save others. In the same way, the casting off of the world and history, which takes place at the same time as the casting off of body-mind, is not something negative. It is directly the cast-off world and history, that is, the awakened world and awakened history, that "advance forward and practice and confirm the self."

Such are the implications of the notion of the oneness of means and end when that notion is applied to the understanding of one's personality and its relationship to other persons and other things. Here we can see Dōgen's challenge to the contemporary issues of ecology and history. The crucial point of this dynamic mutuality between the self and others, and humans and the world, is to forget one's self, or body-mind casting off. Only when one forgets one's own self, and one's body-mind are cast off, is self-awakening-qua-awakening-others fully realized. This is not the "Kingdom of ends," but the "Kingdom of dependent origination."

II

Dōgen on Buddha-nature

THE BUDDHIST COSMOLOGICAL STANDPOINT

The aim of this essay is to discuss Dōgen's idea of the Buddha-nature, which may be regarded as a characteristic example of his religious realization based on overcoming his doubt concerning Tendai thought of original awakening in terms of the doctrine of the oneness of practice and attainment. In the opening section of the "Busshō" ("Buddha-nature") fascicle of the *Shōbōgenzō*, Dōgen quotes the following passage from the *Nirvāna Sūtra: Issai no shujō wa kotogotoku busshō o yū su: Nyorai wa jōjūnishite henyaku arukoto nashi*, "All sentient beings without exception have the Buddha-nature: Tathāgata [Buddha] abides forever without change."[1] This well expresses the fundamental standpoint of Mahayana Buddhism. In the passage, two important themes are emphasized: That all sentient beings have the Buddha-nature, and that the Tathāgata abides forever without change. These two themes are inseparable.

Against this traditional reading, Dōgen dares to read the passage as follows: *Issai wa shujō nari; shitsuu wa busshō nari; Nyorai wa jōjūnishite mu nari, u nari, henyaku nari,* "All is sentient being, whole-being (all beings)[2] is the Buddha-nature; Tathāgata is permanent, nonbeing, being, and change." Since gramatically speaking, this way of reading is unnatural and might even be termed wrong, why does Dōgen read it in this manner? It is because this is the only way for Dōgen to express clearly what he believes to be the fundamental standpoint of

Mahayana Buddhism. It is more important for him to rightly and correctly convey the Buddhist truth than to be grammatically correct. The crucial point in Dōgen's reading is the four Chinese characters of the first part of this passage—*shitsu u bu[tsu]shō*—traditionally read "[All sentient beings] *without exception have* the Buddha-nature," which he changes to read, "*Whole-being is* the Buddha-nature." This change of reading is possible because the Chinese character *u* means both "to be" and "to have." Why did Dōgen believe that this unusual way of reading more appropriately expresses the Buddhist truth? To answer this question I must explain the traditional interpretation of the sentence.

First, the term *shujō*, or *sattva* in Sanskrit, means all the sentient, that is, sentient beings that are in samsara, or the round of birth-and-death. Buddhist texts show that the term *shujō* is interpreted in one of two ways: in its narrow sense, it refers to human beings, and in its broad sense, to sentient beings. Accordingly, *Issai no shujō wa kotogotoku busshō o yū su* means that not only human beings but also all other sentient beings have the Buddha-nature. Buddha-nature (*busshō* in Japanese, *buddhatā* in Sanskrit) refers to Buddhahood, or the nature that enables humans to become buddha, that is, to attain enlightenment. The second part of the passage, *Nyorai wa jōjūnishite henyaku arukoto nashi*, "Tathāgata is permanent, with no change at all," expresses the eternal, unchangeable truth to which a buddha awakens.

Here one can see that in Buddhism, human beings and other sentient beings are similar in that they have the Buddha-nature and the capacity for attaining enlightenment. In this understanding, however, Buddhism must imply a basic dimension common to human beings and other sentient beings. This common dimension may be said to be *shōmetsusei* (Skt. *utpādanirodha*), the generation-extinction nature. Human's "birth-and-death" (*shōji*) is a form of generation-extinction that is common to all sentient beings. Although the problem of birth-and-death is regarded in Buddhism as the most fundamental problem for human existence, Buddhism does not necessarily approach this as the problem of birth-death in the human dimension, but rather as the problem of generation-extinction in the broader dimension of sentient beings.

Unless we are liberated from the very nature of generation-extinction common to all sentient beings, we human beings cannot rightly be liberated from the human problem of birth-death. This is the reason why, in Buddhism, it is emphasized that humans are in samsara, the endless round of transmigration from one form of life to another, and why people can be said to attain nirvāna only by freeing themselves from this endless round.

According to traditional Buddhist doctrine it is said that *shujō* transmigrate through six realms of existence: *naraka-gati* (the realm of hell), *preta-gati* (the realm of hungry ghosts), *tiryagyoni-gati* (the realm of animals), *asura-gati* (the realm of fighting spirits), *manusya-gati* (the realm of human existence), and *deva-gati* (the realm of heavenly existence). The concept of transmigration was derived from pre-Buddhistic Brahmanism and was a reflection of the worldview at that time. We need not take the number *six* for the realms of existence literally. What is essential in this connection is that these six kinds of sentient beings, including human existence, are all interpreted as transmigrating in *one and the same dimension,* the dimension of generation-and-extinction. Here one can see the deanthropocentrism in the Buddhist understanding of the basic human problem and the salvation from it. An old Japanese poem says:

Listening to the voice of a singing mountain bird,
I wonder if it is my [dead] father
Or my [dead] mother.

This poet expresses his feeling of solidarity with all sentient beings as they endlessly transmigrate from one form of life to another. A bird thereby may have been one's father or mother, brother or sister in a previous life. This feeling of solidarity is inseparably connected with the realization of the generation-extinction common to all sentient beings.

In the West and in the East as well, the Buddhist idea of transmigration is not always understood as occurring in one and the same dimension as discussed above, but rather is often misunderstood as a transmigration simply from humans to animal and from animal to other forms of life in such a way that one views the whole process of transmigration with oneself as the center—without an awareness of its deanthropocentric character. But an understanding of transmigration that does not fully realize its deanthropocentric character is inadequate, because in that understanding there is no common basis between human and nonhuman forms of life, a basis without which transmigration is impossible. Deanthropocentrism in this connection means to transcend the dimension of human birth-and-death, thereby arriving at the deeper and broader dimension of the generation-and-extinction of sentient beings. Transmigration as samsara is emphasized in Buddhism simply because the human problem of birth-death is believed to be fully solved only in the deanthropocentric or transanthropocentric dimension, that is, the dimension of generation-extinction common to all sentient beings. And nirvāna as the emancipation from samsara is understood to be attained only on this wider basis.

Accordingly, regarding the deanthropocentric character of the Buddhist idea of transmigration, the following two points must be observed. First, the Buddhist idea of transmigration has nothing to do with animism, a belief in which an *anima* exists apart from human bodies and things, and animates them (although the poem cited above might be understood to suggest an animistic idea). The Buddhist idea of transmigration is based neither on a belief in the independent existence of spirit, or soul, nor on the idea of the stream of life, but on the realization of *generation-and-extinction at each and every moment.* In reality endless transmigration is inseparably connected with the realization of momentary generation-and-extinction. Here one can see the endlessness of transmigration as regards temporality.

Secondly, the so-called six realms of transmigratory existence are not to be interpreted as meaning that the six different worlds stand somewhat side by side. Rather, for human beings this world is understood to be the human world in which animals and the like are living. For animals, however, this world is the animal world in which human beings are living as well. In this sense it is not that there are six worlds existing somewhere concurrently, but that the boundless horizon of generation-extinction opens up, in which six kinds of transmigration are taking place. This shows the boundlessness of transmigration in its spatiality.

Thus, transmigration in terms of deanthropocentrism is endless and boundless in time and space. This endless and boundless dimension is nothing but the dimension of generation-extinction, in which, as indicated by the term *shujō,* humans and other sentient beings are not discriminated from each other. This means that Buddhism does not give a special or superior position to humans over and against other sentient things with regard to the nature and salvation of humans.

In this respect Buddhism is quite different from Christianity. As the Genesis story shows, Christianity assigns to humans the task of ruling over all other creatures and ascribes to humans alone the *imago dei* through which they, unlike other creatures, can directly respond to the word of God. Human death is understood as the "wages of sin," the result of one's own free acts, that is, rebellion against the word of God. Here one can see anthropocentrism among creatures in Christianity. Accordingly, in Christianity there is a clear distinction between humans and other creatures regarding their nature and salvation, with the former having priority over the latter. This anthropocentric nature is essentially related to Christian personalism, in which God is believed to disclose himself as personality and in which a dialogical I–Thou relation between humans and God is essential.

Then, does not Buddhism establish any distinction between humans and other creatures? Is it that, in Buddhism, humans have no special significance among creatures? The very realization of deanthropocentrism is possible only to human existence, which has self-consciousness. In other words, it is by transcending the human limitation that one comes to realize human birth-death as an essential part of a wider problem, that is, the problem of generation-extinction common to all sentient beings. This self-transcendence is impossible apart from self-consciousness on the part of human beings. Like human beings, animals, *asura,* and so on are all undergoing transmigration, equally confined by the nature of generation-extinction. Unlike human existence, however, other sentient beings cannot know transmigration as transmigration. Since only a human, who has self-consciousness, can realize the nature of generation-extinction as such, this becomes a "problem" to be solved rather than a "fact."[3] When a "fact" becomes a "problem," the possibility of solving the problem is also present, that is, the possibility to be liberated from transmigration. Because of this peculiarity of humans, Buddhism emphasizes the need for us to practice Buddhist discipline to attain enlightenment while each of us, though transmigrating endlessly through other forms of life, exists *as a human.* "The rare state of a human" is, in Buddhism, highly regarded; one should be grateful to be born a human, for it is more difficult to be born a human than for a blind turtle to enter a hole in a log floating in an ocean. Unlike other creatures, a human is a "thinking animal,"[4] a being endowed with the capability of carrying out the Dharma. Here one can see the Buddhist notion of humans' special position among all sentient beings. In this sense, Buddhism may be said to be anthropocentric as well.

Further, the realization of transmigration is a personal realization for oneself (ego), not for human existence in general. Apart from one's self-realization there can be no "problem" of birth-and-death, generation-and-extinction. Likewise, only through one's self-realization can one attain nirvāna by solving the problem of generation-extinction, that is, the problem of samsara.

Buddhism is, it must be noted, primarily concerned with the liberation of human existence. In this respect it does not differ from Christianity. Yet what Buddhism believes to be the fundamental problem for human existence, that is, the problem of humans' birth-and-death, can be solved not through a personalistic relationship with the word of God, but, as described above, only when the very nature of generation-extinction common to all sentient beings is resolved. What has been said up to now about the human dimension and the living dimension and their differences may be described as in Figure 2.1.

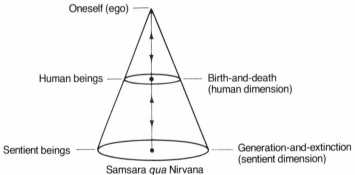

Figure 2.1

It should be clear that while both Christianity and Buddhism are concerned primarily with the salvation of human existence, their *grounds* for salvation differ:[5] in Christianity it is personalistic, whereas in Buddhism it is cosmological. In the former, the personal relationship between a human and God is axial, with the universe as its circumference; in the latter, personal suffering and salvation reside in the impersonal, boundless, cosmological dimension that embraces even a divine–human relationship.[6]

The Buddhist position indicates that if one attains enlightenment by freeing oneself from generation-extinction, all sentient beings simultaneously and in like manner are enlightened by being liberated from generation-extinction. This is simply because generation-extinction itself, common to humans and other creatures, is thereby overcome, and the true Reality is now disclosed universally. According to a Buddhist tradition, upon his enlightenment Śākyamuni exclaimed: "Wonderful, wonderful! How can it be that all sentient beings are endowed with the intrinsic wisdom of the Tathāgata?"[7] Even though one believes one has oneself attained enlightenment, if, from his point of view, other creatures are not enlightened as well, one's enlightenment is not genuine. With one's realizing the Buddha-nature, the possibility of which is possessed by every person, all sentient beings attain their Buddha-nature. This is the meaning of the above-quoted phrase from the *Nirvāna Sūtra,* "All sentient beings have the Buddha-nature."

Dōgen's Notion of "Whole-being Buddha-nature"

What is Dōgen's position in relation to this traditional understanding? Why does he reject it, and why does he read the phrase from the *Nirvāna Sūtra* in his peculiar way? Against the ordinary reading of the passage, "All *sentient* beings without exception *have* the Buddha-nature," Dōgen reads it, especially the four Chinese characters *shitsu u busshō* as follows: "Whole-being *is* the Buddha-nature." According to the traditional reading, it is understood that all sentient beings have the Buddha-nature within themselves as the potentiality of becoming a buddha. Naturally this reading implies that, although all sentient beings are at this moment immersed in illusion, they can all be enlightened sometime in the future because of their potential Buddhahood. The Buddha-nature is then understood as an object possessed and aimed at to be realized by the subject (sentient beings). In this understanding, dichotomies of subject and object, potentiality and actuality, within and without, present and future, and so on are implied. This results in a serious misunderstanding of the basic standpoint of Buddhism. The traditional understanding of the Buddha-nature not only does not represent the right Dharma of Buddhism that Dōgen mastered and confirmed in himself, but is in fact a violation of it. Thus he rejected the ordinary way of reading the passage, with all the above implications, and gave a new reading, even though it meant breaking grammatical rules, to clarify the right Buddha Dharma. As a result he reads *shitsuu wa busshō nari* to mean "Whole-being is the Buddha-nature."

This involves a complete, radical reversal concerning the Buddha-nature's relation to sentient beings (see Figure 2.2).

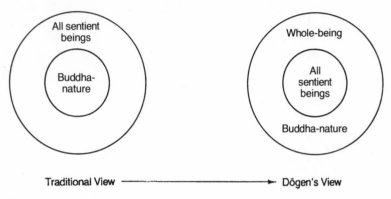

Traditional View ────────────────► Dōgen's View

Figure 2.2

For, in Dōgen's understanding, the Buddha-nature is not a potentiality, like a seed, that exists within all sentient beings. Instead, all sentient beings, or more exactly, all beings, living and nonliving, *are* originally Buddha-nature. It is not a potentiality to be actualized sometime in the future, but the original, fundamental nature of all beings. In order to elucidate these two different understandings of the Buddha-nature and to clarify Dōgen's unique position, the following four points must be carefully observed: first, the deanthropocentric nature of Buddhism; second, the nonsubstantial character of the Buddha-nature; third, the nonduality of whole-being and the Buddha-nature; fourth, the dynamic idea of impermanence-Buddha-nature.

The Deanthropocentric Nature of Buddhism

As stated earlier, in Buddhism the problem of birth-and-death, the fundamental problem of human existence, is not necessarily treated as a birth-death (*shōji*) problem merely within the human dimension, but as a generation-extinction (*shōmetsu*) problem within the total sentient dimension. It is in this deanthropocentric, sentient dimension that the Buddhist idea of transmigration (samsara) and emancipation from it (nirvāna) are understood. By emphasizing "Whole-being is the Buddha-nature," Dōgen carries the deanthropocentrism of Buddhism to its extreme by going beyond the sentient dimension. Whole-being, needless to say, includes sentient as well as nonsentient beings.

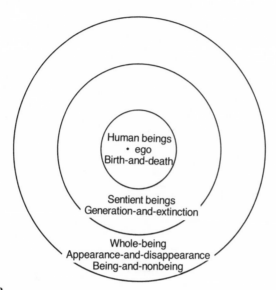

Human beings
• ego
Birth-and-death

Sentient beings
Generation-and-extinction

Whole-being
Appearance-and-disappearance
Being-and-nonbeing

Figure 2.3

For Dōgen, the dimension of whole-being is no longer that of generation-extinction, but that of appearance-disappearance (*kimetsu*) or being-nonbeing (*umu*). The term *generation-extinction* is here used to indicate biological producing and dying out, whereas the term *appearance-disappearance* signifies coming to be and ceasing to be and refers to both living and nonliving beings. Thus it is used synonymously with *being-nonbeing* (see Figure 2.3). The sentient dimension, though transanthropocentric, has a life-centered nature that excludes nonliving beings. The "being" dimension, however, embraces everything in the universe, by transcending even the wider-than-human "life-centered" horizon. Accordingly the being dimension is truly boundless, free from any sort of centrism, and deepest precisely in its deanthropocentric nature. If we add the being dimension to Figure 2.1, we come to have Figure 2.4, which in turn is a three-dimensional representation of Figure 2.3.

When Dōgen emphasizes whole-being in connection with the Buddha-nature, he definitely implies that a person can be properly and completely emancipated from samsara, the recurring cycle of birth-and-death, not in the sentient dimension, but in the being dimension. In other words, it is not by overcoming generation-extinction common to all sentient beings, but only by transcending appearance-disappearance, or being-nonbeing common to all beings, that the human birth-death problem can

be completely solved. Dōgen finds the *basis* for humans' liberation in a thoroughly cosmological dimension. Here Dōgen
reveals a most radical Buddhist deanthropocentrism.

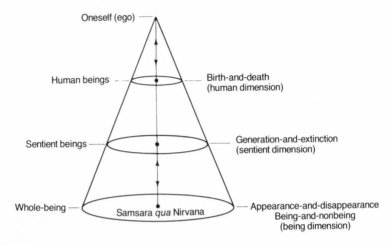

Figure 2.4

Accordingly, one may readily understand why Dōgen refus-
es the ideas of permanent ego, or *ātman,* and of organicism. In
the "Busshō" fascicle of the *Shōbōgenzō,* Dōgen severely attacks
the Senika heresy[8] as not representing the genuine Buddhist
standpoint. That heresy emphasizes the immutability of *ātman,*
or selfhood, and the perishability of the body, a view whose
Western equivalent may be the Platonic immortality of the soul
or the Cartesian thinking ego. In the same fascicle he also
refutes the false view of those who think that "the Buddha-
nature is like the seeds of grasses and plants; when this receives
the Dharma rain and is nourished by it, sprouts shoot forth,
branches and leaves and flowers and fruits appear, and these
fruits have seeds within them."[9] This is a teleological, or organi-
cist, view of the Buddha-nature. The Aristotelian ideas of
dynamis and *energeia,* and various Renaissance philosophies,
might perhaps be cited in comparison.

Thoroughly rejecting these two views, Dōgen often emphasizes that "nothing throughout the whole universe has ever
been concealed (*henkaifusōzō*)."[10] This clearly refers to the complete disclosure of whole-being (*shitsuu*), including human, sentient, and nonsentient beings within the limitless universe,
which is radically deanthropocentric and constitutes the ultimate ontological ground.

The Nonsubstantial Character of Buddha-nature

Dōgen's idea, "Whole-being (*shitsuu*) is the Buddha-nature," as discussed above, opens up a limitless dimension for the Buddha-nature. In Dōgen, the Buddha-nature, the ultimate Reality, is realized precisely in this infinite and ontological dimension in which all beings can exist respectively as they are. The idea of the Buddha-nature may suggest Spinoza's idea of God as Substance that is also called "nature" and that is absolutely infinite, with finite beings as His "modes." However, despite real similarities between them, Dōgen's idea of the Buddha-nature is radically different from Spinoza's idea of God, precisely because Dōgen's Budda-nature is not a substance.

In the "Busshō" fascicle Dōgen says, "What is the essence of the World Honored One's [Śākyamuni's] words, '*All sentient beings without exception have the Buddha-nature*'? It is his utterance, his Dharma teaching of 'What is it that thus comes?'"[11] The question "What is it that thus comes?" is found in the conversation that took place at the first meeting between the sixth patriarch, Hui-neng (J. Enō, 638–713), and Nan-yüeh Huai-jang (J. Nangaku Ejō, 677–744) as recorded in the *Ching-tē ch'üan-tēng lu* (J. *Keitoku dentōroku*), volume 5. The Patriarch asked:

"Whence do you come?"
"I come from Tung-shan."
"What is it that thus comes?"
Nan-yüeh did not know what to answer. For eight long
    years he pondered the question, then one day it dawned
    upon him, and he exclaimed,
"Even to say it is something does not hit the mark."

The question, "*What* is it that *thus* (*immo ni*) comes?"[12] (*kore shimobutsu immorai*)[13] that Huai-jang took eight years to solve refers to the Buddhist Truth, and in Dōgen's case, to the essential point of the words "Whole-being is the Buddha-nature." Even the first question "*Whence* do you come?" is not an ordinary question. Zen often indicates the ultimate Reality beyond verbal expression by interrogatives as well as by negatives such as "nothingness" and "emptiness." An interrogative "what" or "whence" is that which cannot be grasped by the hand, that which cannot be defined by the intellect; it is that which can never be objectified: it is that which one can never obtain, no matter what one does. Indeed, "what" or "whence" is unknowable, unnameable, unobjectifiable, unobtainable, and therefore limitless and infinite. Since the Buddha-nature is limitless and boundless, without name, form, or color, it can be well, indeed best, expressed by such an interrogative. This is the reason Dōgen finds the essence of his idea "Whole-being is the Buddha-nature" precisely in the question "*What* is it that thus comes?"

This does not mean, however, that for Dōgen Buddha-nature is *something* unnameable and unobtainable, *something* limitless and boundless. If the Buddha-nature were *something* unnameable, it would not be truly unnameable, because it would be something *named* "unnameable." If the Buddha-nature were *something* limitless, it would not be really limitless, because it would be *limited* by or distinguished from something limited. Therefore, for Dōgen the Buddha-nature is not *something* unnameable, but *the unnameable*. Yet at the same time *the unnameable is the Buddha-nature*. The Buddha-nature is not *something* limitless, but *the limitless,* yet at the same time *the limitless is the Buddha-nature*. This simply means that for him the Buddha-nature is *not "something" at all,* even in a negative sense such as something unnameable, something limitless, and so forth. In other words it is not *substantial* at all. Accordingly, an interrogative such as *what* or *whence* does not *represent* the Buddha-nature. If it did, then the Buddha-nature would have to be *something* existing *behind* this "what," and being represented by "what." Since the Buddha-nature is not substance, "what" is immediately the Buddha-nature, and the Buddha-nature is immediately "what."

This being so, the question "What is it that thus comes?" is completely a question, and the word *what* is also thoroughly an interrogative. Yet at the same time, *what* is not a sheer interrogative, but is the Buddha-nature. Again, "What-is-this-that-thus-comes" is not a mere question, but is a realization of the Buddha-nature.

Spinoza's idea of God as Substance is of course not something. Since in Spinoza God is the Substance of so-called substances, He is really infinite and the one necessary being. However, Spinoza's idea of God as Substance—though it might be called "what" from the side of relative substances and finite beings—cannot *in itself* be properly called "what," because "Substance" is, according to Spinoza's definition, that which is in itself and is *conceived* through itself; it can be *conceived* independently of the conception of anything else.[14] In other words, for Spinoza, God may be said to be "what" when it is viewed from the outside, from the side of relative substances and finite beings, but it is not that "what" is God. This is precisely because in Spinoza, God is Substance, which is conceived through itself.

The difference between Dōgen's idea of the Buddha-nature and Spinoza's idea of God as Substance may be clearer if we take into account their relations to things in the universe. In Spinoza the One God has, insofar as we know, two "attributes," thought (*cogitatio*) and extension (*extensio*); particular and finite things are called the "modes" of God, which depend upon, and are conditioned by, the divine and infinite being. This clearly shows the monistic character of Spinoza's idea of God as that from which everything else is derived and by which everything else is conceived. Yet the very ideas of "attribute" and "mode" involve a duality between God and the World—in Spinoza's terminology, between *natura naturans* (the active nature) and *natura naturata* (the passive nature)—a duality in which the former has priority. In sharp contrast to this, Dōgen's Buddha-nature is not *natura naturans* that is distinguished from *natura naturata*, that is, the created world. Accordingly, particular things in the universe are not modes of Buddha-nature. Nor is there any exact equivalent to Spinoza's idea of "attribute" in Dōgen's idea of Buddha-nature, because the idea of "attribute" is meaningless in a nonsubstantial Buddha-nature.

Then, what significance do particular things and particular qualities have for the Buddha-nature? Since the Buddha-nature is nonsubstantial, no particular thing or particular quality in the universe corresponds to, or is represented by, Buddha-nature. In terms of mode and attribute, for Dōgen each particular thing is a mode of "what"; each particular quality is an attribute of "what." A pine tree, for instance, is not a mode of God as Substance, but a mode of "what," namely a mode without modifier. Therefore, a pine tree is really a pine tree in itself, no more and no less. This refers to the pine tree's "*thus* comes" in the above "What-is-this-that-thus-comes?" Again, thought is not an attribute of God as Substance, but an attribute of "what," an attribute not attributed to anything. Accordingly, thought is just thought in itself, no more and no less. This again refers to the thought's "*thus* comes."

When the sixth patriarch asked Huai-jang, "*What* is it that *thus* comes?," the question directly pointed to Huai-jang himself as an independent and individualized personality that will not allow surrogation. Huai-jang is not a creature determined by God as Substance. He may be said to be something coming from "what," something determined without a determinator. Determination without a determinator is self-determination, freedom, and selfhood, which are but different terms for the Buddha-nature. If Huai-jang had realized himself as that which *"thus* comes" from "what," he would have realized his Buddha-nature. It took Huai-jang eight years to solve this question and say, "Even to say it is *something* does not hit the mark."

Huai-jang in himself is "What-is-this-that-thus-comes." However, this is not the case only for him. You and I as well are precisely "What-is-this-that-thus-comes." Trees and grasses, heaven and earth, are equally "What-is-this-that-thus-comes." *Cogitatio* and *extensio,* mind and body, are respectively "What-is-this-that-thus-comes." Everything without exception in the universe is "What-is-this-that-thus-comes." This is precisely the meaning of Dōgen's "Whole-being *is* the Buddha-nature." It is for this reason that Dōgen recognized in the sixth patriarch's question "What is it that thus comes?" the essence of his idea, "Whole-being is the Buddha-nature."

Like Dōgen's idea of the Buddha-nature, Spinoza's idea of God is eternally infinite, absolutely self-sufficient, self-determining, and self-dependent. However, for Spinoza, the monist par excellence, the relationship between the One Substance and the multiplicity of finite beings is understood *deductively.* In marked contrast to this, in Dōgen the relationship between Buddha-nature and all finite beings is not deductive, but *nondualistic,* precisely because the Buddha-nature is *not* One Substance. All beings without exception are *equally* and *respectively* "What-is-this-that-thus-comes." Even God as the One Substance in Spinoza's sense cannot be an exception to this. In other words, from Dōgen's point of view, God as the One Substance is, prior to being designated as such, "What-is-this-that-*thus*-comes." Thus there can be no difference, no deductive relation, between God and finite beings in the universe. This all-embracing, even-God-or-Substance-embracing "What-is-this-that-thus-comes" in itself is the Buddha-nature in the sense of Dōgen's words, "Whole-being is the Buddha-nature."

Accordingly, in Dōgen the Buddha-nature is neither transcendent nor immanent. One of the characteristics of Spinoza's philosophy lies in the immanent character of his idea of God— *Deus sive natura* (God or nature). Spinoza rejected the orthodox theological doctrine of a transcendent personal God who creates and rules the world with will and purpose. He emphasized God as the infinite cause of the necessary origination of all entities. In this sense, Spinoza's position is much closer to Buddhism in general, and to Dōgen in particular, than to orthodox Christianity. However, as Richard Kroner points out in speaking of Spinoza, "All individuality is finally swallowed up by the universality of the One God who alone truly Is."[15] This may be the reason Spinoza's system is called "pantheism." In Dōgen, however, the statement "Whole-being is the Buddha-nature" does not indicate that all beings are *swallowed up* by the Buddha-nature. Instead, he stresses that "throughout the universe nothing has ever been concealed," every particular thing in the universe manifests itself in its individuality simply because the Buddha-nature is not a substance, but a "what." For Dōgen, all beings are "swallowed up" *bottomlessly* by the Buddha-nature; yet at the same time the Buddha-nature is also "swallowed up" *bottomlessly* by all beings. This is because whole-being (*shitsuu*) and the Buddha-nature are nondualistic, and therefore the Buddha-nature is neither immanent nor transcendent (or both immanent and transcendent). Thus, despite frequent misunderstandings to the contrary, one may readily notice that Dōgen is not a pantheist, however pantheistic his words may appear at first glance. Indeed, he is as unpantheistic as he is nontheistic.

THE SIGNIFICANCE OF "NO-BUDDHA-NATURE"

*Nonduality of Whole-being (*shitsuu*) and the Buddha-nature*

With the idea that "Whole-being is the Buddha-nature," Dōgen carries the nonanthropocentric nature of Buddhism to its ultimate end, by transcending the dimension of generation-extinction (traditionally considered the realm of human transmigration and the basis for human liberation from it) to the dimension of appearance-disappearance, or the dimension of being-nonbeing that is common to all beings, living or nonliving. Again, for Dōgen, only on this infinite, ontological basis common to all beings can the human problem of birth-and-death be resolved.

In other words, for Dōgen, the human problem of birth-and-death can be properly and completely resolved and the Buddha-nature fully realized only by moving to and then breaking through this infinite dimension of being-nonbeing. But "breaking through" does not imply a mere transcendence or "going beyond" the dimension of whole-being (being-nonbeing). Even this transcendence must be negated. Thus the "going beyond" the dimension of whole-being is simultaneously a "return to" that very dimension, so that whole-being (*shitsuu*) is truly realized as whole-being (*shitsuu*).

However, Dōgen's is not different from the traditional interpretation in the respect that only through human self-consciousness is one's radical transcendence to the dimension of being-nonbeing possible. For the human problem of birth-and-death is essentially a subjective problem with which each person must individually and consciously cope. Buddhist deanthropocentrism, in Dōgen's case as well, is connected inseparably with its emphasis on one's self (ego) as the subject of self-consciousness. Dōgen insists that, to attain the Buddha-nature, one must transcend one's egocentrism, anthropocentrism, and sentient being-centrism, and thereby ground one's existence in the most fundamental plane, that is, in the being dimension, which is the dimension of Dōgen's *shitsuu*, that is, whole-being. The realization of the impermanence of *shitsuu* is absolutely necessary for the attainment of the Buddha-nature.

Accordingly, if one attains the Buddha-nature in oneself by basing one's existence in the being dimension, and by then freeing oneself from the being-nonbeing nature (impermanence) common to all beings, then everything in the universe attains the Buddha-nature as well. For at the very moment of one's enlightenment, the being-nonbeing nature itself is overcome. It is for this reason that Buddhist sūtras often say, "Grasses, trees, and lands, all attain Buddhahood," or "Mountains, rivers, and the earth totally manifest the Dharmakaya (Dharma body)." These passages taken objectively without one's own existential awakening seem absurd, at best pantheistic. Dōgen emphasizes *dōji-jōdō,* "simultaneous attainment of the Way," which refers to the notion that everything in the universe attains enlightenment simultaneously at the moment of one's own enlightenment—an enlightenment that opens up the universal horizon of the Buddha-nature. If one cannot rightfully speak of the attainment of Buddha-nature by mountains, rivers, lands, and the like, one cannot be said to realize the Buddha-nature.

This is a crucial point for a thorough realization of the Buddha-nature through emancipation from the birth-and-death cycle of samsara. Although always latent in the Mahayana tradition, this point was clearly realized and explicitly expressed in Dōgen's "Whole-being *is* the Buddha-nature." More important in this connection, however, is that unlike the dimensions of human beings and sentient beings, the dimension of whole-being (*shitsuu*), which Dōgen takes as the basis for the Buddha-nature, is *limitless*. There is no "centrism" of any sort at all in this dimension. Further, the Buddha-nature that is realized by freeing oneself from the being-nonbeing nature common to all beings is nonsubtanstial. Therefore, even if Dōgen emphasizes "Whole-being is the Buddha-nature," he does not mean by this an immediate identity between all beings and the Buddha-nature; rather the identity is established only through the realization of the limitlessness of the being dimension and the nonsubstantiality of the Buddha-nature—in short, only by the realization of "what."

This means a complete turnover of the immanent view of the Buddha-nature, which Dōgen doubly denies; first, by transcending the sentient dimension to the being dimension, he denies the immanence of the Buddha-nature within sentient beings; secondly, by emphasizing the nonsubstantiality of the Buddha-nature, he denies its immanence as the one cause of the world, that is, like Spinoza's idea of God. This double negation of the immanent view of the Buddha-nature brings about a radical reversal in the traditional interpretation of the Buddha-nature. It is the logical conclusion to the idea of the Buddha-nature latent in the Mahayana tradition, not just a mere explication of its implicit elements. This implies the nonduality of all beings and the Buddha-nature, a Buddha-nature that is neither immanent nor transcendent. "*The Buddha-nature is always whole-being,* because whole-being is the Buddha-nature,"[16] says Dōgen.

To avoid humans' natural tendency to objectify and to substantialize everything, and to make clear the nonduality of whole-being and the Buddha-nature, Dōgen emphasizes two things: (1) the idea of "no-Buddha-nature"—to clarify the nonsubstantiality of the Buddha-nature, and (2) the bottomlessness of whole-being—to eliminate its being objectified.

1. In the "Busshō" fascicle Dōgen often emphasizes the idea of *mubusshō,*[17] no-Buddha-nature, by quoting and reinterpreting various words and conversations of old Zen masters. In one such case he quotes Ta-kuei, or Kuei-shan Ling-yu (J. Isan Reiyū, 771–853), "All sentient beings have no Buddha-nature," and says:

Śākyamuni preaches that "all sentient beings without exception have the Buddha-nature." Ta-kuei preaches that "all sentient beings have no Buddha-nature." The words "have" and "have not" are totally different in principle. Doubts will understandably arise as to which utterance is correct. However, in the Buddha Way, "all sentient beings have no Buddha-nature" is alone preeminent.[18]

In Dōgen the idea of "no Buddha-nature" is not understood as peculiar to Ta-Kuei alone:

> Thus the utterance "no-Buddha-nature" is something that reverberates far beyond the patriarchal chambers of the Fourth Patriarch. It was seen and heard in Huang-mei, circulated freely in Chao-chou, and was exalted in Ta-kuei. You must without fail devote yourself to the truth of 'no-Buddha-nature,' never remitting your efforts."[19]

Those who remember Dōgen's emphasis that "whole-being is the Buddha-nature" may be surprised by these words. Dōgen's comment on Ta-kuei's words is also striking.

> The truth of Ta-kuei's words is the truth of "all sentient beings have no Buddha-nature." That is not to say that Ta-kuei's no Buddha-nature is boundless and uncertain. Right in the sūtras he embodies in himself this truth is received and maintained. You should probe further: How could all sentient beings be Buddha-nature? How could they have a Buddha-nature? If a sentient being were to have a Buddha-nature, he would belong with the devil-heretics. It would be bringing in a devil, trying to set him on top of a sentient being.[20]

This is a complete negation of the traditional doctrine that maintains that the Buddha-nature is possessed by sentient beings. If we penetrate Dōgen's standpoint, however, these words not merely are surprising but have deep meaning. Dōgen's idea of "no-Buddha-nature" does not indicate the opposite of Buddha-nature, but "no Buddha nature" in its *absolute* sense, which is free from both "Buddha-nature" and "no Buddha-nature." Here we find another example of Dōgen's peculiar way of reading traditional texts. In the same "Buddha-nature" fascicle he quotes the following conversation between the fifth patriarch, Hung-jen, and Hui-neng, later to be the sixth patriarch, at their first meeting:

> "Where do you come from?"
> "I am a man of Ling-nan [in the southern part of China, then considered uncivilized]."

"What have you come for?"

"I've come to become a buddha."

"*Reinanjin mubusshō* (people of Ling-nan have no Buddha-nature). How could you attain Buddhahood?"

"Though men have souths and norths, Buddha-nature does not."[21]

Commenting on this conversation, Dōgen dares to say:

This utterance does not mean that people of Ling-nan have no Buddha-nature, or that they do have a Buddha-nature; he means, "man of Ling-nan, you are no-Buddha nature." *How could you attain Buddhahood?* means "What buddha are you expecting to attain?"[22]

Traditionally, the term *mubusshō* meant sentient beings have no Buddha-nature within themselves. However, Dōgen is not concerned with *having or not having* the Buddha-nature but with the *Buddha-nature in itself,* which is nonsubstantial. When we concern ourselves with having or not-having the Buddha-nature, we thereby objectify it in a positive or negative way. Since the Buddha-nature is an unobjectifiable and unobtainable "what," it is entirely wrong to talk objectively about whether or not one *has* the Buddha-nature. With Hung-jen, Dōgen emphasizes: "You say no (Buddha-nature) because Buddha-nature is emptiness."[23]

He also stresses:

As for the truth of the Buddha-nature: the Buddha-nature is not incorporated prior to attaining Buddhahood; it is incorporated upon the attainment of Buddhahood. The Buddha-nature is always manifested simultaneously with the attainment of Buddhahood. This truth should be deeply, deeply penetrated in concentrated practice. There has to be twenty or even thirty years of diligent Zen practice.[24]

If one realizes that sentient beings are fundamentally the Buddha-nature, there is no need to emphasize "having the Buddha-nature." It suffices simply to say that sentient beings are sentient beings. To say sentient beings have the Buddha-nature is like adding legs to a snake, which is why Dōgen says:

How could all sentient beings be Buddha-nature? How could they have a Buddha-nature? If a sentient being were to have a Buddha-nature, he would belong with the devil-heretics. It would be bringing in a devil, trying to set him on top of a sentient being.

Continuing, Dōgen says, "Since Buddha-nature is just Buddha-nature, sentient beings are just sentient beings"[25]—a definite statement referring to his idea of "no-Buddha-nature." The Buddha-nature is absolutely the Buddha-nature, and sentient beings are absolutely sentient beings. Yet, in this realization, the Buddha-nature and sentient beings are not two different things, but simply two aspects of one and the same living reality. Practically speaking, the Buddha-nature is realized as such simultaneously with enlightenment. It is an illusion to think that the Buddha-nature is or is not endowed in sentient beings apart from enlightenment. This is why, against the ordinary reading, Dōgen reads *Reinanjin mubusshō* as "People from Ling-nan, no-Buddha-nature," meaning that those people in themselves are freed from dichotomous thoughts as to whether or not they have the Buddha-nature. This freedom, no-Buddha-nature itself, is the genuine realization of Buddha-nature.[26] Hence Dōgen emphasizes that both a preaching of having the Buddha-nature and a preaching of having no Buddha-nature involve a defamation of Buddhism. Dōgen's idea of "no-Buddha-nature" clearly indicates the nonsubstantiality of the Buddha-nature by rejecting both the "eternalist" view, which substantializes and is attached to the idea of the Buddha-nature, and the "nihilistic" view, which also substantializes and is attached to the idea of no Buddha-nature.

2. For Dōgen, just as the Buddha-nature is nonsubstantial, whole-being (*shitsuu*) is nonobjectifiable, limitless, and groundless.

As stated earlier, Dōgen emphasizes "Whole-being (*shitsuu*) is the Buddha-nature" by changing the ordinary reading of the passage in the *Nirvāna Sūtra,* which had been traditionally read as "All sentient beings (*shujō*) without exception have the Buddha-nature." In this case Dōgen broadens not only the meaning of the term *Buddha-nature,* but also that of the term *sentient beings* (*shujō*). In the "Busshō" fascicle, immediately after saying "Whole-being is the Buddha-nature," he continues, "I call one integral entity of whole-being 'sentient beings.' Just when things are thus, both within and without sentient beings (*shujō*) is in itself the whole-being (*shitsuu*) of the Buddha-nature."[27] This means that Dōgen broadens the meaning of *shujō,* which traditionally referred to living or sentient beings, to include nonliving beings or nonsentient beings. In other words, he ascribes life to nonliving beings, sentiments to nonsentient beings, and ultimately mind and the Buddha-nature to all of them. Thus he states:

As for all "sentient beings," in the Buddha Way all things possessed of "mind" are called sentient beings (*shujō*). That is because mind is, as such, sentient being. Things not possessed of mind are equally sentient beings, because sentient beings all are being Buddha-nature. Grass and trees, states and lands, are mind. Because they are mind, they are sentient beings. Because they are sentient beings, they are being Buddha-nature. Heavenly bodies are mind. Because they are mind, they are sentient beings. Because they are sentient beings, they are being Buddha-nature.[28]

Thus we see that for Dōgen, sentient beings (*shujō*), whole-being (*shitsuu*), mind, and the Buddha-nature are ultimately identical.

However strongly Dōgen emphasizes the idea "Whole-being is the Buddha-nature," the concept of whole-being (*shitsuu*) is not a counterconcept to nonbeing. It is whole-being in its absolute sense, which is beyond and freed from the opposition between being and nonbeing. This is clearly shown in the following:

You must understand, the "being" that the Buddha-nature makes *whole-being* is not the being of being and nonbeing. *Whole-being* is a buddha's words, a buddha's tongue, the pupils of buddhas' and patraiarchs' eyes, the nostrils of Zen monks. Nor does the term *whole-being* mean emergent being; nor is it original being, or mysterious being, or anything of the like. And it is of course not conditioned being or illusory being. It has nothing to do with such things as mind and object, substance and form.

It is noteworthy to point out that in this passage Dōgen insists that "whole-being" (*shitsuu*) does not mean "original Being," such as might be interpreted as an equivalent to the Heideggerian "Sein." Such a comparison between "original being" and Heidegger's notion of "Sein" is instructive, because the original Being is that which discloses itself as the place in which beings exist. Heidegger establishes *ontologische Differenz* (ontological difference), which essentially differs from *ontische Differenz* (ontic difference, that merely distinguishes one being from another). By establishing *ontologische Differenz*, Heidegger thematically questions the sense of *Sein* (Being), the idea of which is latent in the everyday experience of various beings (*Seiendes*). He thereby constructs *Fundamental-Ontologie* to elucidate the significance of *Sein des Seienden* (Being of beings) that is concealed in everyday understanding. In contrast to this, Dōgen does not make an *ontologische Differenz*, not because he is unaware of the essential difference between Being and beings, but simply because he deliberately denies the idea of *Sein* ontologically distinguished from *Seiendes*. Hence his emphasis on the idea of "no-Buddha-nature."

A question, however, must remain here. Why, in Dōgen, is *shitsuu*, all beings or whole-being, referred to in the plural form while *shitsuu* is said to be identical with the Buddha-nature? If whole-being is not *Sein* in the Heideggerian sense, is not then whole-being the ground of *Weltanschaung* in which everything, including God, nature, human, life, and so on, is systematically grasped? Definitely not, as Dōgen's previously quoted words on whole-being already clearly show. Then what is "all beings," or whole-being (*shitsuu*)? Beings (*Seiendes*) are, needless to say, not Being (*Sein*), and vice versa. However, *all beings* are just *all beings*, no more and no less; *nothing* is outside of them. For *all beings*, there is no possibility even for *ontologische Differenz*. All beings are really and absolutely *all beings*—through the mediation of *nothing*. This is precisely the meaning of "Whole-being is [or all beings are] the Buddha-nature."

In Heidegger as well, Nothingness is essential in his quest for Being. *Sein selbst* (Being itself) or *Sein als solches* (Being as such), we are told, must be held down into Nothingness, it must appear as nothing, in order to be.[29] In Dōgen, however, it is the *Seiendes als solches* (beings as such) that must appear as nothing in order to be. This is because the dimension of whole-being (*shitsuu*) is limitless and bottomless without a further embracing, deeper dimension, without the ultimate ground, even in the Heideggerian sense of *Sein als solches*, or in the traditional Buddhist sense of the Buddha-nature, from which all beings come to be present (*anwesen*).

This may be clearer when we take into account Dōgen's remarks on the term "thus" (*immo*), which appears in the words "What-is-this-that-*thus*-comes," words that Dōgen takes as an adequate expression of the Buddha-nature. In the "Immo" fascicle, based on Huai-jang's words, Dōgen emphasizes that *immo* is unobtainable, not-*immo* is unobtainable, both *immo* and not-*immo* are unobtainable. This clearly shows that in the words "What-is-this-that-thus-comes," "thus" (*immo*) is not simply affirmative. Rather, it is neither affirmative nor negative. The genuine "thus" is the kind of "thus" freed from both affirmation and negation. Accordingly, when Dōgen says that the essence of "Whole-being is the Buddha-nature" is well expressed in the words "What-is-this-that-thus-comes," whole-being appears in this sense of "thus." And the very fact that all beings "thus" appear from "what" indicates "Whole-being is the Buddha-nature." Zen's household expressions, "Willows are green; flowers are red," "Mountains are really mountains; waters are really waters," simply indicate this. We may fully concur: "I am really I; you are really you." Yet at this very moment—all beings are the Buddha-nature. *Seiendes als solches* "thus" come to be present (*anwesen*) from "what." Only when the Heideggerian idea of *ontologische Differenz* is overcome can Dōgen's idea of "*Whole-being* is the Buddha-nature" be truly understood.

IMPERMANENCE AND NONSUBSTANTIALITY

The Dynamic Idea of Impermanence-Buddha-nature

I have stated that Dōgen on the one hand insists that "whole-being is the Buddha-nature" and on the other emphasizes "no-Buddha-nature." This he does to reject the common view that objectifies and substantializes all beings and the Buddha-nature, and to clarify their nondualistic and dynamic oneness. Dōgen's characteristic idea of "no-Buddha-nature" (*mubusshō*) already serves this purpose, as it denies both the eternalist view and the nihilistic view of the Buddha-nature. However, to make definitely clear the nondualistic and dynamic oneness of all beings and the Buddha-nature, Dōgen goes further by saying "*mujō* [impermanence] is the Buddha-nature."

In Hegel, the contradistinction of Being and Nothing sets the dialectic in motion, and the unity of Being and Nothing is Becoming (*Werden*). In Dōgen, *mujō-busshō* (impermanence-Buddha-nature) is the unity of Buddha-nature and no-Buddha-nature. *Mujō* (*anitya* in Sanskrit, impermanence, mutability, transiency) has been one of the key concepts of Buddhism from its very beginning, one of the three basic Buddhist principles or Dharma seals (*sanbōin*)[30]—"Whatever is phenomenal is impermanent." In Buddhism the impermanence or mutability of phenomena had been emphasized in contrast with the permanence or immutability of the Buddha-nature, or the Tathāgata (Buddha). Dōgen, however, insists that impermanence is the Buddha-nature. He makes the following remark concerning Hui-neng:

The Sixth Patriarch taught his disciple Hsing-ch'ang (J. Gyōshō), "Impermanence is in itself Buddha-nature. Permanence is, as such, the (dualistic) mind which discriminates all dharmas, good or bad."[31]

This again may sound surprising to the ear of one who holds to a stereotyped understanding of Buddhism, according to which the task of Buddhism is to emancipate oneself from impermanence, or samsara, and to enter nirvāna by attaining the Buddha-nature. However, if nirvāna is sought for simply *beyond* impermanence, it is not true nirvāna, because it stands against impermanence and thereby is still related to and limited by impermanence. The true nirvāna is attained only by emancipating oneself even from nirvāna as transcendence of impermanence. In other words, it is realized by a complete return from nirvāna to the world of impermanence through liberating oneself from both impermanence and permanence, from both samsara so-called and nirvāna so-called. Therefore, genuine nirvāna is nothing but the realization of impermanence as impermanence. If one remains in nirvāna by transcending samsara, one must be said to be still selfish, because one loftily abides in one's own enlightenment apart from the sufferings of other samsara-bound sentient beings. True compassion can be realized only by transcending nirvāna to return to and work in the midst of the sufferings of the ever-changing world. This is the characteristic realization of Mahayana Buddhism, which emphasizes, "Do not abide in samsara or nirvāna." This complete no-abiding is true nirvāna in the Mahayanist sense. Hui-neng's words quoted above are one Zen expression of this idea.

When Dōgen quotes Hui-neng to the effect that "*mujō* [impermanence] in itself is the Buddha-nature," he carries the Mahayanist standpoint to its logical conclusion. As stated before, by stressing "Whole-being is the Buddha-nature," Dōgen goes beyond the dimension of sentient beings to that of beings, and makes explicit the implication of Mahayana Buddhism that even nonliving, nonsentient beings can attain Buddhahood. As discussed earlier, the dimension of beings is that of appearance-disappearance, or being-nonbeing. This dimension, embracing all beings, sentient or nonsentient, may be said to be the most thoroughgoing dimension of *mujō* (impermanence). In other words, it is only in Dōgen's emphasized dimension of whole-being" that the time-honored Buddhist idea of *mujō* is fully and completely realized, because not only sentient beings but also all beings, sentient and nonsentient, are without exception impermanent. It is precisely through the realization of impermanence in this sense that one can properly state of one's own enlightenment that grasses, trees, and lands disclose the Buddha-nature.

Not only that, but by emphasizing "Whole-being is the Buddha-nature," Dōgen radically turned over the traditional view of the Buddha-nature. The dimension of whole-being was limitless and bottomless, to the extent that it cannot properly be called a measurable dimension. For Dōgen, who grounded his own existence in this dimensionless dimension of whole-being, there is a mutual interpenetration between the Buddha-nature and all beings: the Buddha-nature is neither immanent nor transcendent in relation to all beings (see Figure 2.5).

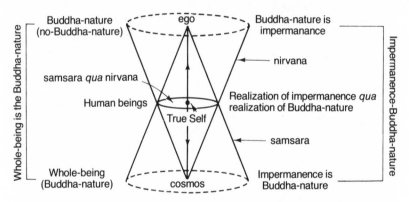

Figure 2.5   *The dynamic and nondualistic structure of 'Whole-being is the Buddha-nature' or impermanence-Buddha-nature.*

Figure 2.5 is a further and final development of Figures 2.1 and 2.4. Figures 2.1 and 2.4 were each cones. Figure 2.5 shows the crossing or intersection of two opposing cones. The cone that stands upright with whole-being, or "cosmos," as its base and with ego as its point indicates the realm of samsara. On the other hand, the inverted cone with Buddha-nature as its base signifies the realm of nirvana.

The intersection of these two opposing cones, that is, of the realms of samsara and nirvāna, indicates the complete mutual interpenetration between the Buddha-nature and all beings, and the dynamic oneness of the Buddha-nature and impermanence. This mutual interpenetration and dynamic oneness are possible because the Buddha-nature is nonsubstantial (and thus no-Buddha-nature) and because all beings are limitless and boundless. The nonsubstantial character of the Buddha-nature and limitlessness of all beings (which is described above as the "dimensionless dimension of whole-being") are here in Figure 2.5 indicated by the circles in dotted lines as the bases of the two cones. Since the bases of the two cones are nonsubstantial and limitless—or, as it were, bottomless—these two opposing cones can be freely overturned so that neither cone is fixed to either the upright or the inverted position. This "turning over" from samsara to nirvāna, from nirvāna to samsara, as well as the realization of the dynamic oneness of the Buddha-nature and all beings, or the Buddha-nature and impermanence, are possible only through human beings, specifically through a person who attains her or his true Self by awakening to the realization of impermanence *qua* the realization of Buddha-nature. In Figure 2.5 this crucial fact is represented by the middle circle at the intersection of the two cones. The figure especially attempts to show the true Self as the pivotal point of the dynamism of samsara and nirvāna, the realization of impermanence qua the realization of Buddha-nature.

Restated in connection with the idea of impermanence, when Dōgen reaches the dimension of whole-being, impermanence common to all beings is thoroughly realized *as impermanence,* no more and no less. Apart from this thorough realization of impermanence, there is no realization of Buddha-nature. However, in this very realization that underlies Mahayana Buddhism, Dōgen achieves a complete and radical reversal, a reversal from the realization of "Impermanence itself is the Buddha-nature" to the realization of "The Buddha-nature in itself is impermanence." His idea of *mujō-busshō* (impermanence-Buddha-nature), is the outcome of this reversal. It can also be seen in the following passage in which he develops the words of the sixth patriarch.

> Therefore, the very impermanency of grass and tree, thicket and forest, is the Buddha-nature. The very impermanency of humans and things, body and mind, is the Buddha-nature. Nations and lands, mountains and rivers are impermanent because they are Buddha-nature. Supreme and complete enlightenment, because it is the Buddha-nature, is impermanent. Great Nirvāna, because it is impermanent, is the Buddha-nature. Those holding the various narrow views of the Hinayanists, and Buddhist scholars of the sūtras and sastras

and the like, will be suspicious of, surprised and frightened by these words of the Sixth Patriarch. If so, then they belong in the ranks of the devils and heretics.[32]

For Dōgen, impermanence itself is preaching impermanence, practicing impermanence, and realizing impermanence, and this, as it is, is preaching, practicing, and realizing the Buddha-nature.

Spinoza looked at everything under the aspect of eternity (*sub specie aeternitatis*). In marked contrast, Dōgen looked at everything under the aspect of impermanence. In Spinoza, time seems to be effaced or conquered by the one Substance. Transiency is surpassed by the perfect stability of truth in its ultimate sense. But for Dōgen transiency is indispensable; apart from it there is no such thing as eternal substance. Time is realized as "being" that is beyond continuity and discontinuity. Rejecting the eternalist view, Dōgen states:

> To learn, in speaking of substance, there is no flowing for water and no growth and perishing for trees is heresy. Śākyamuni Buddha said, "Such is form; such is substance." Accordingly, flowers opening, leaves falling in themselves are the substance of suchness. Nevertheless, fools think there can be no flower opening, no leaf falling, in the realm of True Dharma.[33]

In emphasizing change and motion, Dōgen is more akin to Hegel than to Spinoza. As Becoming, in Hegel, is the unity of Being and Nothing, *mujō-busshō* (impermanence-Buddha-nature), in Dōgen, is the unity of the Buddha-nature and no Buddha-nature.

One cannot doubt that negation and contradiction are the vital notions in Hegel's account of the dialectic. For Hegel neither pure Being nor pure Nothing is truth, and only Becoming as their unity (*Einheit*) or unseparateness (*Ungetrenntheit*) is their truth. In his *Science of Logic,* referring to Being and Nothing he says:

> The truth is not their lack of distinction, but that they are not the same, that they are absolutely distinct, and yet unseparated and inseparable, each disappearing immediately in its opposite. Their truth is therefore this movement, this immediate disappearance of the one into the other, in a word, Becoming: a movement wherein both are distinct, but in virtue of a distinction which has equally immediately dissolved itself.[34]

This is strikingly similar to Dōgen's idea of *mujō-busshō*. However, despite Hegel's emphasis on the unseparateness and mutual passing over (*Übergehen*) of Being and Nothing, it cannot be overlooked that in his system Being is prior to Nothing. In Hegel, the Beginning (*Anfang*) of everything is Being as such, and his dialectical movement develops itself in terms of Being (thesis), Nothing (antithesis), and Becoming (synthesis). It never involves a movement in terms of Nothing (thesis), Being (antithesis), and Becoming (synthesis). In this way Being as such is the supreme principle of Hegel's metaphysical logic. Insofar as Being is thus given priority over Nothing, however dialectical Becoming may be as the unity, it is not a genuine Becoming but a quasi-Becoming, which is after all reducible to Being, because in Hegel Becoming is a synthesis of Being and Nothing in which Being is always the thesis. In addition, by asserting that there is a final synthesis, his system cut off all further development: it swallowed up the future and time itself. For all its dynamically fluid, dialectical character, his system is consistently supported in an irreversible, one-directional line with Being as the Beginning.

On the other hand, Dōgen's idea of "no-Buddha-nature" is already freed from the contradiction between Buddha-nature and no Buddha-nature. Herein any possible priority of Buddha-nature over no Buddha-nature is overcome. When he goes further and comes to the point of impermanence-Buddha-nature, Dōgen consciously denies any possible trace of final duality, that is, the possible priority of no Buddha-nature over Buddha-nature possibly implied in the very idea of no-Buddha-nature. Hence in the idea of *mujō-busshō*, "impermanence-Buddha-nature," every kind of duality and every sort of priority of one against the other is completely overcome. There is no irreversible relation. Everything is dynamically interrelated yet distinct. Thus Dōgen's idea of "impermanence-Buddha-nature" is not a Becoming that can be reduced either to Being (Buddha-nature) or to Nothing (impermanence). Rather, it is a genuine "Becoming" of which we can, paraphrasing Hegel, legitimately say:

> They [the impermanence of all beings and the Buddha-nature] are not the same. They are absolutely distinct, and yet unseparated and inseparable, each disappearing immediately in its opposite. Their truth is therefore this movement—in a word, Becoming.

Becoming in this sense is seen in the following Dōgen passage:

Moreover, to think the Buddha-nature exists only for the duration of life and cannot exist in death, is an example of small feeble understanding. The time of life is being-Buddha-nature, no-Buddha-nature. The time of death is being-Buddha-nature, no-Buddha-nature.... Therefore, holding to the mistaken views that Buddha-nature exists according to whether or not there is movement, that it is a spiritual force according to whether or not there is consciousness, or that it exists according to whether or not there is perception—this is not Buddhism.[35]

Therefore, "Becoming," in Dōgen's sense, is not a *synthesis* that *presupposes* any duality as its basis, such as Being and Nothing, Buddha-nature and impermanence, and so forth. Rather, this Becoming itself takes place in the boundless, dimensionless dimension of whole-being, which is truly cosmological. This leads us to sum up the essential differences between Hegel and Dōgen as follows:

1. Taking the "absolute Spirit" as its philosophical foundation, the *basis* of Hegel's system is still personalistic, not completely deanthropocentric or cosmological, while the *basis* of Dōgen's system is completely deanthropocentric and cosmological.[36]
2. Accordingly, in Hegel, the development of concept (*Begriff*), though dialectic, is *ultimately* a one-dimensional and closed system; in Dōgen, everything is reversible and mutually interpenetrating, thereby forming an open system. The more cosmological the basis is, the more personalistic the mind, and vice-versa. In other words, if the basis on which one attains the Buddha-nature is limited to the sentient dimension, or more narrowly to the human dimension, that is to say, is limited to a narrow cosmological framework, then the Buddha-nature that is attained on that basis will also be limited in its personalistic depth. Conversely, a realization reached in a broader cosmological framework will be one of greater personalistic depth. This may be termed "cosmo-personalistic."
3. In Hegel, because emphasis is stronger on the final synthesis than on contradictory opposition, an individual finally loses his individuality. This is seen in what he calls the "List der Vernunft" (trick of reason), which manipulates individual figures through passion in his-

tory. Since for Dōgen the Buddha-nature is thoroughly nonsubstantial, all beings are all beings, inseparable from each other yet without losing individuality.

4. Despite his emphasis on "The truth is the Whole" and "The ultimate truth is Subject," there is working in Hegel's system a hidden objectification that *speculates* the whole. In marked contrast to this, Dōgen insists that through Zen *practice*, which for him is zazen (sitting meditation), every objectification is overcome, and dynamic nonduality between subject and object, self and the universe, is fully realized.

5. Again, despite his emphasis on time and history, Hegel's speculative dialectic, which is often called "panlogicism," ultimately turns them into motionless eternity. In Dōgen, however, time is being and being is time. Becoming as impermanence-Buddha-nature involves a paradoxical unity of time and eternity at each and every moment.

All of these differences are based on a completely radical turning over of the priority of Being over Nothing, a turning over that is lacking in Hegel. In Dōgen's case, there is a turning over of the priority of the Buddha-nature over impermanence—a reversal from "Impermanence is the Buddha-nature" to "The Buddha-nature is impermanence." For Dōgen, all beings, impermanence, and the Buddha-nature are identical, with the realization of impermanence as the dynamic axis.

THE IMPORTANCE OF RELIGIOUS PRACTICE

The four items discussed above set forth Dōgen's idea of the Buddha-nature in its ontological structure. However, his position is not exhausted by an ontology of the Buddha-nature or by a philosophy of whole-being. Not solely a thinker, Dōgen was essentially an ardent religious practitioner who emphasized *shikantaza*, just sitting, and devoted himself fully to the Buddha Way. The *mujō* (impermanence) of all things was not, in Dōgen, the nature of the world viewed with a philosophical eye but the pain and suffering of all sentient beings and the universe felt by a religious mind. In fact, it was this impermanence that drove him as a youth to renounce the world and seek the truth. *Mujō-busshō,* "impermanence-Buddha-nature," was the consummation of his final realization that "whole-being is the Buddha-nature."

Dōgen's idea of "Whole-being is the Buddha-nature" cannot be fully understood apart from his idea of the "oneness of practice and attainment." These two ideas constitute the solution, realized in his own enlightenment, for the question or doubt that he encountered as a young monk concerning the Tendai idea of original awakening (*hongaku*) that stands in contrast with acquired awakening (*shikaku*). Why should people engage in religious practice to overcome illusion, if they are already endowed with the Buddha-nature and are originally enlightened?

An emphasis on original awakening that is *a priori*, fundamental to all sentient beings, and eternal, is apt to become pantheistic or mystical, neglecting ethical and religious practice. On the other hand, an emphasis on acquired awakening, which an unenlightened one can attain *a posteriori* only through various stages of practice, is inclined to become idealistic or teleological, setting enlightenment far afield as an end. The relationship between original and acquired awakening is a dilemma in Mahayana Buddhism, particularly in the Tendai school in which Dōgen started his Buddhist studies. It is not, however, a theoretical problem. It is the *practical* problem par excellence.

After struggling seriously with this problem, Dōgen, through Zen practice and his own enlightenment, rejected sheer original awakening as a naturalistic heresy[37] that regards the human mind itself as buddha by identifying the given human consciousness with true awakening. Accordingly, he emphasizes the importance and necessity of practice. At the same time, Dōgen also rejects an idea of a mere acquired awakening as an inauthentic Buddhist teaching that distinguishes practice and enlightenment, taking the former as a means to the latter as an end. Instead he emphasizes the oneness of practice and attainment. Thus, by rejecting both the naturalistic-pantheistic and the idealistic-teleological views of the Buddha-nature, Dōgen breaks through the relativity of original and acquired awakening and opens up a deeper ground that is neither *a priori* nor *a posteriori*. This very ground is the original Awakening in its absolute sense, because it is prior to and liberated from any dualistic thought or any discriminatory view.

For Dōgen it is the "immaculate" Buddha-nature that is realized in zazen, sitting meditation, which he calls "the casting off of body-mind" (*shinjin-datsuraku*). The original awakening as understood by Dōgen is not an original awakening that is looked at and aimed at from the point of view of acquired awakening. Rather, Dōgen's original awakening is deeper than both original and acquired awakening in their relative senses, and takes them as aspects of itself. This is the reason Dōgen emphasizes, "What is to be understood is that one must practice in realization."[38] For Dōgen the Buddha-nature manifests itself regardless of humans' illusions and enlightenment. Both practice and attainment are beginningless and endless. There is nothing standing against the Buddha-nature in its immediacy. Throughout the universe nothing has ever been concealed; all beings ceaselessly manifest the Buddha-nature while they are ever changing.

Accordingly, Dōgen's position of "the oneness of practice and attainment" combined with "Whole-being is the Buddha-nature" completely overcomes the following three dualities:

1. The duality of subject and object. When Dōgen emphasizes "Whole-being *is* the Buddha-nature" instead of "All sentient beings *have* the Buddha-nature," the subject-object structure is already overcome. The Buddha-nature is no longer an object with which one is endowed and that is to be realized by a subject (sentient beings); rather, subject (whole-being) and object (Buddha-nature) are identical—the verb *is* indicating their nondual relationship. Yet their identity is dynamic rather than static, because all beings are limitless and the Buddha-nature is nonsubstantial. Through the realization of impermanence they are dynamically nondualistic. Here the realizer and the realized are one and the same. Even a distinction between creator and creature does not exist, for the realization "Whole-being is the Buddha-nature" is based on a deanthropocentric, cosmological dimension. The oneness of practice and realization, an exceedingly human and personal problem, is realized not on a personalistic basis but on the limitless cosmological basis. Hence there is the simultaneous attainment of a zazen practitioner and everything in the universe. This is also the reason Dōgen emphasizes self-enlightenment *qua* enlightening others.[39]

2. The duality of potentiality and actuality. The Buddha-nature is not a potentiality to be actualized sometime in the future but originally and always the basic nature of all beings. At each and every moment in the ever-

changing movement of all beings including humans, the Buddha-nature manifests itself as "suchness" or "thus-comes." Since "suchness" or "thus-comes" is the Buddha-nature, Dōgen says, as stated before, that "As for the truth of the Buddha-nature: the Buddha-nature is not incorporated prior to attaining Buddhahood. The Buddha-nature is always manifested simultaneously with the attainment of Buddhahood." Therefore, for Dōgen, the distinction of Buddha-nature (potentiality) and Buddha (actuality) is also overcome. The simultaneity of the Buddha-nature and enlightenment (Buddha) is realized only *here and now* at each and every moment. From this point of view, the theological ideas of "participation" and "anticipation" are not acceptable, because, though dialectical, they imply an ultimate Reality beyond "here and now." They seem to be well aware of humans' finitude, but they are lacking a keen realization of impermanence common to all beings, which is fully realized only "here and now" at each and every moment in the ever-changing world.

3. The duality of means and end. Practice in itself, as a means approaching enlightenment as an end, is an illusion. With such a practice one may infinitely approach and approximate but never reach the "end," thereby falling into a false endlessness. In the very realization of the illusory character of such a practice, one may find oneself at the real starting point for life, because in this realization one realizes that the Buddha-nature is not the end but the *basis* of practice. Even in an initial resolution to attain enlightenment, the Buddha-nature fully manifests itself. Dōgen says, "Both the moment of initial resolution and the moment of attaining highest enlightenment are the Buddha Way; beginning, middle, and end equally are the Buddha Way."[40] For Dōgen, religious conduct, that is, initial resolution, practice, enlightenment, and nirvāna, consists of an infinite circle, where every point is its starting point as well as its end.

Accordingly, Dōgen's rejection of a mere acquired awakening, and of a practice-attainment duality, does not involve a negation of ethical and religious practice. Rather it implies a strong emphasis on the importance of pure practice, because for him realization is fully functioning at every step of practice

insofar as practice is undefiled.[41] Practice as such is a manifestation of realization. His apparently contradictory emphasis on
"Have no designs on becoming a buddha"[42] refers to a realm
free of human agency in which practice (zazen) is pure practice.
This pure practice, undefiled zazen, in itself is realization—simply because it is the practice (zazen) of body-mind casting off.

On the other hand, Dōgen's rejection of a sheer original
awakening and emphasis on practice does not deny *authentic*
original awakening as the fundamental basis for practice. It simply denies the notion of a given enlightenment or innate Buddha-nature. It involves a recognition that people are immersed
in the midst of illusion and suffering in this floating world and
that there is no self-existing Reality apart from this fact. Here we
should notice Dōgen's words, "Buddhism has never spoken of
nirvāna apart from birth-and-death."[43] Delusions and suffering
originate from a lack of right and full realization of the impermanence of humans and the world, and from a false idea of Reality
apart from this impermanence. A rejection of the defiled idea of
original awakening conceived as something beyond impermanent phenomena, and a direct realization of impermanence as
impermanence, immediately enable one to awaken to Reality
here and now, liberated from delusions and suffering. This awakening is *originally* functioning precisely in the impermanence of
the world. It is through undefiled practice that this original
Awakening in its authentic sense is awakened.

The oneness of practice and realization is realized only in
the realm of undefiled practice and awakening—practice undefiled by an intention to become a buddha, and awakening undefiled by illusory projective thinking that posits enlightenment as
a goal beyond the realm of impermanence. In other words, only
by being freed from aim-oriented human action, both in practice and in attainment, is Dōgen's idea of the oneness of practice
and attainment realized. However, this undefiled realm is not
static but highly dynamic, because through zazen it opens up
authentic original awakening directly at the feet of one's existence, here and now at each and every moment.

Practically speaking, in Dōgen this freedom from aim-oriented human action indicates faith in the Buddha Way, religious spirit, and compassion. This is expressed clearly in the
following passages taken from his writings:

> One who practices the Buddha Way above all should have
> faith in the Buddha Way.[44]

To begin with, the practice of the Buddha Dharma is not done for one's own sake. And of course it is not for the sake of fame and wealth. One should simply practice the Buddha Dharma for its own sake.[45]

The resolve to attain supreme enlightenment is the issuance and act of a vow to save all sentient beings prior to one's own salvation.[46]

As for the buddhas and patriarchs, from the very first awakening of their religious mind they take a vow to gather in all the various Buddha Dharmas. Therefore, in their zazen they do not forget or forsake any sentient being, down even to the tiniest insect. They give them compassionate regard at all times, vowing to save them all and turning over to them every merit they acquire.[47]

However, the realm of undefilement, with its accompanying faith and compassion, is not merely the goal but the starting point of Buddhist life, because without the realization of faith and compassion one cannot have a real point of departure for this life. And only in the undefiled realm in which the oneness of practice and enlightenment is realized is the idea of "Whole-being is the Buddha-nature" as well rightly realized.

TIME AND BUDDHA-NATURE

Dōgen's idea of the "oneness of practice and attainment" necessarily leads us to an examination of his view of *time,* because that idea overcomes another important duality—time and eternity. His view of time in connection with the Buddha-nature is clearly seen in still another example of his peculiar way of reading traditional texts.

In the "Busshō" fascicle Dōgen quotes the following passage from the *Nirvāna Sūtra:*

Busshō no gi o shiran to omohaba masani jisetsu no innen o kanzubeshi: Jisetsu moshi itareba busshō genzen su.

If you wish to know the Buddha-nature's meaning, you should watch for temporal conditions. If the time arrives, the Buddha-nature will manifest itself.[48]

This traditional reading implies waiting for the time of the Buddha-nature's manifestation sometime in the future through present practice: unless the time comes, the Buddha-nature is not manifested, however one may engage in practice. This reading presupposes the Buddha-nature as a potentiality like a seed contained within living beings, a view Dōgen severely rejects. Accordingly he changes the reading: (*tōkan jisetsu innen*) "You are directly knowing temporal conditions" instead of "You should watch for temporal conditions," and (*jisetsu nyakushi*) "the time is *already* arrived" instead of "*if* the time arrives."[49] Dōgen's aim is clear. He rejects such an attitude as anticipation of the Buddha-nature's future manifestation and clarifies the presence of the Buddha-nature. There is no time that is not the right time.

Dōgen's emphasis on the idea of "Whole-being is the Buddha-nature" may be regarded as referring to spatiality. The idea developed into "no-Buddha-nature" and then into "impermanence-Buddha-nature," which implies temporality. As indicated earlier, the dimension of all beings was that of appearance-disappearance, or mutability. However, this does not mean that first there is time, and then within this time, for example, spring comes. Nor is it that there is a time named spring, and then, in it, flowers bloom. Rather the flower blooming in itself is the coming of spring, that is, time called "spring." Apart from the facts of flowers blooming, birds singing, grass growing, breezes blowing, there is not spring. Apart from mutable phenomena of the world there is no time. Dōgen says, "Times have color such as blue, yellow, red, and white."[50] He also says:

> Mountains are time and seas are time. If they were not, there would be no mountains and seas. So you must not say there is no time in the immediate now of mountains and seas. If time is destroyed, mountains and seas are destroyed. If time is indestructible, mountains and seas are indestructible."[51]

There is no time apart from the mutability or appearance-disappearance of things in the universe. Nor is there anything apart from time. Thus emphasizing *uji* (being-time), Dōgen says, "Time, just as it is, is being, and being is all time."[52]

Dōgen does not, however, simply identify being and time. Their common denominator is mutability, or impermanence. For Dōgen all beings without exception are impermanent; just for this reason all beings are the Buddha-nature, for he rejects an immutable Buddha-nature beyond impermanence. Here we have seen a radical overturning of the traditional understanding of the Buddha-nature. Similarly, Dōgen makes a radical change in the common understanding of time. For him, time does not simply flow.

> You should not only learn that flying past is the property inherent in time. If time were to give itself to merely flying past, it would have to have gaps. You fail to experience the passageless-passage of being-time and hear the utterance of its truth, because you are learning only that time is something that goes past. The essential point is: every entire being in the entire world is, each time, an (independent) time, even while making a continuous series. Inasmuch as they are being-time, they are my being-time. Being-time has the virtue of passage-less-passage.[53]

Against the ordinary understanding, for Dōgen, time is flying, yet not flying; flying-*qua*-not-flying is time's passageless-passage. Passageless-passage as flying-*qua*-not-flying is always the *present* in which the Buddha-nature manifests itself. In other words, the Buddha-nature always manifests itself as time, specifically as present time.

Accordingly, with the realization of mutability, or impermanence, as the dynamic axis, being and time are identical. The realization of universal impermanence involves the unity of spatiality and temporality. And just as all beings are the Buddha-nature, all times are the Buddha-nature. This is well expressed by the Zen maxim, "Every day is a good day." Dōgen himself expressed the same realization in the following poem shortly after his return from Sung China:

> Morning after morning the sun rises from the east,
> Every night the moon sinks in the west;
> Clouds disappearing, mountain ridges show themselves,
> Rain ceases, surrounding mountains are low.

When Dōgen emphasizes a new reading, "You are directly knowing temporal conditions," instead of the traditional reading, "You should watch for temporal conditions," he strongly rejects such ideas as anticipation, hope, and expectation that look for eternity beyond the present moment. Even an idea of anticipation or hope that involves a dialectic of "prior to" and "not yet" is not an exception, because the very dialectic is based on the future-oriented idea of divine will or a supreme Being. Dōgen denies the continuity of time and emphasizes the independence of each point of time, as seen in his following words:

Once firewood turns to ash, the ash cannot turn back to being firewood. Still, one should not take the view that it is ashes *afterward* and firewood *before*. You should realize that although firewood is at the dharma-stage of firewood, and that this is possessed of before and after, the firewood is beyond before and after. Ashes are at the stage of ashes, and possess before and after. Just as firewood does not revert to firewood once it has turned to ashes, man does not return to life after his death. In light of this, it being an established teaching in Buddhism not to speak of life becoming death, Buddhism speaks of the unborn. It being a confirmed Buddhist teaching that death does not become life, it speaks of nonextinction. Life is a stage of time and death is a stage of time, like, for example, winter and spring. We do not suppose that winter becomes spring, or say that spring becomes summer.[54]

This indicates the complete discontinuity of time that is realized through negating a transition from one state to another, the immortality of the soul, and eternal life after death. Life is absolutely life, death is absolutely death; spring is absolutely spring, summer is absolutely summer; each in itself is no more and no less—without the slightest possibility of becoming. This refers precisely to Dōgen's idea of "directly knowing" (*tōkan*) temporal conditions. When we directly know temporal conditions at each and every moment, there is nothing beyond time, nothing apart from it. Thus Dōgen says, "The way to watch for temporal conditions is through temporal conditions."[55] There is no room for God as the ruler of time and history, the one Substance, or even the Buddha-nature. To realize time as time is to attain the Buddha-nature. For Dōgen, time is the Buddha-nature, and the Buddha-nature is time.

This is the reason he changes the reading of the phrase *jisetsu nyakushi* from "*if* the time arrives" to "the time is *already* arrived." In Dōgen's realization it is not that the fullness of time occurs at a particular time in history, but that any moment of history is the fullness of time, because for him at every moment time fully manifests itself. This is inseparably connected with his idea of the complete discontinuity of time and the independence of each moment. The criticism may be voiced that time and history are spatialized by such ideas and thereby lose their meaning. But conversely, the idea of anticipation, or waiting for the fullness of time in the future, however dialectic it may be, is not entirely freed from a naturalistic view of time. This is because the idea of anticipation is still lacking the thorough realization of the discontinuity of time and is, in the final analysis, based on the nature of time (continuity) as conceived by humans.

Time and space are, however, completely contradictory. Space is fully realized as space only through the negation of time, which is in turn realized as the negation of space. Likewise, time is fully realized as time only through the negation of space, which is in turn realized as the negation of time. Accordingly, the negation of space as well as the negation of time are necessary for the full realization of space; and the negation of time as well as the negation of space are necessary for the full realization of time. For Dōgen the complete discontinuity of time, that is, the negation of temporality, is not a mere spatialization of time, but rather an essential element for the full realization of time itself. Only by the realization of the complete discontinuity of time and of the independent moment, that is, only by the negation of temporality, does time become real time. For Dōgen, there is no time that is not the fullness of time:

> 'If [the time] arrives' is the same as saying '[time] is already arrived.' If the time is already here, the Buddha-nature does not have to come. Therefore, the time being already arrived is in itself the immediate manifestation of the Buddha-nature. Or 'This truth is clear all of itself.' There has never yet been a time not arrived. There can be no Buddha-nature that is not Buddha-nature manifested right here.[56]

However, in spite of the complete discontinuity of time and independent moment, time flows. This is *kyōryaku*, that is, passageless-passage or movement as flying-*qua*-not-flying. Therefore, time's passage is not one-directional but completely reversible.

> Being-time has the virtue of passageless-passage: there is passageless-passage from today to tomorrow, from today to yesterday, from yesterday to today, from today to today, from tomorrow to tomorrow. This is because passageless-passage is a virtue of time. Past time and present time do not overlap one another, or pile up in a row, yet Ching-yüan is time, Huang-po is time. Ma-tsu and Shih-t'ou are times too. As self and other are both times, practice and realization are times; entering the mud, entering the water, is equally time.[57]

There are great similarities between Dōgen's view of time and Heidegger's. Both of them emphasize the identity of being and time. In Heidegger, through the analysis of *Dasein* (human being) in terms of *Sorge* (care), *Angst* (dread), and being-unto-death, temporality is regarded as the essential nature of human existence. In Dōgen it is through humans' self-consciousness that the problem of life-and-death, generation-and-extinction, and being-and-nonbeing, in short, the problem of impermanence, is realized as the problem to be solved. However, at least the following three differences must be noticed:

1. In Heidegger, temporality is grasped particularly through the analysis of human existence, while in Dōgen impermanence is realized emphatically as the universal nature of all beings in the universe. This is because Dōgen grounds his existence on the radically deanthropocentric, cosmological dimension, whereas Heidegger is not altogether freed from anthropocentrism, though he emphasizes transcending toward the world.

2. In Dōgen, the realization of the impermanence of all beings in terms of a dimension that is limitless and bottomless makes clear not only that being is time but also that time is being. On the other hand, in Heidegger it is clear that being is time but not clear that time is being, even in the thought of his later period.[58]

3. Dōgen's idea of "impermanence-Buddha-nature" results in the realization of simultaneous enlightenment for humans and nature. His idea of reversible "passageless-passage" involves the realization of the contemporaneity of an infinite past and an infinite future in terms of the Buddha-nature; progression is regression, and regression is progression—in the awakening to "what." We cannot, however, find the exact equivalent of these ideas in Heidegger.

In Dōgen, the impermanence of the universe and the passageless-passage of time are inseparable. The mediating point of these is sustained practice and realization. His ideas of the oneness of being and time, and the fullness of time at each and every moment, are based on severe religious practice, especially zazen. At the culminating point of religious practice, "Whole-being is the Buddha-nature" is fully realized. Through zazen all beings in the universe are enlightened and all times in history manifest eternity. Yet this takes place here and now in the absolute present. Apart from the here and now, apart from the casting off of body-mind in the present, this cannot take place. Time elapses from present to present. Things in the universe are mutually interpenetrating, with self and others being undifferentiated yet distinct. This is Dōgen's world of the manifestation of the Buddha-nature. It must, however, be repeatedly emphasized that this is not merely the goal but the starting point of Buddhist life.

In the "Sansuikyō" fascicle, Dōgen quotes the words of Fujung Tao-k'ai (Fuyō Dōkai, n.d.), "A stone woman bears a child at night," to indicate that beginning springs from the Absolute and free subjectivity. "A stone woman" refers to the undifferentiated "what" as the Buddha-nature. "Bears a child" may be taken as differentiated multitude coming out of the undifferentiated "what." It happens "at night" because it is beyond analytic reasoning. The words excellently symbolize the beginning of all things and freedom in Zen.

Freedom in Zen, particularly in Dōgen, is different from that in Spinozism. In Spinoza, God as the one Substance is free because he is *causa sui* (self-cause) and self-determined, while humans can be free by seeing themselves as part of God's self-determined being. On the other hand, as has been repeatedly stated, since Dōgen's idea of the Buddha-nature is nonsubstantial, empty, and no-Buddha-nature, humans themselves are *causa sui* and completely free in the sense of "What-is-this-that-thus-comes." "A stone woman bears a child at night" is simply another expression of this. However, the "night" is not the same as "the night in which...all cows are black," so stated by Hegel as criticism of Schelling's idea of the undifferentiated identity. Hegel criticized Schelling in that manner because for the latter the law of identity, A = A, is supreme, whereas the distinction between subject and object is formal and relative. In Dōgen, on the contrary, the distinction between subject and object, self and others, becomes clear through the realization of all beings' limitlessness and the Buddha-nature's nonsubstantiality. One statement, "Whole-being is the Buddha-nature," may be rendered into two inseparable statements, "Whole-being is absolutely whole-being" and "The Buddha-nature is absolutely the Buddha-nature."

In this sense, the "night" in which "a stone woman bears a child" is much closer to "a bright night of nothingness of dread"[59] in Heidegger's philosophy. By referring to "onto-theology," Heidegger rejects the whole Western metaphysical tradition and emphasizes nothingness instead of substance. Beings in totality are opened up through the "night of nothingness of dread." However, Heidegger's emphasis on the nothingness of dread does not necessarily lead him to the completely deanthropocentric, cosmological dimension in which alone the impermanence of all beings in the universe is fully realized. Only in this dimensionless dimension is it possible to have a complete, radical reversal from "Impermanence is the Buddha-nature" to "The Buddha-nature is impermanence," or from "Being is time" to "Time is being." "A stone woman bears a child at night" indicates the cosmo-personalistic freedom based on the realization of this reversal. It is self-determination without a determinator that takes place at each and every moment of the absolute present with the boundless cosmological dimension as its basis. This freedom is realized in the infinite circle of religious conduct in which practice and attainment are not two but one.

Let me conclude this lengthy discussion on Dōgen's idea of the Buddha-nature by quoting the following conversation between Zen master Ch'ang-sha Ch'ing-ts'en (J. Chōsha Keishin, n.d.) and Minister Chu (J. Jiku Shōsho, n.d.), which Dōgen discusses near the end of the "Busshō" fascicle:

"An earthworm is cut. It becomes two. Both of them move. In which part, I wonder, would the Buddha-nature reside?" The master said: "Hold no illusions."[60]

III

Dōgen's View of Time and Space

THE MEANING OF
"ONE PERSON PRACTICING ZAZEN AT ONE TIME"

Dōgen's view of time and space cannot be understood apart from his standpoint of Buddha-nature. It also cannot be grasped aside from his standpoint of continuous practice. Unless we speak from within the standpoints of Buddha-nature and continuous practice, any discussion of Dōgen's view of time and space, however finely detailed, must remain casual and uncertain. The standpoint of Buddha-nature is really the standpoint of "whole-being Buddha-nature" (*shitsuu-busshō*), or, if we investigate it further, the standpoint of "impermanence-Buddha-nature" (*mujō-busshō*). Apart from this standpoint, Dōgen's doctrines of "being-time" (*uji*) and "nothing concealed in the entire universe" (*henkaifusōzō*) probably cannot be understood correctly. The standpoint of continuous practice is the standpoint of the "unceasing circulation of continuous practice" (*gyōji-dōkan*) or the "spontaneous manifestation of continuous practice" (*gyōji-genjō*). Apart from this standpoint, Dōgen's doctrines of the "absolute now" (*nikon*) and the "true person revealed in and through the whole universe throughout the ten directions" (*jinjippōkai shinjitsu jintai*) cannot be grasped correctly.

Dōgen's standpoints of Buddha-nature and continuous practice are based primarily on *subjectivity* that was forged in his encounter with and overcoming of his doubt concerning Tendai original-enlightenment thought and his formulation of the doctrine of the oneness of practice and attainment. The emphasis on subjective experience is reflected in the significance of Dōgen's statements "The Buddha-Dharma is originally in the *self*"[1] and "To learn the Buddha Way is to learn one's own *self*."[2] Yet, since Dōgen also says, "To learn one's self is to forget one's self. To forget one's self is to be confirmed by all dharmas,"[3] to study the *self* is nothing other than to be confirmed by *all dharmas*. This is the meaning of "whole-being Buddha-nature." That is, in the standpoint of the Buddha-nature, the one side, the realization of the absolute self expressed as "Right here there is no second person!"[4] is attained *simultaneously* with the other side, the realization that the entire world is this very self, expressed as "The entire world is the Dharmakaya of the self."[5] Stated another way, the standpoint of whole-being Buddha-nature is not simply the standpoint of being-Buddha-nature. It is rather the standpoint of no-Buddha-nature. Moreover, the standpoint of no-Buddha-nature is not simply the opposite of the standpoint of being-Buddha-nature. Dōgen enjoins us to "just set aside the nothingness of 'being and nothingness,' and ask 'What is this Buddha-nature?'"[6] thus taking the standpoint of impermanence-Buddha-nature as the true standpoint of Buddha-nature. It is also "the fundamental reason of the Way: that our *self* is *time*."[7] Dōgen's view of time and space speaks from within such a standpoint of Buddha-nature.

So how did Dōgen view time and space? Consider the following passage:

> When even just one person, at one time, sits in zazen, he becomes, imperceptibly, one with each and all of the myriad things, and permeates completely all time, so that within the limitless universe, throughout past, future and present, he is performing the eternal and ceaseless work of guiding beings to enlightenment. It is, for each and every thing, one and the same undifferentiated practice, and undifferentiated realization.[8]

This one sentence of the "Bendōwa" fascicle fully expresses by itself the foundations of Dōgen's views of time and space. Although there may be only one person practicing zazen at one time (the zazen of the self right here at this very moment), if it is truly the zazen of the oneness of practice and attainment, the zazen of original attainment–wondrous practice, or the zazen of the casting off of body-mind, it becomes imperceptibly one with all dharmas (the myriad things of the universe) and penetrates completely to *each and all* times (all moments of time). This is because in the zazen of the oneness of practice and attainment, or the zazen of the casting off of body-mind, the ordinary self (the self-centered self) is liberated from itself, and the self-liberating awakening boundlessly extends throughout the ten directions of the universe. The self that practices zazen right here at this very moment is practicing zazen in the unfolding of a self-liberating awakening that is continuously circulating. All beings that exist in the universal field of limitless space are awakened as discrete or distinctive beings. At the same time, the aspect of all beings ever changing in the moment-to-moment, life-and-death process in the flow of limitless universal time is equally awakened as discrete and distinctive. We say, "Beings are awakened." But this refers to an awakening that has no *subject,* because it is the awakening of self-liberating realization in the unfolding of self-liberating awakening. It is awakening without a subject that awakens to something. Therefore, it is also an awakening without an object that is awakened. It is an awakening that has no object. That is why Dōgen says in the "Busshō" fascicle, "The entire world is completely free of all dust as objects to the self."⁹

Because it is awakening that is truly beyond the dichotomy of subject and object, the self that has cast off body-mind through zazen in the circulation of such an awakening *"becomes, imperceptibly, one* with each and all of the myriad things, and *permeates completely* all time." All beings in universal space and all times in universal time are each awakened to their distinctiveness. Yet they are "permeating imperceptibly and completely" into the self-liberating "zazen practiced by one person at one time." The world of self-fulfilling samadhi is thereby spontaneously manifested. This, in itself, is neither the world of being-Buddha-nature nor the world of no-Buddha-nature. It is the world of impermanence-Buddha-nature. Right here, the world of impermanence-Buddha-nature is ever unfolding, in which all impermanent beings and all impermanent times are each realized in their distinctiveness and yet penetrate each other thoroughly and without obstruction in limitless universal time and universal space. Because of this, Dōgen writes (as quoted above):

He is performing the eternal and ceaseless work of guiding beings to enlightenment. It is, for each and every thing, one and the same undifferentiated practice, and undifferentiated realization.

All beings circulating in the unlimited universe and all time extending throughout past, present, and future are all spreading the Buddhist teaching of original attainment without losing their individuality and particularity. All are equally identical in terms of undifferentiated practice and undifferentiated realization. This is not a world of fixed and static reality. It is the fullest dynamic world, which is limitlessly unfolding in the ten directions of the universe and in which each and every particularity in time and space thoroughly and mutually penetrates and circulates through each other in each moment. This is precisely the world of "one person practicing zazen at one time."

When Dōgen says, "Time, just as it is, is being, and being is all time,"[10] that does not express a philosophical realization of the identity of being and time. It expresses the identity of being and time in the self-fulfilling samadhi of "one person practicing zazen at one time," or zazen of the self right here at this very moment. *Uji* (being-time), in one sense, is literally "a certain time" (pronounced *aru toki*). "Sometimes standing on the highest mountain peak, sometimes walking on the deepest ocean floor"[11] means that at a certain time there is standing on the highest mountain peak, and at a certain time there is walking on the deepest ocean floor, beyond before and after and without continuity. However, *uji*, in another sense, is really "Being is time" or "Time that is identical with all beings." That is, a certain time standing on the highest mountain peak and a certain time walking on the deepest ocean floor, while different moments of time, are both completely permeated with "one person practicing zazen at one time." Therefore, there is no obstruction between them. Furthermore, "one person practicing zazen at one time" is not only completely permeating all times. It is also imperceptibly being one with each and all of the myriad things. Thus, the being of the highest mountain peak and the being of the deepest ocean floor, while completely different beings, are equally permeating imperceptibly the zazen of the self at this very moment. Therefore, they are mutually nonobstructive. Dōgen appropriately expresses this by saying, "You must see through each and every particular thing of the entire universe as each and every time. The mutual nonobstruction of each and every thing is just like the mutual nonobstruction of each and every time."[12]

Put in terms of space, it is the nonobstruction of each and every thing (*jijimuge*). Put in terms of time, it is the nonobstruction of each and every time (*jijimuge*).[13] But it is not that there are two kinds of nonobstruction. There is only one nonobstruction, and everything is nonobstruction. In the world of self-fulfilling samadhi in which "one person practices zazen at one time," the nonobstruction of each and every thing in itself is the nonobstruction of each and every time. We must see through this truth of being-time. Therefore, while "a certain time" is "a certain time," it is *being*-time (*uji*)—"time is already being." On the other hand, while "a certain being" is "a certain being," it is being-*time* (*uji*)—"beings are all time." This can be expressed only in the *nonobstruction* of self-fulfilling samadhi. It cannot be expressed apart from "one person practicing zazen at one time." The truth of being-time is only realized in the standpoint of the self-liberating self practicing zazen at this very moment, or the self of the oneness of practice and attainment. Here, the *self* is *being* and the *self* is *time*. Just before the above passage from the "Uji" fascicle, Dōgen says, "The configuration of my-self makes up the entire universe."[14] This indicates that the *self* is *being*. In the same passage, he also clearly maintains that the *self* is *time*, when he states that "projecting the configuration of my-self I see that. Such is the fundamental reason of the Way: that the Self is time."[15] *Uji* is not realized apart from the self-liberating self, or the self of the casting off of body-mind and the body-mind that have been cast off. In this sense *uji* cannot be sufficiently grasped from the standpoint of being-time. *Uji* must be grasped from the standpoint of *muji*, that is nothingness-time. It is only when grasped from the standpoint of *muji*, or nothingness-time, that *uji*, being-time, can be truly grasped as *uji*, being-time.

THE TRUTH OF BEING-TIME

Above we said that the standpoint of being-time, which Dōgen expresses as "time is already being, and beings are all time," is possible only in the self-liberating self of self-fulfilling samadhi. Based on this, when inquiring further about Dōgen's view of time and space, we must clearly establish at least the following three points.

1. Each and every being as it is realizes all other beings, and each and every time as it is realizes all other times. It is in and

through the self that being and time in the above sense are
identical. This is the truth of being-time.

Each and every being and each and every time has a particularity irreplaceable by any other being. Dōgen refers to this as
"abiding in a dharma-stage" (*jū-hōi*):

> You should realize that although firewood is at the dharma-
> stage of firewood, and that this is possessed of before and
> after, the firewood is beyond before and after. Ashes are in
> the stage of ashes, and possess before and after.... Life is a
> stage of time, and death is a stage of time.[16]

But in the dharma-stage—each and every stage that is beyond
before and after—everything is spontaneously presenting itself.
Because of this, if we discuss life and death at the present
moment, at the same time that "life is a stage of time, and
death is a stage of time," it is also the case that "life is the manifestation of the total dynamic working (*zenki*) [of all dharmas],
and death is the manifestation of the total dynamic working [of
all dharmas]."[17] The notions that each and every thing is abiding in a dharma-stage and that each and every thing is the
manifestation of the total dynamism of all dharmas are not
contradictory but identical with one another. In this regard we
are not simply referring to life and death. We are referring to all
beings and all times. Therefore while firewood abides in the
dharma-stage of firewood, it is the manifestation of the total
dynamism of all dharmas, and while ashes abide in the dharma-stage of ashes, they are the manifestation of the total
dynamism of all dharmas. While yesterday abides in the dharma-stage of yesterday, it is the manifestation of the total
dynamism of all dharmas. While each and every being and
each and every time abide in the dharma-stage of their own
particularity, they are *equally* the manifestation of the total
dynamism of all dharmas. Therefore, (1) all beings are mutually
nonobstructive; (2) all times are mutually nonobstructive; and
(3) all beings and all times are mutually nonobstructive and
mutually interpenetrating. This is well expressed in the following passages (italics added):

> Although the principle of 'life is the manifestion of the
> total dynamism' covers all the world and all space, without
> concern for beginning or endings, not only does it not even
> hinder [any] 'life as the manifestation of the total
> dynamism,' it does not even hinder [any] 'death as the

manifestation of the total dynamism.' Although when 'death is the manifestation of the total dynamism,' it covers all the world and all space, not only does it not impede [any] 'death as the manifestation of the total dynamism,' it does not even impede [any] 'life as the manifestation of the total dynamism.' Therefore, life does not impede death; death does not impede life. All the world and all space exist equally within life and within death.[18]

There is passageless-passage (*kyōryaku*) from today to tomorrow, there is passageless-passage from today to yesterday, there is passageless-passage from yesterday to today.[19]

You must study each and every grass and each and every phenomenon in the entire world...it is by virtue of this very time that *being-time* appears at *all times* and that *being-a-grass* and *being-a-phenomenon* alike are *time*. *All beings of the entire universe are in time at each and every moment.* You should seriously consider whether or not *any* being in the entire universe lies outside this very moment of *time*.[20]

All beings in the entire universe are linked together as time's occurrence at each and every moment.[21]

Furthermore, the dynamic total relationship without obstruction between being and time cannot be separated from "the self"—the self of the casting off of body-mind, expressed as "The whole universe throughout ten directions in the light of this very self,"[22] and "There must be time in my-self. I already am and time does not slip away."[23]

2. Each and every being does not sequentially turn into or become (*naru-seiseisuru*) another being, and in the same way, each and every time does not continuously pass away (*utsuru-keikasuru*) into another time. Rather, each and every being is the spontaneous manifestation (*genjō*) of all beings while maintaining its particular dharma-stage, and in the same way, each and every time makes a passageless-passage (*kyōryaku*) to other times while maintaining its particular dharma-stage at this very moment.

As noted above, each and every being (for example, firewood), because it is the manifestation of the total dynamism of all dharmas while abiding in its own dharma-stage, cannot be seen as sequentially turning into, or *becoming*, another being (for example, ashes). The relationship of one being and another being is not a process of *becoming* (*seisei*) but a spontaneous manifestation (*genjō*). Dōgen expresses this by saying,

"You must realize the truth of the birth of a child.... You should study not only that the child comes from the parent but also that the parent comes from the child. You must also study and thoroughly investigate that the moment of the arising of parent and child is the practice and attainment of the manifestation of childbirth."[24] But, although the relationship of one being and another being is a spontaneous manifestation, the spontaneous manifestation itself is not understood as an event in a linear, sequential temporal dimension. As already noted, all of being-time is grasped from the standpoints of the self-liberating self, the oneness of practice and attainment, or the unceasing circulation of continuous practice in "one person practicing zazen at one time." Therefore, it is understood in a dimension that transcends the ordinary dimension of time and space. So, at this point, the child is the total spontaneous manifestation of the self-liberating self, and the parent is the total spontaneous manifestation of the self-liberating self. It is the same with firewood and ash. Dōgen also says, "Practice always possesses the capacity of spontaneously manifesting the entire universe."[25] Thus, not only the spontaneous manifestation of particular beings, but the spontaneous manifestation of the entire world including all beings, are realized precisely by virtue of the capacity of authentic discipline and continuous practice.

In the same way, each and every time (for example, yesterday), because it is simultaneously the manifestation of the total dynamism of all times while abiding in its own dharma-stage, cannot be correctly seen as passing into another time (for example, today). The relationship of one time and another time must be seen not as a matter of passing away (*keika*), but as *passageless-passage* (*kyōryaku*). To see it as merely passing away is to understand time as simply *flying by*. But Dōgen says:

> You must not understand time only as flying by. You must not study flying by as the only function of time. If time had only the one function of flying by, there would have to be a gap in time. If someone does not heed the way of being-time, it is because he sees it only as something that is slipping away.[26]

Then what is "heeding the *way of being-time*?" It is to know that being-time has the function of passageless-passage. Therefore, Dōgen says:

There is passageless-passage from today to tomorrow, there is passageless-passage from today to yesterday, there is passageless-passage from yesterday to today, there is passageless-passage from today to today, and there is passageless-passage from tomorrow to tomorrow.[27]

Passageless-passage does not necessarily exclude flying by or passing away. It does not simply negate the irreversibility of time. Rather, these aspects are contained within it. Passageless-passage encompasses a tracing back to the origin along with flying by. Furthermore, as in "passageless-passage from today to today," it includes a self-deepening and inner circulation of time itself. While passageless-passage, in one sense, is always irreversible, it bears the reversal of all time from a transtemporal dimension. This is the function of passageless-passage that is not limited by passing away. The freely nonobstructive function of passageless-passage extending throughout yesterday, today, and tomorrow as well as past, present, and future is really the spontaneous manifestation of the self-liberating self through the zazen of the oneness of practice and attainment. "As self and other are both times, practice and attainment are time."[28]

However, spontaneous manifestation is not only the spontaneous manifestation of being. As Dōgen says, "Spontaneous manifestation is spontaneously manifested as the whole earth, the entire universe, all times, and all dharmas";[29] it is spontaneously manifested in terms of everything in time and space. That is the reason, for Dōgen, that everything is the spontaneous manifestation of true suchness (*genjōkōan*). But the special form constituting the spontaneous manifestion of time may be seen as the passageless-passage of time.

In order to clarify the truth of being-time, if we temporarily use the term *spontaneous manifestation* only for being, and *passageless-passage* only for time, then we may express the following: The spontaneous manifestation of being in the entire universe is as it is the passageless-passage of time throughout all times, and the passageless-passage of time throughout all times is as it is inseparable from the spontaneous manifestation of being in the entire universe. But although the spontaneous manifestation of being and the passageless-passage of time are indistinguishable from one another, this signifies neither that the spontaneous manifestation of being in the entire universe is a sequential appearance in a temporal process nor that the passageless-passage of time throughout all times is simply the transition of life-to-death of beings in space. To interpret these aspects in such a way would be to confuse spontaneous manifestation (*genjō*) with becoming (*seisei*) and passageless-passage (*kyōryaku*) with passing away (*keika*). Spontaneous manifestation is different from becoming and transcends a sequential life-to-death transition. Also, passageless-passage is different from passing away, and transcends a unidirectional process. Both of them express the dynamism in which all dharmas are totally presencing in each and every particular dharma-stage. Therefore, in the spontaneous manifestation of only a single being, the entire universe is fully realized; also, in the passageless-passage of only a single time, all times are universally realized. We must not overlook that each and every being unfolding in being spontaneously manifests itself directly at this very place, and that each and every time is precisely the very moment of the absolute now.

3. The truth of being-time is never realized apart from this very place (absolute here) and this very time (absolute now). This, however, does not obstruct the manifestation of particular things in all the places of limitless universal space, as expressed by Dōgen as "Nothing throughout the whole world has ever been concealed."[30] And since he says that "as the time right now is all there ever is, each being-time is without exception entire time,"[31] the absolute now contains limitless universal time.

Because the truth of being-time is always realized from the standpoints of the oneness of practice and attainment, self-fulfilling samadhi, or impermanence-Buddha-nature, it constitutes a nonobjectifiable subjectivity. It is a standpoint of the self-liberating Self that has overcome, the distinction of self and other. All objectification of space is overcome and the absolute here—this very place—is realized. All objectification of time is negated, and the absolute now—this very moment—is realized. Apart from this very place there is no oneness of practice and attainment, and aside from this very moment it cannot be said that "impermanence is itself Buddha-nature." This is the reason why Dōgen refers to what sixth patriarch Hui-neng asked Nan-yüeh Huai-jang, "What is it that has thus come? [What thus appears at this place?]" and says, "You must not doubt the truth of liberation at this very place."[32] Again, that is the reason he says that when you correctly study the Dharma, "the Way of the Tathāgata is spontaneously manifested at this very moment."[33] But although he mentions this very place and this very moment, they do not refer to a merely particular point occupied in space or a merely particular point flowing in time. Rather, at this very place and this very moment, space itself and time itself are emancipated. All beings and all times liberated from the limits of time and space are distinctively manifested. If a person says that he has liberated the self, and yet the mountains, rivers, and the great earth are not liberated, then this person's liberation is not a genuine one. When the self is liberated, mountains, rivers, and the great earth are simultaneously liberated. That is why Dōgen says, "The whole universe throughout the ten directions is in the radiance of the Self."[34] That is also the reason he says, "The practice of Buddha is the same as the practice of the entire universe and all sentient beings. If it is not practice with all other things, it is not yet the practice of Buddha."[35] In the same way Dōgen says, "At the very moment of the arousing of the resolve for enlightenment, the resolve for enlightenment is aroused throughout the entire universe."[36] At the very moment the self resolves to seek enlightenment, the self shares the resolve for enlightenment with all beings in the entire universe. Again he says, "All sentient beings at all moments past, present, and future in the whole universe throughout the ten directions are all Buddhas of the past, present, and future of the whole universe throughout the ten directions."[37] All sentient beings at all times of the past, present, and future are understood to attain enlightenment simultaneously with the enlightenment of the self. From the standpoint of the absolute now, the meaning of the simultaneity of practice and the simultaneity of attainment—which Dōgen refers to as "For each and every thing, one and the same undifferentiated practice, and undifferentiated realization,"[38]—is truly realized throughout the two aspects of time and space.

Therefore, it is natural for Dōgen to make the following revision of the passage from the *Nirvāna Sūtra* in the "Busshō" fascicle. The original is:

> Buddha said, 'If you wish to know the Buddha-nature's meaning, you should watch for temporal conditions. If the time arrives, the Buddha-nature will manifest itself.'[39]

Dōgen's interpretive reading is:

> The passage, 'If the time arrives,' means 'the time is already here' and there could be no room to doubt it.[40]

He further interprets, "'If the time arrives' is the same as saying 'it has already arrived.'"[41] From the standpoint of the absolute now, Dōgen completely rejects as the naturalist heresy (*jinen-gedō*) the viewpoint that thinks, "You await a future time when the Buddha-nature will become manifest," and maintains that "continuing your practice this way, the time of the Buddha-nature's manifestation will be encountered naturally. If the time does not come, then whether you go to a master in search of the Dharma, or negotiate the Way in concentrated practice, it is not manifested."[42] All *times* are the *temporal occasion* of the manifestation of Buddha-nature, so that a *time* that does not have the significance of *temporal occasion* does not exist at any point in the flow of limitless universal time. Such a temporal condition is not accelerated and matured by anything outside of itself. That is why Dōgen says, "The way to watch for temporal conditions is through temporal conditions."[43]

Just as all times are the occasion of the manifestation of the Buddha-nature, all beings are the Buddha-nature. When Dōgen refers to "whole-being Buddha-nature," the term *Buddha-nature* is not merely about *being*. At the same time, the term cannot be separated from time in the sense of the temporal occasion for the manifestation of the Buddha-nature. *Whole-being* is *Buddha-nature* at the same time that *Buddha-nature* is *time* in the sense that it is temporal conditions, as expressed in the passage "If you wish to know the Buddha-nature's meaning you should know that it is precisely temporal conditions themselves."[44] Being and time are identical in terms of the Buddha-nature. To put it more correctly, being and time are identical in terms of the *manifestation* (*genzen*) of the Buddha-nature. This is the truth of being-time. Moreover, for Dōgen, Buddha-nature in the end is neither being-Buddha-nature nor nothingness-Buddha-nature, but impermanence-Buddha-nature. Therefore, in the awakening of impermanence-is-itself-Buddha-nature, the truth of being-time as the nonduality of being and time must be said to be realized.

BEING, TIME, AND SELF

Dōgen's view of time and space seen in terms of the truth of being-time in the above discussion, as already frequently noted, is realized inseparably from the standpoint of the Self casting off body-mind, or the self-liberating Self. This Self is simultaneously "the Self prior to the universe sprouting any sign of itself" (the Self prior to the creation of the universe) and the "Self" that constitutes the whole universe throughout the ten directions at all times (the world of universal time and universal space) as the whole body of the Self. In that case, while all subjects and objects are mutually reversible, the subject is always the subject and the object is always the object. Self and other are nondual but do not lose the distinction between them; and being and time are identical yet differentiable. It is only on this basis that the world of truly free and nonobstructive creation is manifested.

In the standpoint of the ordinary self (the self-centered self) prior to the casting off of body-mind, self and other, and subject and object, are opposing dimensions, and therefore everything is objectified as centering around the self. This is also the world bound by time and space. When we question the meaning of original awakening and acquired awakening, Dharma-nature and practice, from the standpoint of this ordinary self, they are differentiated from one another by objectification. Original awakening is regarded as a reality that is not mediated by acquired awakening, and the Dharma-nature is looked on as the goal based on practice. But for the self-liberating Self that has cast off body-mind, the distinction of self and other, and subject and object, is overcome at its root by the complete dissolution of self-centeredness, and the world of identity in which self and other are nondualistic is realized. In this experience, the boundaries of time and space are also dissolved, and the circulation of awakening extending throughout the limitless ten directions is attained. As noted above, it is awakening without a subject who awakens, and awakening without an object that is awakened. It is self-awakening in which self-awakening self-awakens self-awakening. The self-liberating Self, or the Self of the casting off of body-mind, is nothing other than the circulation of this awakening. This is the awakening originally beyond the distinction of subject and object that is limitlessly circulating in the ten directions. Moreover, according to the passage "The true Person revealed in and through the whole universe throughout the ten directions is itself the Self,"[45] the circulation of awakening extending throughout the ten directions is truly "the *Self*." It is the Self prior to all selves, the Self that is not the ordinary self. This *Self* is not the self realized in time and space, but the Self through which limitless time and limitless space are in themselves realized, or the Self as the foundation for the realization of time and space.

Dōgen calls this "the Self prior to the universe sprouting any sign of itself,"[46] or "the Self prior to the *kalpa* [aeon] of the great void."[47] But although the Self is more primordial than the arising of the universe, it has no previous existence that is independent or separable from the universe. Rather, as the Self that is the *foundation* of the arising of time and space, it is *spontaneously manifested everywhere* throughout limitless universal space and *makes passageless-passage at all times* of limitless universal time. When Dōgen says, "The whole universe throughout the ten directions is this particular true person; life and death, and coming and going are the true person,"[48] the true person is none other than this Self. Dōgen also says, "The place of the turning of the Dharma-wheel is the domain of mutuality and the time of mutuality. It is the body of the true person although there are distinctions among the various spheres."[49] This means that in the place of the turning of the Dharma-wheel throughout everywhere in universal space and at all times in universal time, although there are distinctions among the various spheres, these spheres are all the Self, or the body of the true Person. The Self is truly the "place of turning the Dharma-wheel." This is above all the Self of this very place at this very time. That is the reason Dōgen says, "You at this very moment and I at this very moment are the persons who realize the body of the true Person in the whole universe throughout the ten directions. You should learn the Way by not overlooking this point."[50] Therefore, "the Self prior to the universe sprouting any sign of itself" is *you at this very moment,* and "the self prior to the *kalpa* of the great void" is *I at this very moment.* It is "one person practicing zazen at one time"—the Self that practices zazen at this very moment. The Self that pactices zazen here at this very moment is simultaneously turning the Dharma-wheel everywhere in the universe at all times. This is no different than the above-quoted statement:

> When even just one person, at one time, sits in zazen, he becomes, imperceptibly, one with each and all of the myriad things, and permeates completely all time, so that within the limitless universe, throughout past, future, and present, he is performing the eternal and ceaseless work of guiding beings to enlightenment. It is, for each and every thing, one and the same undifferentiated practice, and undifferentiated realization.

The dynamism of the Self that contains everything in universal time and universal space is fully manifested at this point.

The following passage is cited to discuss *being* in terms of the dynamism of the "Self." In "Eihei zenji goroku" (the recorded sayings of Dōgen at Eiheiji Temple), volume 5 of *Dōgen oshō kōroku,* in citing a *mondō* between Sōzan and Tokujōza, Dōgen says, "The donkey sees the well, the well sees the donkey, the well sees the well, the donkey sees the donkey."[51] This is Dōgen's own view concerning the following question: Referring to a sentence from "The Golden Light Sutra" (*Suvarnaprabhāsa Sūtra*), "The true Dharmakaya of the Buddha is like the vast, empty sky but, just as the moon reflects itself on the water, it manifests forms in response to the object,"[52] Sōzan asked Tokujōza, "Can you explain the meaning of just such a response?" In Dōgen's view, the donkey appears as the subject (the self), and the well as the object (the other). That the true Buddha-body "manifests a form in response to the object" is not a phenomenon in which the donkey as subject merely sees the well as the object. Rather, it is simultaneously a phenomenon in which the well as the object sees donkey as subject. At this point there is reciprocity of guest (object) and host (subject) liberated from self-centeredness. Reality transcending objectification and conceptualization is fully realized. But however reciprocal the guest and host may be, and however interchangeable subject and object may be, it is not the case that the subject stops being the subject and the object stops being the object. The reverse is true. At this point, the subject is always realized as the subject, and the object is always realized as the object. That is the reason Dōgen says, "The well sees the well, the donkey sees the donkey." This is the manifestation in which the subject is realized distinctively as the subject, and the object is realized distinctively as the object. If that is not the case, then subject and object cannot be manifested interchangeably either. In the reciprocity of guest and host, the particularity of each and every guest and host is not lost or fused. The reciprocity of guest and host is established on the basis of their distinctiveness. This is the spontaneous manifestation of being. This dynamic spontaneous manifestation of being is realized because the true Dharma-body of the Buddha (the Self that has cast off body-mind) is "like the empty sky" and is "the Self prior to the *kalpa* of the great void," or "the Self prior to the universe sprouting any sign of itself." Here again, what is called "manifesting a form in response to something" is realized.

When Dōgen says, "The donkey sees the well, the well sees the donkey, the well sees the well, the donkey sees the donkey," the consistent point is the function of "seeing." This is seeing without a subject that sees or an object that is seen. It is seeing that cannot be called ordinary seeing. It is seeing in the sense of not-seeing. It is only in this sense, referred to as "the well sees the well, the donkey sees the donkey," that a completely nonobjectifiable subjective seeing is realized. In the free reciprocity that maintains the distinctiveness of subject and object referred to as the donkey and the well, the function of absolute seeing is consistent. At this point, the self that sees the world objectively is radically turned over. Although the function of absolute seeing is the seeing of not-seeing, indeed, precisely because it is so, it is seeing that sees seeing. Or, seeing sees seeing. It is also the truth of "manifesting a form in response to something." The reciprocity of guest and host that maintains their distinctiveness is the "response." "The donkey sees the well, the well sees the donkey" is certainly the spontaneous manifestation of being. But in understanding the relation of subject and object in just this way, the spontaneous manifestation of being cannot be fully realized. To take it further, it is only when we understand "the well sees the well, the donkey sees the donkey" that the spontaneous manifestation of being is fully realized.

Now, we must discuss the passageless-passage of *time* in exactly in the same way in which we discussed the spontaneous manifestation of *being*. As previously quoted, Dōgen says, "There is passageless-passage from today to tomorrow, from today to yesterday, from yesterday to today, from today to today, and from tomorrow to tomorrow. This is because passageless-passage is the distinctive function of time." He also says in the "Den'e" fascicle:

> The robe of the right transmission of the buddhas and patriarchs is not arbitrarily transmitted from buddha to buddha. It is the robe transmitted from the former buddha to the later buddha, and from the ancient buddha to the contemporaneous buddha. In order to transform the Way, to transform the buddha, and to transform the past, present, and future, there is a right transmission from past to present, from present to future, from present to past, from past to past, from present to present, from future to future, from future to present, and from future to past. It is the right transmission only between a buddha and a buddha.[53]

The question of being raises the basic issue of the two dimensions of subject and object, but the question of time raises the issue of the threefold aspect of past, present, and future. These issues, however, are fundamentally the same. What is the passageless-passage of time? What is the true transmission of the Dharma that "transforms the Way and transforms the buddha?" Passageless-passage is not only the passing from yesterday to today, and from today to tomorrow, or the right transmission from past to present, and from present to future. That cannot be said to transform the Way. In that case, time is objectified in a form that is understood as an irreversible process proceeding unidrectionally. That is, the self sees time as something external by its standing *apart* from time conceived of as a process proceeding unidirectionally. But, we do not stand outside of time. The self and time are inseparable. It is only when seen not from the outside but from the inside that time is realized as nondualistically united with self. Or, to put it more accurately, it is only when it is grasped from *neither the inside nor the outside*. Here, the Self is not the ordinary self (the self-centered self) that objectifies time, but the self-liberating Self. Time realized from neither the inside nor the outside as nondualistic with the self-liberating Self is not merely irreversible time that proceeds unidirectionally, but reversible time. This simultaneously includes the direction of tracing back to the origin, referred to as "from tomorrow to today, and from today to yesterday," or "from future to present and from present to past." The Dharma-wheel of time turns itself, with the self-liberating Self as the hub or turning place. It is only because of this that the dynamic passageless-passage of time is realized beyond the passing away of time.

But this alone is not a full realization of the passageless-passage of time. However reversible time may be, that does not mean that the particularity of each and every aspect of yesterday, today, and tomorrow or of past, present, and future is dissolved into a monolithic uniformity. This is exactly the same as the fact that however much the reciprocity of guest and host is realized, referred to as "the donkey sees the well, the well sees the donkey," it does not indicate a merging of the particularity of each and every aspect of guest and host into a false unity. Guest and host are reciprocal, yet their distinctiveness is maintained. That is to say, subjective seeing not based on anything outside of itself is manifested, as expressed by "the well sees the well, the donkey sees the donkey." The exact same realization as this occurs in terms of the passageless-passage of time. Dōgen says of this, "You must realize that there is passageless-passage without anything outside of itself."[54] He then explains, "For example, the passageless-passage of spring always makes passageless-passage in-and-through spring. Although passageless-passage is not just spring, since it is the passageless-passage of spring, *passageless-passage attains the Way now at the very time of spring.*"[55] Here, "*transforming* the Way and *transforming* the buddha" are determined by the passageless-passage of time. Therefore, however reversible time may be, in order to realize time's reversibility there must be *passageless-passage without anything outside of itself,* as expressed by "passageless-passage from today to today, and from tomorrow to tomorrow." Also, there must be a *right transmission only between a buddha and a buddha,* as expressed by "There is a right transmission from past to past, from present to present, and from future to future." This indicates that the passageless-passage of time is fully realized only when the total dynamism of time is grasped, such that not only is the irreversibility of time seen as reversible, but each and every aspect of time is seen as making passageless-passage in and of itself without anything outside of itself.

DYNAMISM OF IMPERMANENCE-BUDDHA-NATURE

Above, the spontaneous manifestation of being and the passageless-passage of time were discussed separately. But these originally are just two aspects of one and and the same truth of being-time. As previously discussed, the truth of being-time cannot be realized apart from the standpoints of the oneness of practice and attainment, the unceasing circulation of continuous practice, or self-fulfilling samadhi. These standpoints are also inseparable from the standpoints of the Self that has cast off body-mind, the Self prior to the universe sprouting any sign of itself, or the Self prior to the *kalpa* of the great void. In that case, we have two dynamisms. One is the dynamism of the spontaneous manifestation of being, in which the reciprocity of guest and host, called "the donkey sees the well, the well sees the donkey," is founded on the subjective awakening to the distinctiveness of guest and host, called "the well sees the well, the donkey sees the donkey." The other is the dynamism of the passageless-passage of time, in which the complete reversibility of time, called "passageless-passage from yesterday to today, and from today to tomorrow, as well as from tomorrow to today, and from today to yesterday," is realized through the passageless-passage of each and every time not based on anything outside of itself, called "passageless-passage from yesterday to yesterday, from today to today, and from tomorrow to tomorrow." These two dynamisms (the dynamism of the spontaneous manifestation of being and the dynamism of the passageless-passage of time) are equally grounded on the dynamism of the standpoint of the oneness of practice and attainment, or the Self that has cast off body-mind.

The standpoint of the oneness of practice and attainment is realized when practice and attainment are grasped in their inseparable identity. This cannot mean, however, that practice and attainment are a direct identity unmediated by the realization of some negation. Rather, as the oneness of practice and attainment was realized through the overcoming of young Dōgen's doubt concerning original awakening, attainment as ground and practice as condition form a nonduality, or oneness, mediated through the realization of no-Buddha-nature or impermanence-Buddha-nature. As Dōgen says, "Thus, even while one is directed to practice, he is told not to anticipate realization apart from practice";[56] the time of practice is only for diligent practice without any anticipation of attainment beyond practice itself. It is only practice practicing practice. Dōgen also says, "At the time of attainment, attainment spontaneously manifests itself as attainment without obstruction."[57] The time of attainment is only attainment, and practice is not a prerequisite to attainment. It is only attainment attaining attainment. In this way, the absolute nature of both practice and attainment is clearly realized. Referring to the spontaneous manifestation of being, this corresponds to the distinctiveness of guest and host, expressed as "the well sees the well, the donkey sees the donkey." And referring to the passageless-passage of time, this corresponds to passageless-passage not based on any thing outside itself, expressed as "passageless-passage from today to today, and from tomorrow to tomorrow." The oneness of practice and attainment is established precisely when attainment is realized conforming to the absolute nature of practice, and practice is realized conforming to the absolute nature of attainment. Here is the dynamism of the oneness of practice and attainment as expressed by the passage "As it is *already* realization in practice, realization is endless; as it is practice in realization, practice is beginningless."[58] We can say that without the realization of this dynamic oneness of practice and attainment, the reciprocating nature of guest and host in terms of being, and the reversibility of past, present, and future in terms of time, cannot be realized.

For Dōgen, the dynamism of the oneness of practice and attainment is deeply based on the realization of impermanence-Buddha-nature. As mentioned before, Dōgen strongly rejects the standpoint of being-Buddha-nature while emphasizing whole-being Buddha-nature.

> How could all sentient beings be Buddha-nature? How could they have a Buddha-nature? If a sentient being were to have a Buddha-nature, he would belong with the devil-heretics.... Since Buddha-nature is just Buddha-nature, sentient beings are just sentient beings.[59]

Here we see the absolute quality of the Buddha-nature as Buddha-nature, and the absolute quality of sentient beings as sentient beings. To directly connect Buddha-nature and sentient beings is to belong with the devil-heretics. Futher, Dōgen quotes the words of Po-chang in rejecting no-Buddha-nature along with being-Buddha-nature:

> To preach that sentient beings have Buddha-nature is to disparage Buddha, Dharma, and Sangha. To preach that sentient beings have no Buddha-nature is also to disparage Buddha, Dharma, and Sangha.[60]

What is Dōgen's own standpoint? Nothing other than the standpoint of impermanence-Buddha-nature as in "impermanence is itself Buddha-nature." Dōgen says:

> Therefore, the very impermanency of grass and trees, thicket and forest, is itself the Buddha-nature. The very impermanency of men and things, body and mind, is the Buddha-nature. Nations and lands, mountains and rivers are impermanent because they are Buddha-nature.[61]

He goes on to say:

> Supreme and complete enlightenment, because it is the Buddha-nature, is impermanent. Great nirvāna, because it is impermanent, is the Buddha-nature.[62]

How surprising these words are! Dōgen says that enlightenment (*satori*) is impermanent because it is Buddha-nature; nirvāna is the Buddha-nature *because* it is the impermanent. The dynamism of Dōgen's subjective realization reaches the fullest point here. The dynamism of the Self that contains all of universal space and universal time is none other than the dynamism of impermanence-Buddha-nature. Therefore, both the dynamism of the complete and spontaneous manifestation of being and the dynamism of the complete passageless-passage of time attain this dynamism of impermanence-Buddha-nature.

The realization of impermanence-Buddha-nature covers limitless universal space and penetrates limitless universal time. Each and every thing in universal space and each and every moment in universal time cannot be separated from this realization. There is not one thing that is not turned in terms of impermanence-as-it-is-Buddha-nature and Buddha-nature-as-it-is-impermanence based upon this realization:

> All kinds of beings [all the particularities of existence] which are being-time in darkness and light [the invisible and visible worlds] are the spontaneous manifestation and passageless-passage of *my* utmost exertion. You should realize that without *my* utmost exertion at this very moment, there would be neither the spontaneous manifestation nor the passageless-passage of a single dharma or a single thing.[63]

This is precisely the world in which the dynamism of impermanence-is-itself-Buddha-nature unfolds. The world of creation takes place based upon the spontaneous manifestation of *my* utmost exertion and the passageless-passage of *my* utmost exertion. The *Self* in this sense is not the ordinary self (the self-centered self). It is the self-liberating Self that has extricated itself from self-centeredness, the Self of the casting off of body-mind. Or, to put it another way, it is the Self prior to the universe sprouting any sign of itself or the Self prior to the *kalpa* of the great void. Each and every thing and each and every time of the universe can be neither spontaneously manifested nor making passageless-passage without the "utmost exertion" of the Self prior to the universe sprouting any sign of itself, or the Self prior to the *kalpa* of the geat void. We must, however, not forget that this Self is directly the Self that at this very moment is "one person pacticing zazen at one time." In this regard, Dōgen also says, "The rotation of east, west, north, and south is the arising and dissolution of this very Self."[64] And again, "This very moment of being-time in myself is itself being-time."[65]

This is, at the same time, the world of self-fulfilling samadhi and the world of the spontaneous manifestation of true suchness (*genjōkōan*). In this world, turning the mountains, rivers, and the great earth into the Self as well as turning the Self into the mountains, rivers, and the great earth takes place.[66] It is also expressed as, "We cause the mountains, rivers, earth, sun, moon, and stars to practice and conversely the mountains, rivers, earth, sun, moon, and stars cause us to practice."[67] This is the world of the nonobstruction of things and things that "is turning both self and other."[68] Dōgen also says:

> Even if there is resolve, practice, and attainment for a *mere instant,* this very mind itself is the Buddha; even if there is resolve, practice, and attainment in an infinitesimal entity, this very mind itself is the Buddha; even if there is resolve from immeasurable *aeons ago,* this very mind itself is the Buddha.[69]

Also:

> The mountains and waters of this very moment are the manifestations of the Way of the primordial Buddha.... Because they are active prior to the kalpa of the great void, they are alive at this very moment.[70]

Time freely makes passageless-passage transcending the unidirectionality of past, present, and future and directly realizing an identity of the present moment and eternity. This is the world of the nonobstruction of times and times. If we speak from within the standpoint of the spontaneous manifestation of being-time, this has to be said:

> The complete realization of all times as all beings leaves no dharma left over.[71]

The nonobstruction of times and times in limitless universal time as it is, is *fully realized* as the nonobstruction of things and things in limitless universal space. Outside of this there is not one other thing left over. In the dynamism of the Self, the nonobstruction of things and things and the nonobstruction of times and times are identical and result in one single nonobstruction. This is the truth of impermanence-Buddha-nature, expressed by "Impermanence is itself the Buddha-nature." The world of being-time realizes that the nonobstruction of things and things itself is the nonobstruction of times and times, and the nonobstruction of times and times is the nonobstruction of things and things. This is the world of creation in the deepest sense.

The world in which we live is the world of the spontaneous manifestation of true suchness. It is the world making passageless-passage at this very moment. It is always the world of impermanence, but because it is ever impermanent, it is an ever-creative world.

Appendix: Dōgen's View of the Interpenetration of the Three Tenses of Time—a Further Clarification

Past, present, and future are clearly different modes of time and are usually understood to move unidirectionally from past though present to future. At this point, however, we must ask ourselves, Where do we stand when we understand time in this way? From what perspective do we talk about the different modes of past, present, and future? Do we not stand somewhat outside of time in talking about three different tenses of time and the unidirectional movement from past through present to future? Are we not objectifying and thereby conceptualizing time in a way severed from concrete and direct experience? Such a view must be said to represent an unreal understanding of time based on objectification and conceptualization. In reality, as we talk about past, present, and future as three different tenses moving unidirectionally, we are always and fundamentally standing *in the present*. Apart from the present, we have no foothold to stand upon.

This present, however, is not a present tense merely considered to stand side by side or parallel with past and future, that is, the present in the relative sense. Rather, it is the present in the absolute sense in that it embraces past, present, and future from their deeper basis. It is not the present seen before us objectively, but the present in which we are existentially living. In living reality, past is realized as past in the "present," present is realized as present in the "present," and future is realized as future in the "present." This "present" is not a temporal present but a transtemporal present. We can thus distinguish two levels of temporality. When Dōgen discusses passageless-passage from today to today, he is referring to this transtemporal present, and when he discusses passageless-passage from, for instance, today to tomorrow, he is referring to the temporal present and temporal future. Elsewhere (in chapter 4), I call the dimension of transtemporal present encompassing all three tenses from their deeper basis the "vertical dimension" of time, and the dimension of temporal past, present, and future moving unidirectionally, the "horizontal dimension" of time.

Once we realize the passageless-passage from today to today in the vertical dimension, naturally we also realize the passageless-passage from yesterday to yesterday as well as the passageless-passage from tomorrow to tomorrow. This is because the realization of absolute now (*nikon*), the interpenetrating foundation that makes possible the passageless-passage from today to today, opens up completely the vertical dimension of time as such. This dimension encompasses, and therefore refers equally, to any particular point of the horizontal dimension of time regardless of how it appears to be separate from other tenses. The horizontal dimension of time indicates the extension of time, whereas the vertical dimension of time signifies the depth of time. We are always living at the intersection of the horizontal and the vertical dimensions, that is, between temporality and transtemporality. *Nikon*, the absolute now, is nothing but the now realized at this intersection.

How is the bottomless depth of the vertical dimension of time opened up? It occurs by cutting through the horizontal dimension of time in terms of the concentrated meditative practice of zazen. This cutting through involves the complete negation of the egocentric self, that is, the casting off of body-mind. And this, in turn, implies a realization of the beginninglessness and endlessness of time that exists even in the horizontal dimension. Through the negation of the egocentric self and the clear realization of the beginninglessness and endlessness of time, one can then transcend the horizontal dimension of time and jump into the vertical depth of time whereby one awakens to absolute nothingness as the true Self. As the horizontal dimension of time is now seen without particular beginning or end, the vertical dimension of time is a depth without a particular bottom. As a bottomless depth it cannot be objectified, but can be reached only nonobjectively through the existential realization of no-self, which is indeed the true Self. This true Self as no-self is qualitatively different from the ego-self. Based on its own self-centered preoccupations and fixations, the ego-self makes a fixed distinction between past, present, and future in the horizontal dimension, and tends to see their movement simply as a matter of unidirectionality and irreversibility. However, the true Self, which Dōgen calls "the Self prior to the universe sprouting any sign of itself," is prior to time and space and thus embraces and manipulates past, present, and future from its bottomless depth—from the absolute present, *nikon*.

Since, in *nikon*, time is realized as completely beginningless and endless from the bottomless depth, all times are understood not simply as moving unidirectionally but as interpenetrating each other in all possible directions without obstruction. This is why Dōgen talks about movement from tomorrow to today, from today to yesterday, as well as from yesterday to today and from today to tomorrow. This complete interpenetration of the three tenses of time is possible in the horizontal dimension of time only in and through the realization of the true Self as no-self, which is identical with the nonobjectifiable bottomless depth of the vertical dimension of time. Although past, present, and future are distinctively different tenses of time in the horizontal dimension, once they are grasped in light of the absolute present that is realized at the bottomless depth of the vertical dimension of time, they come to be understood not only to move forwardly but also to move backwardly. Thus they are reciprocal and even reversible. In other words, with the realization of no-self at the absolute present as the pivotal point, past and future are realized in terms of their mutuality and interpenetration, that is, their reciprocity and reversibility.

Let me explain this point in regard to concrete experience as seen in Christianity. Repentance, or *metanoia*, is an important religious practice in Christianity. If we give up our will completely in our heartfelt repentance and stay open to God's will by saying, "Not as I will, but as Thou will" (Matthew 26:39), we may be redeemed from our past sinful deed. Of course, this does not mean that our past deed becomes undone. The past deed was completed as it was, and it cannot be taken away. But the meaning of that past deed for our present life may be changed dramatically through our repentance and God's forgiveness. This means that the present deeply affects the past retrospectively.

I have commented elsewhere on the relation between previous action and current redemption:

At this point some may say that it is only a change of meaning, not a change of fact, that is merely a cognitive change and not a real change. We must ask ourselves at this point, however, if there are any pure facts apart from a certain meaning for us. Meaning and fact are inseparable in our actual life. A sheer fact devoid of meaning is an abstract idea, not a real fact. Accordingly, we can say with justification that through our repentance and God's forgiveness the meaning of our past deed to our life at this moment may be retroactively changed. Our past deed is now regrasped in light of God's forgiveness. Otherwise, such a religious practice as repentance or *metanoia* is either meaningless or self-deception.[72]

Our repentance and God's forgiveness take place not in the horizontal dimension of time but in the vertical, or transtemporal, dimension of time that is opened up by entering into the I–Thou relation, that is, the divine–human relationship. Further, in Christianity repentance in the present is oriented by anticipation of the last judgment at the end of history. The futural end of history is not only a goal that one hopes will be reached eventually, but the finality of the *eschaton* that orients present and past in light of the last judgment. In this manner we can see a sort of interpenetration between past, present, and future in Christianity.

In Buddhism, however, we see an even more radical form of the interpenetration of the three tenses. This is because, unlike Christianity, Buddhism has no notion of God, the ruler, working beyond or behind the process of history—no notion of one God, but the realization of absolute nothingness or emptiness on the vertical, transtemporal dimension as the basis of karma and transmigration.

The Buddhist notions of karma, volitional act or deed, and transmigration through the cycles of existence originated in the pre-Buddhist Hindu tradition. The Hindu view of karma is largely deterministic, or fatalistic, in that one's past deed, for good or evil, determines one's way of existence in the present and future as well. Although he accepted the traditional notion of karma, Gautama Buddha is primarily concerned with how to be emancipated from karma and transmigration. The Buddha teaches the doctrine of *anātman*, no-self, which emphasizes that the notion of an enduring or substantial self as the agent of karma is an unreal illusion, and that we must awaken to nonsubstantiality, or the utter lack of own-being of the ego-self. If we awaken to the truth of no-self at this present moment, we can be emancipated from the deterministic power of karma and can be creative toward the future. Karma in Buddhism is both conditional and generative. As D. T. Suzuki once stated:

> Our present life is the result of the karma accumulated in our previous existence, and yet in our practical life the doctrine of karma allows in us all kinds of possibilities and all chances of development.[73]

Although karma works deterministically on the horizontal dimension of time, once the vertical, or transtemporal, dimension is opened up as one awakens to the truth of no-self, that person is no longer a slave to karma but becomes its master. This means that on the basis of the realization of the true self as no-self at the bottomless depth of the vertical dimension of time, the present act can emancipate one's self from past karma and create new karma that will affect the future as, for instance, in the form of a vow. Consider the Four Great Vows of Mahayana:

> However innumerable the beings are, I vow to save them;
> However inexhaustible the passions are, I vow to extinguish them;
> However immeasurable the Dharmas are, I vow to master them;
> However incomparable the Buddhist truth is, I vow to attain it.

The vows referring to the future orient our present life and give new meaning to the past. But some may feel that an arrogance is implied here, because the vows to save *innumerable* beings and to extinguish *inexhaustible* passions seem unrealistic or unattainable for us as finite beings. Such vows may appear arrogant and unreachable if they are pronounced from within the framework of finite time. However, as stated before, in Buddhism time is understood to be without beginnning and without end, and the beginninglessness and endlessness of time on the horizontal dimension must be clearly realized in order to open up the vertical and transtemporal dimension and to awaken to no-self, which is the true Self. Since Buddhism has no notion of one God as the ruler of history, and time is understood as without beginning and end, past, present, and future are realized to be completely interpenetrating, as exemplified by the Buddhist teachings of the emancipation from karma. Seen from the standpoint of a master of karma liberated from fixation with only the horizontal view of time, the vows are not arrogant. They reflect the highest and most sublime aspirations of one who realizes that his or her enlightenment interpenetrates with the aspirations of all beings at all times.

In Dōgen's thought the interpenetration of past, present, and future as understood in the Buddhist awakening to no-self is precisely talked about in terms of *kyōryaku*, passageless-passage, and *fuden no den*, transmission of nontransmission. The passagelessness or nontransmission that is realized at the bottomless depth of absolute nothingness in the vertical dimension of time makes possible a reciprocal and reversible passage or transmission of the three tenses experienced in the horizontal dimension without losing the distinctiveness of past, present, and future. In Dōgen's notion of *uji* (being-time), the complete interpenetration of each moment of *time* without hindrance is just another aspect of the complete interpenetration of each *being* without hindrance. And for Dōgen, the reality of *uji* is realized by the true Self, or the self-liberating Self who has broken through time and space through the casting off of body-mind and who has realized the oneness of practice and attainment. For Dōgen, the true Self is realized at this very place and at this very moment (*nikon*).

As stated before, the interpenetration of past, present, and future is realized in Christianity as well in terms of the practice of repentance, or *metanoia*. Fundamentally speaking, however, Christianity is future oriented, being more concerned with the whither (*telos*) of history than the whence (origin) of history, because the realm of history itself is understood as divine providence in which the will of God is to be finally fulfilled. For Christianity history is a forward movement in which the interpenetration of past, present, and future is allowed to occur to a certain—though not to a complete—degree through the mercy of God.

On the other hand, Buddhism is more concerned with the whence (origin) of time and history than the whither (*telos*) of time and history, as seen in a typical Zen question, "What is your original face before your parents were born?" and in Dōgen's emphasis on the self as "the Self prior to the universe sprouting any sign of itself." In Buddhism, however, the whence (origin) of time and history is not understood to be merely a counterpart to the whither (*telos*) in the horizontal dimension of finite time. It is the whence (origin) not in the temporal sense but in the transtemporal, ontological (or vertical) sense, in that it is the whence that is beyond the very distinction between whence and whither in the temporal sense.[74] This is because, as repeatedly stated, in Buddhism time is understood as completely beginningless and endless, and there is no sense of God as the ruler of the universe and history. Instead, everything, including beginning and end, and past and future, is interdependent, that is, coarising and coceasing in terms of the law of *pratitya-samutpāda* (dependent origination). Accordingly, Buddhism is neither past-oriented nor future-oriented but absolute-present-oriented. Thus the interpenetration of past, present, and future is fully realized by "the Self prior to the universe sprouting any sign of itself" at this very place and at this very moment (*nikon*).

IV

The Problem of Time
in Heidegger and Dōgen

INTRODUCTION

The intention of this essay is to clarify the affinities and differences in the views of time of Martin Heidegger and Dōgen. Martin Heidegger is no doubt one of the most original and profound thinkers in our century. Overcoming the whole history of Western metaphysics as the history of the "Forgottenness of Being" (*Seinsvergessenheit*),[1] Heidegger tries to open up a new horizon of thinking in which the meaning of Being as such (*Sein als solches*) is disclosed through the realization of Nothingness. In his earlier work, *Sein und Zeit*, he did so by analyzing Dasein (human existence) and its anxiety in the face of death, and emphasizing temporality as the essential nature of human existence. In his later writings, although a significant turn (*Kehre*) from the earlier work cannot be overlooked, the problem of Being (*Seinsfrage*) is persistently investigated, and the nature and meaning of time is continuously scrutinized in connection with the problem of Being.

Dōgen is a Zen master in medieval Japan who, although traditionally credited as the founder of Japanese Sōtō Zen, concerned himself not with the establishment of any new sect but rather with the return to the Buddha Dharma (Buddhist truth) originally awakened to and expounded by Gautama Buddha. He does so not only by criticizing all existing forms of Buddhism in Japan as inauthentic, but also by radically reinterpreting the traditional understanding of Mahayana Buddhist scriptures and teachings. In this attempt, the problem of time constitutes one of his serious concerns, for the impermanency, or transiency, of humans and nature and its overcoming were the central issues for his philosophy and religion.

In Heidegger's thought, Being and time are inseparable. In what way they are inseparable is an issue that must be clarified, especially because Heidegger's thinking changes significantly from his early work, *Sein und Zeit* (*Being and Time*), to his later work, particularly his lecture "Zeit und Sein" ("Time and Being"). On the basis of this understanding of the inseparability of Being and time, Heidegger tries to overturn radically the whole history of Western metaphysics and return to Being as such as the ultimate Reality that has been obscured for many centuries by "metaphysical" thinking. Dōgen, on the other hand, as early as in thirteenth-century Japan, also emphasized the inseparability of Being and time in terms of *uji,*[2] that is, "being-time," though from a different angle. How Dōgen understands the inseparability of Being and time, and what he means by *uj,* must be also elucidated. At any rate, it is undeniable that although Heidegger and Dōgen lived in entirely different geographical areas and different historical ages with different spiritual backgrounds, Western and Buddhist, there is a striking similarity in their emphasis on the inseparability of Being and time. At the same time it is equally important to see the subtle yet essential differences between them in this regard. Accordingly, the clarification of the affinities and differences in the views of time of Heidegger and Dōgen would contribute something important to the ongoing East–West encounter and dialogue by virtue of which we are trying to deepen our understanding of humans and the world.

HEIDEGGER AND THE PROBLEM OF DEATH

What separates Heidegger from traditional Western philosophy and brings him much closer to Buddhist thinking is his emphasis on the problem of death as the essential issue for understanding human existence and Being. With the notable exception of Plato, who, in his depiction of the death of Socrates, talks about the immortality of the soul after physical death and emphasizes "practicing dying," while living, as the supreme task for the philosopher, the problem of death in the Western philosophical tradition had been almost completely neglected or at least has been regarded as a secondary issue for humans.[3] This can be well illustrated by Spinoza, who states that "a free man thinks of nothing less than of death, and his wisdom is not a meditation upon death, but upon life."[4] Although influenced by Kierkegaard and Nietzsche, in spite of them Heidegger takes the problem of death most seriously in the Western philosophical tradition and grasps human existence as being-unto-death (*Sein zum Tode*).[5] In his inauguration lecture, "Was ist Metaphysik?," given at Freiburg University in 1929, Heidegger defines Dasein as "Being held out into Nothingness" (*Hineingehaltenheit in das Nichts*).[6] His fundamental experience is that of Nothingness, "*eine Grunderfahrung des Nichts.*" He emphasizes that "anxiety (*Angst*) reveals the Nothing (*das Nichts*),"[7] and the greatest anxiety is the anxiety before death. In Heidegger, only through the fundamental experience of Nothingness can one go beyond and transcend the totality of beings and arrive at Being itself. In other words, only through the fundamental experience of Nothingness does Being reveal itself. This is perhaps the reason why Heidegger talks about the "clear night of the Nothing of anxiety" (*die helle Nacht des Nichts der Angst*)[8] rather than "the dark night of the Nothingness of anxiety."

In Heidegger, time is called the "preliminary name" (*Vorname*) of Being,[9] because for him Being is always comprehended in the purview of time. In *Sein und Zeit,* fundamental ontology is the ontological analysis of Dasein, which analyzes Dasein in terms of temporality and interprets Being in terms of the transcendental horizon of time. The core of Heidegger's fundamental experience is a primordial experience of time in being-unto-death. Dasein is not merely in time, but exists temporally. The temporality of Dasein is nothing but one's own way of being revealed in being-unto-death. The primordial experience of time is not realized by the change of times, nor by the transiency of myriad things, but is appropriated only through the encounter with one's own death. One's own being reveals itself as temporality, and such temporality is time itself, or fundamental time. In other words, time is the fundamental structure of Dasein by virtue of which you "become what you are" (*Werde, was du bist*)[10] through the encounter with death.

In his later writings Heidegger talks about the "fourfold" (*Geviert*),[11] which itself is gathered into original simplicity and One-ness. In this fourfold, four aspects of Being—earth, sky, gods, and mortals—mirror each other. Yet in this mutual mirroring each is properly itself. "This event of mirroring [each other] liberates each unto its own proper self, yet binds what is thus liberated in the One-ness of their essential mutuality."[12] And it is precisely in this fourfold that mortals, that is, human beings, dwell. While animals simply stop living (verenden), human beings alone, properly speaking, can die, for "to die" means to be able to know death as death. Human existence is the domain of the mortal simply because mortals are capable of death as death (den Tod als Tod vermögen).[13] For Heidegger, however, mortals are understood in a manner free of the conception of the human being as the rational living being. Mortals must die the death of a rational living being. They must die the death of the transcendental will as the basis of Erleben—the strengthening or intensification of life. This is the reason why Heidegger states that "the rational living beings must first become mortals."[14] This does not, however, mean that rational living beings exist separately from mortals simply because the mortals' mortality reveals itself. Mortals fundamentally dwell within the fourfold. This is the place of gathering and the death of the transcendental will functioning at the base of the rational unity of "living being" and "reason," which includes even the will to power in the Nietzschean sense. Referring to the deaths of mortals in the fourfold, Heidegger states that "death is the shrine of Nothing.... As the shrine of Nothing death harbors within itself the perceiving of Being"[15] Death is not any "being" whatsoever, but the shrine of Nothing that manifests the mystery of Being itself.

Throughout the long history of Western metaphysics, *death as death* has never been questioned on its own terms. Rather, death has always been regarded from a perspective other than death—for instance, from the perspective of the immortality of the soul (Plato), or from that of the will of God (Christianity) or pure practical reason (Kant) or the will to power (Nietzsche). It is Heidegger who, for the first time in Western history, grasps death not from any perspective other than death but precisely as death by saying that mortals are capable of death as death and that death is the shrine of Nothing.

DŌGEN AND THE PROBLEM OF DEATH

For Dōgen, as well, the problem of death is the most serious one. He emphasizes that "clarifying birth, clarifying death, is the matter of greatest importance for a Buddhist."[16] From the outset Buddhism regards death (*marana*) as one of the four types (also including birth, old age, and sickness) of the suffering or dissatisfaction (*dukkha*) that characterize human existence. The four marks of Dharma that distinguish Buddhism from other faiths are that (1) all conditioned things are impermanent, (2) all things are nonsubstantial, without "self-being," (3) all existences are characterized by suffering, and (4) nirvāna is quiescence. Nirvāna, the goal of Buddhist practice, is attained by the full realization of impermanency and nonsubstantiality of all things. In addition to these basic Buddhist teachings, Dōgen was deeply impressed by the impermanence of humans and the world, due to the tragedies he personally experienced. At the age of two Dōgen lost his father, and at the age of seven, his mother. According to the traditional biography of Dōgen, *Kenzeiki*, as he watched the smoke ascending from the incense at his mother's funeral service, he was profoundly moved by the transiency of human life and the impermanence of all things in the universe.[17] It was this awareness of impermanence and death that moved him to seek the Way and made him determined to enter the Buddhist monkhood. For Dōgen the lucid understanding of life and the thorough penetration into death, which is possible only on the basis of a total understanding of the meaning of impermanence and death, was the alpha and omega of religion.[18] It is through this realization of the impermanence of everything in the universe that Dōgen came to be concerned with the problem of time as well as the problem of Buddha-nature.

To understand Dōgen's view of life and death properly, we must clearly notice the following four points. First, for Dōgen, as for Buddhism in general, life and death or birth and death are not two different entities, but are inseparably interconnected in human reality. This is why, in the "Shōji" ("Birth and Death") fascicle of his *Shōbōgenzō*, Dōgen emphasizes that "it is a mistake to think you pass from birth to death."[19] To view life as passing from birth to death is nothing but an outsider's view in which we observe our own life and death objectively and conceptually from without. If we grasp our life and death not from the outside but nonobjectively from within, we realize that life and death are not two different things, but rather that we are living and dying at one and the same time. In this nonconceptual, existential understanding, there is no living apart from dying and there is no dying apart from living. Living and dying are like two sides of one sheet of paper, and are two different verbal expressions of one and the same reality. Usually, however, people are not clearly aware of this human reality and think that they pass from birth to death. Since such an unreal understanding of human reality is the cause of suffering, Buddhism strongly admonishes us to be aware of this human reality of living-dying transmigration as samsara, the realization of which is essential to attain nirvāna.

Not only in Dōgen in particular, but also in Buddhism in general, samsara is understood to be without beginning and without end. At the same time, in samsara, living-dying is taking place at each and every moment. In fact, at each and every moment, we are fully living and fully dying. Since samsara is the beginningless and endless process of living-dying at each moment, it itself is realized as Death in the absolute sense. If one existentially realizes the beginningless and endless process of samsara itself as real Death *at this moment,* this realization of samsara as real Death turns into the realization of nirvāna as real Life. This is why Dōgen says, "You must realize birth-and-death is in and of itself nirvāna. Buddhism has never spoken of nirvāna apart from birth-and-death."[20] The beginningless and endless living-dying transmigration (samsara) constitutes the basic problem innate in human existence. In and through the clear existential realization of the beginninglessness and endlessness of transmigration at this moment, the emancipation from transmigration (nirvāna) is attained. Accordingly, the realization of the beginninglessness and endlessness of transmigration is a turning point from samsara (problem) to nirvāna (its solution).

Second, however, in Dōgen the above-quoted statement from "Shōji," "It is a mistake to think you pass from birth to death," is emphasized also because life (or birth) is absolute life (or birth) and death is absolute death. There is utterly no passage between them, as can be seen from the statements immediately following the quotation cited above:

Being *a situation of [timeless-] time (hitotoki no kurai),* birth is already possessed of before and after. For this reason, in the Buddha Dharma it is said that birth itself is no-birth. Being *a situation of [timeless-] time* as well, cessation of life also is possessed of before and after. Thus it is said, extinction itself is nonextinction. When one speaks of birth, there is nothing at all apart from birth. When one speaks of death, there is nothing at all apart from death. Therefore, when birth comes, you should just give yourself to birth; when death comes, you should give yourself to death. Do not hate them. Do not desire them.[21] [Italics added]

The same idea is clearly stated in another important fascicle, "Genjōkōan":

Once firewood turns to ash, the ash cannot turn back to being firewood. Still one should not take the view that it is ash *afterward* and firewood *before.* You should realize that although firewood is *at the dharma-situation* of firewood, and that this is possessed of before and after, the firewood is beyond before and after. Ashes are *at the dharma-situation* of ashes, and possess before and after. Just as firewood does not revert to firewood once it has turned to ash, man does not return to life after his death. In light of this, it being an established teaching in Buddhism not to speak of life becoming death, Buddhism speaks of the unborn. It being a confirmed Buddhist teaching that death does not become life, it speaks of nonextinction. Life is *a situation of [timeless-] time* and death is *a situation of [timeless-] time,* like, for example, winter and spring. We do not suppose that winter becomes spring, or say that spring becomes summer.[22]

For Dōgen, *in reality* there is no "becoming" from firewood to ash, from winter to spring, and likewise, from birth to death. This notion of "becoming" is a human projection based on the conceptualization and objectification of the relationship of the two items involved. The relationship of the two items so conceptualized and objectified in terms of becoming is an unreal, conceptual construction projected from outside. In the nonconceptual and nonobjective understanding of firewood and ash from within themselves, one should say in the manner of Dōgen:

Although firewood is possessed of before and after, it is beyond before and after (*zengo saidan seri*): although ash is possessed of before and after, it is beyond before and after.

Dōgen calls this reality "firewood being at the dharma-situation [*hōi ni jūsu*] of firewood" and "ash being at the dharma-situation of ash." Exactly the same thing can be stated of birth and death. Birth is already possessed of before and after, but, being beyond before and after, birth itself is called "no-birth"; death (cessation of life) is possessed of before and after, but, being beyond before and after, death itself is called "nonextinction."

In this regard, Dōgen also states that life (birth) is a situation of (timeless-) time and death is a situation of (timeless-) time.

DŌGEN'S VIEW OF EMANCIPATION

The third point in clarifying Dōgen's understanding of life and death deals with the question, How do these two apparently contradictory actualities—that life (or birth) and death are simultaneously nondual and absolutely distinct—go together? What does Dōgen mean by "being at a dharma-situation" (hōi ni jūsu) and "being a situation of (timeless-) time" (hitotoki no kurai)? It is through breaking through, or emancipation (tōdatsu) from, life and death, or through the casting off of body-mind (shinjin-datsuraku),²³ that these two apparently contradictory existential actualities go together. And Dōgen's notions of "being at a dharma-situation" and "being a situation of (timeless-) time" indicate the "situation" of a thing that is emancipated from human conceptualization and objectification, and is realized in its own presencing (genjō).²⁴ A dharma-situation and a situation of (timeless-) time are not situations of relative character limited by time and space, body and mind, but are realized as a dharma-situation and a situation of (timeless-) time by breaking through time and space and by casting off body-mind.

As for emancipation (tōdatsu), Dōgen states in the "Zenki" ("Total Dynamic Functioning") fascicle:

'Emancipation' means that life emancipates life, and that death emancipates death. For this reason, there is deliverance from birth and death, and immersion in birth and death. Both are the Great Way totally culminated. There is discarding of birth and death, and there is saving from birth and death. Both are the Great Way totally culminated. Realization is life, life is realization. When [the Great Way] is realized, it is nothing but life's total realization, it is nothing but death's total realization.²⁵

In the total culmination of the Buddhist Way, all dualities, including the basic duality of birth and death, are completely broken through. Accordingly, from life's point of view each thing—death included—is life's total presencing; while from death's point of view each thing—life included—is death's total presencing. This is why, quoting the Chinese Zen master Yüan-wu K'o-ch'in (J. Engo Kokugon, 1063–1135), Dōgen emphasizes:

Life is the manifestation of the total dynamism [of the universe]; death is the manifestation of the total dynamism [of the universe].

As this phrase makes clear, in Zen awakening the following four aspects are included: (1) the whole universe does not hinder either life or death, because both life and death are equal manifestations of the total dynamism of the whole universe; (2) life does not impede death; death does not impede life; (3) the whole universe and its total dynamic function occur and are presencing equally within life and death; and (4) the manifestation of the whole universe's total dynamic functioning occurs within what is neither life nor death.

In this regard, (4) is especially important. For Dōgen emphasizes that both life and death are equal manifestations of the total dynamics of the universe and that life and death do not impede one another, simply because he clearly realizes through his own emancipation (*tōdatsu*) that *life is no-life* and *death is no-death*. Only through the realization of *what is neither life nor death*, that is, only through the realization of *sūnyatā*, are the unhindered mutual penetration of life and death, and their unhindered mutual penetration with the whole universe as described in (1), (2), and (3), properly grasped. A dharma-situation and a situation of (timeless-) time for each and every thing is realized in this total dynamic working of the universe.

The fourth point in Dōgen's understanding is that nirvāna is accordingly not to be realized apart from life and death. Rather, life-and-death transmigration as such, if its nonsubstantiality is clearly grasped through *tōdatsu*, is realized to be nirvāna. This is why Dōgen states:

To think that birth-and-death is something to be eliminated is a sin of hating the Buddha Dharma.[26]

For a person to seek Buddha apart from birth-and-death would be like pointing the cart thills northward when you wish to go south to Yüeh, or like facing south to see Ursa major [in the northern skies]; the cause of birth-and-death would increase all the more, and he would leave completely the Way to deliverance.[27]

Just understand that birth-and-death itself is nirvāna, and you will neither hate one as birth-and-death, nor cherish the other as being nirvāna. Only then can you be free of birth-and-death.[28]

In his writings, Dōgen repeatedly emphasizes the identity of life-and-death and nirvāna, or Buddha Dharma.

Life-and-death are the everyday practice of the Buddhist Way.[29]

Life-and-death and coming-and-going are the body of the true Person. This indicates that although the so-called life-and-death is transmigration for the unenlightened, it is the emancipation for great sages.[30]

This present birth-and-death itself is the life of Buddha. If you attempt to reject it with distaste, you are losing thereby the life of Buddha. If you abide in it, attaching to birth-and-death, you also lose the life of Buddha, and leave yourself with [only] the appearance of Buddha. You only attain the mind of Buddha when there is no hating [of birth-and-death] and no desiring [of nirvāna].[31]

In the above, I have tried to clarify Dōgen's view of life-and-death through an examination of four interrelated aspects of his religious realization: first, the nonduality of life-and-death, or birth-and-death, in terms of samsara; second, life-and-death are each absolute, as a dharma-situation and a situation of [timeless-] time; third, these two apparently contradictory aspects go together through the emancipation from, or break-ing through (tōdatsu) of, life-and-death; fourth, life-and-death (or birth-and-death) itself is the life of Buddha—samsara is nirvāna. It is precisely on the basis of this understanding of life-and-death that Dōgen discusses uji (being-time), that is, the identity of being and time. As Dōgen clearly states in the begin-ning of the "Uji" fascicle:

'Uji' [being-time] means that time, just as it is, is being, and being is all time.[32]

Being and time are completely inseparable from one another and identical in Dōgen's view. Any and every being is time, and any and every time is inseparable from being. Thus Dōgen says:

Mountains are time and seas are time. If they were not, there would be no mountains and seas. So you must not say there is no time in the immediate now [nikon] of mountains and seas. If time is destroyed, mountains and seas are destroyed. If time is indestructible, mountains and seas are indestruc-tible. Within this true dharma, the morning star comes to appear, the Tathāgata [the Buddha] comes to appear, the eye-pupils [the essence of Buddha Dharma] come to appear, the holding up of the flower comes to appear. This is time. Were it not time, things would be not-so.[33]

This identity of being and time, however, is not an identity realized objectively from the point of view of the ego-self. Nor is it an identity realized through philosophical insight. It is an identity awakened through the emancipation from, or breaking through of, all self-centeredness, that is, through the casting off of body-mind in religious practice, which for Dōgen usually means sitting meditation. It is a deeply religious awakening, yet it is not transcendent or supernatural—nothing divine, as distinguished from the human, is included. For Dōgen, the identity of being and time, that is, the "principle of *uji*," is realized by "the Self prior to the universe's sprouting any sign of itself" (*chinchō mibō no jiko*)."[34] In other words, it is realized by the true Self, which is not self. This Self that extricates itself from body and mind, from life and death, from being and nonbeing, from time and timelessness, is at once the whole universe and the whole expanse of time. This is why Dōgen emphasizes that the "Self is time,"[35] and "the whole universe throughout the ten directions itself is Self."[36] It is precisely in the awakening of this Self that the identity of time and being is legitimately and fully realized.

*   *   *

If we take *Sein und Zeit* as the point of comparison in trying to uncover the relationship between the respective understandings of Heidegger and Dōgen on the problem of death and the identity of Being and time, the considerable affinity between them is overshadowed by the unmistakable differences in their positions. When, however, we take the later Heidegger after the *Kehre*, or "turn," into account, we see much closer and more interesting similarities between them. Even so, it seems to me, there are subtle yet essential differences between Heidegger and Dōgen in their understandings of time, being, death, nothing, the world, and ultimate Reality. In the following pages, I will (1) compare Heidegger's early thought, as reflected in *Sein und Zeit*, with Dōgen's thought; (2) clarify how Heidegger turned from his early thought to that of his later period, especially as regards his understanding of Being and time; and (3) elucidate the affinities and differences between the later Heidegger and Dōgen.

EARLY HEIDEGGER AND DŌGEN

As already mentioned, unlike most Western philosophers Heidegger confronts the problem of death with utmost seriousness and grasps human existence as being-unto-death (*Sein zum Tode*). Death is understood by him to be an inescapable wall toward which Dasein rushes (*anlaufen*) and from which Dasein is thrown back (*zurückgeworfen wird*).[37] Further, death, which draws everything into Nothingness, is not understood simply as an event that happens at some point in the personal history of each Dasein, but rather characterizes the authentic way of existing of one's own Dasein (*das eigentliche "Wie" meines "Da"*).[38] Death is not only an end of Dasein in which Dasein, together with everything, expires, but it is also the beginning (*Anfang*) of Dasein, because Dasein returns to itself and can appropriate itself "authentically" only by being thrown back upon itself through its encounter with death. In this regard, there is a significant similarity between Heidegger and Dōgen, since the latter also emphasizes the realization of impermanence and death as the indispensable entryway to the attainment of the true Self.

In Heidegger, however, death is grasped from the side of Dasein as the possibility of becoming Nothing and as the possibility of making Dasein be itself authentically. In marked contrast, for Dōgen, death is not understood as the end of life in any sense, or as a *possibility* of becoming Nothing or of returning to the authentic Self, but is grasped as an *actuality* at the core of one's present existence. For Dōgen, living and dying are inseparable, and the process of living-dying (samsara) is beginningless and endless. Furthermore, we are fully living and fully dying at each and every moment. When Dōgen speaks of *shōjikorai* (coming-and-going of life-and-death), he indicates the aforementioned beginningless and endless process of living-dying. And, it is worthy to note, for Dōgen this *shōjikorai*, that is, the beginningless and endless process of living-dying (samsara), in itself is *shinjitsunintai*, that is, "the body of the true Person," which is another term for Buddha or nirvāna. Why is the beginningless and endless process of living-dying itself the body of the true Person? Why is samsara itself nirvāna? Because as noted earlier, for Dōgen (as for Buddhism in general), the beginningless and endless process of living-dying (samsara) itself is realized as Death in the absolute sense. When one existentially realizes the beginningless and endless process of samsara itself as real Death *at this present moment,* this realization of samsara as real Death turns into the realization of nirvāna as real Life. This is why, as quoted earlier, Dōgen says, "Buddhism has never spoken of nirvāna apart from life and death."³⁹ In Dōgen's view, not only life and death but also samsara and nirvāna are nondual, because all possible conceptualization and objectification, as well as the dualistic matrix that is their concomitant, are broken through (*tōdatsu*) or cast off (*datsuraku*).

On the other hand, although in the being-unto-death of the early Heidegger there occurs a kind of transformation from the Nothingness of the self to the Being of the self through Dasein's "anticipatory resoluteness" (*vorlaufende Entschlossenheit*)⁴⁰ toward death as a possibility, Being and Nothingness are divided into two by the wall named "death." For Heidegger, death is an inescapable and yet impenetrable wall that the will can neither evade nor pass beyond. Accordingly, in the final analysis, death is looked at as being "over there," not right here and now, immediately. In other words, death is objectified and represented (*vorgestellt*) and is not understood to be presencing.

Furthermore, in Heidegger's understanding, the primordial temporality of Dasein (*die ursprüngliche Zeitlichkeit des Dasein*),⁴¹ which is the temporality constituting being-unto-death, is realized in the realization of death as described above. And this primordial temporality is ecstasy (*Ekstase*), and in itself and for itself (*an sich und für sich selbst*) is "outside-of-itself" (*Aussersich*). This "standing-outside" of itself, or transcendence, opens up an ecstatic horizon in which alone Being as such reveals itself. This transcendence is essentially different from transcendence in the speculative idealism represented by Kant, Hegel, and others, since the standpoint of speculative idealism lacks an existential realization of death and nothingess. Heidegger, on the contrary, characterizes Dasein's transcendence not only in terms of being-unto-death, but also as a "holding oneself out into the nothingness" (*ein Sichhineinhalten in das Nichts*).⁴² Neverthless, strictly speaking, since in Heidegger death is to some extent grasped "over there" and objectified, the horizon opened up in Dasein's *Ekstase* is not completely free from conceptualization and objectification. For this reason, Heidegger's notion of *Ekstase* differs significantly from Dōgen's notion of *tōdatsu*, as does his usage of the concept of horizon.

For Dōgen, who cast off body-mind (*shinjin-datsuraku*) and broke through (*tōdatsu*) time and space, as mentioned earlier, it is not only that life and death do not impede one another, but also that being and time do not hinder one another. Rather, "time, just as it is, is being, and being is all time."[43] For in *tōdatsu*, all conceptualization and objectification, together with all possible *vorstellendes Denken* (representational way of thinking), is overcome. Thus Dōgen states:

> As the time right now is all there ever is, each being-time is without exception entire time. A being-grass and a being-form are both times. Entire being, the entire world, exists in time of each and every now. Just reflect: right now, is there an entire being or an entire world missing from your present time or not?[44]

Although for Heidegger the world is opened up to Dasein on the basis of *Ekstase*, that is, the ecstatic horizon in which Dasein realizes itself as "being-in-the-world" (*In-der-Welt-sein*), his thinking is limited by a phenomenological approach in his Dasein-analysis. Accordingly, time is interpreted primarily in terms of the temporality of Dasein, not in terms of the temporality of Being itself (*Sein selbst*). Further, in the presence of Dasein's anxiety in the face of death, Being reveals itself through the annihilation of the Nothing. However, the nihilation of the Nothing is still rather negative in Heidegger's thought. For in its process of presencing (*Anwesen*), *Sein* conceals itself in a negative manner even while revealing.

In marked contrast, for Dōgen:

> Nothing throughout the whole world has ever been concealed.[45]

This is because his standpoint is completely free from objectification, as can be seen in the following statements:

> The entire world is completely free of all dusts as objects to the Self. Right here, there is no second person!"[46]

> Whole-being (*shitsuu*) is in itself completely and totally emancipated suchness.[47]

> Buddha-nature is always whole-being, because whole-being is the Buddha-nature.[48]

This does not, however, mean that in Dōgen there is no notion of concealment at all. In one sense, samsara, the process of living-dying transmigration, is a total concealment of nirvāna, or Buddha-nature. From the standpoint of Dōgen's awakening, however, this total concealment in itself is a total disclosure of nirvāna. The concealment (samsara) itself is the disclosure (nirvāna). Accordingly, the above statement, "Nothing throughout the whole world has ever been concealed," does not indicate a mere disclosure, but a *complete* nonconcealment of Buddha-nature that is beyond the duality of concealment and disclosure. It is on the basis of this complete nonconcealment that Dōgen understands the identity of Being and time. In the "Uji" fascicle he states:

> Rats are time. So are tigers. Sentient beings are time, and buddhas are, too. This time realizes the entire world by being a creature with three heads and eight arms [the figure of the ashura or fighting demon, unenlightened existence in general], and realizes the entire world by being a sixteen-foot golden body [Śākyamuni Buddha in his standing attitude]. Thus, entirely worlding the entire world with the whole world (*jinkai o motte jinkai o kaijin suru*) is called penetrating exhaustively (*gūjin suru*).... One does nothing but penetrate exhaustively entire time as entire being.[49]

HEIDEGGER'S "TURN" AND DŌGEN

The point of transition from Heidegger's early period to his later one is frequently referred to as the *Kehre*, or "turn." This is most typically illustrated by the shift of focus from "Being and time" to "time and Being." This transition, however, should not be taken simply to indicate a reversal in the direction of Heidegger's point of view. As Heidegger himself states in his letter to William J. Richardson:

> The thinking of the reversal (*Kehre*) *is* a change in my thought. But this change is not a consequence of altering the standpoint, much less of abandoning the fundamental isssue of *Being and Time*.[50]

> The reversal is above all not an operation of interrogative thought; it is inherent in the very matter designated by headings: "Being and Time," "Time and Being." For this

reason, the passage cited from the "Letter on Humanism" reads "Here the Whole is reversed." "The Whole": this means the matter [involved] in "Being and time" "time and Being." This reversal is in play within the matter itself.[51]

The ecstatic-horizonal temporality delineated in *Being and Time* is not by any means already the most proper attribute of time that must be sought in answer to the Being-question.[52]

Thus we see that the turn is deeply rooted in the very matter of Being/time and centers around the problem of temporality. In other words, the turn does not indicate a reversal in direction from Being and time to time and Being with the same concept of time as an axis, but, on the contrary, points to the overcoming of a subjectivistic approach to temporality in the early work. Accordingly, the meaning that time has in the question about the meaning of Being is changed.

Time, which is addressed as the meaning of Being in *Being and Time,* is itself not an answer, not a last prop for questioning, but rather itself, the naming of a question. The name "time" is a preliminary word for what was later called "the truth of Being."[53]

In his lecture "Zeit und Sein," Heidegger himself states:

Being—a matter, but not a being.
Time—a matter, but nothing temporal.

We say of beings: they are. With regard to the matter, "Being" and with regard to the matter "time," we remain cautious. We do not say: Being is, time is, but rather: there is Being [*Es gibt Sein*] and there is time [*es gibt Zeit*]. For the moment we have only changed the idiom, with this expression. Instead of "it is," we say "there is," "It gives."[54]

The use of "It gives" to express the nature of Being and of time does not, however, simply imply a change of idiom. Rather, it indicates that which holds both Being and time toward each other and perdures through their relation. This "It gives" is named "Appropriation" (*Ereignis*).[55] Appropriation is neither Being nor time. It indicates the "and" in "Being *and* time" or "time *and* Being," because it "determines both, time and Being, in their own, that is, in their belonging together."[56]

Accordingly, the turn is not a change of the standpoint, but rather constitutes a return to the root source of Being and time.

This is the step back (*Schrittzurück*) in which the "meaning of time, as yet unthought, which lies in Being as presencing, is anchored in a still more original relation."[57]

It is difficult to find an exact equivalent of Heidegger's turn in Dōgen's thought. This is because in his experience of emancipation (*tōdatsu*), or casting off of body-mind (*shinjin-datsuraku*), which occurred at the age of twenty-six under the guidance of Chinese Zen master Ju-ching (1163–1228), Dōgen completely overcame all conceptualization and objectification and awakened to the Dharma. Herein Dōgen realized the complete nonduality of life and death, being and nothing, delusion and enlightenment, impermanency and Buddha-nature. With this fundamental experience of *tōdatsu*, Dōgen's liberation was complete. Having thus "arrived" at the goal of his religious quest, Dōgen was thereafter utterly free from any notion of being "on the way," a notion that is often emphasized by Heidegger.

In Dōgen's writings, however, there are some passages that remind us of the turn in Heidegger.

> To practice and confirm all things by conveying one's self to them, is illusion: for all things to advance forward and practice and confirm the self, is enlightenment. [Those] who greatly enlighten illusion, are buddhas. [Those] who are greatly deluded about enlightenment, are sentient beings.... When buddhas are genuinely buddhas there is no need for them to be conscious that they are buddhas. Yet they are realized buddhas, and they continue to realize buddha.[58]

> To learn the Buddha Way is to learn one's own self. To learn one's self is to forget one's self. To forget one's self is to be confirmed by all dharmas. To be confirmed by all dharmas is to effect the casting off of one's own body and mind and bodies and minds of others as well. All traces of enlightenment [then] disappear, and this traceless enlightenment is continued on and on endlessly.[59]

The phrases "to practice and confirm all things by conveying one's self to them" and "for all things to advance forward and practice and confirm the self" constitute a complete turn in the direction of approach. The former indicates an approach from the self toward things, and the latter an approach from all things toward the self. This turn, or "shift," however, is not a reversal within the same dimension. There is an essential difference of dimension between the former and the latter. The former indicates the dimension of illusion, because by an approach from the self toward things, one can know things only from his or her subjective point of view, that is, only from the outside, not from within—thus, things are not known in themselves. On the other hand, the latter signifies the dimension of enlightenment, because an approach from all things toward the self provides clear knowledge of things in themselves without any subjective distortion. To attain enlightenment, one must overcome the self-centered approach involved in the dimension of illusion and move to the all-things-centered approach. Again, to do so one must "forget one's self." This forgetting one's self is not a psychological forgetting but a total abnegation, or "death," of the ego-self. It is nothing but a breaking through (*tōdatsu*) or casting off of body-mind (*shinjin-datsuraku*).

For Dōgen, however, an approach from all things toward the self does not exclude, but rather includes, an approach from the self toward things. Unenlightened sentient beings reject an approach from all things toward the self as an illusion and take an approach from the self toward things alone as real. They are "deluded about enlightenment." On the other hand, enlightened beings, that is buddhas, take even "an approach from the self toward things" in the light of "an approach from all things toward the self." Thus they "enlighten illusion." This means that the self is "confirmed by all dharmas [things]." Accordingly, a genuinely enlightened one is not, or need not be, conscious of her or his enlightenment, because a *genuinely* enlightened one is beyond the consciousness of being enlightened. Herein, both the self and all things are truly enlightened and confirmed.

Heidegger's turn, on the other hand, is not at all a shift from the dimension of illusion to that of enlightenment. Nevertheless, it may be said to be a turn from "an approach from the self toward Being" to "an approach from Being toward the self." For, before the turn, Being is understood to be revealed primarily through the phenomenological analysis of Dasein (the human self). Whereas after the turn, by giving up the Dasein-centered approach, Being is understood to reveal itself from a deeper root source called the "Appropriation" (*Ereignis*), or the "It" that "gives." In this regard, we can see some parallel between Dōgen's emphasis on an approach from all things toward the self as opposed to an approach from the self toward things, and Heidegger's turn, in which the disclosure of Being itself is seen as more primordial than Dasein-analysis as an indispensable path toward Being. We should not, however, overlook that Being or its source—"Appropriation" (*Ereignis*) in Heidegger's thought—is not identical with the Self in Dōgen. For Dōgen, all things "advance forward and practice and confirm the self." That is, all things are in reality the Buddha-nature and true Self. This is why Dōgen emphasizes that "the whole-being is the Buddha-nature,"[60] and "the whole universe throughout the ten directions is the Self."[61]

THE LATER HEIDEGGER AND DŌGEN

The affinities and differences between the later Heidegger and Dōgen can perhaps be clarified through discussing the following four questions.

1. Is Heidegger's Thought Transanthropocentric?

The point of the epoch-making significance of Heidegger's philosophy in the history of Western thought, and the point that in turn also opens up a great common horizon with Eastern—especially Buddhist—philosophy is the attempt by Heidegger to establish his philosophy on the basis of the realization of death. Modern Western philosophy since Descartes has been an anthropocentric and subjectivistic philosophy based on reason, thinking, consciousness, sensation, experience, and the like. It is this modern philosophy of subjectivism that Nietzsche criticizes in his book, *Human, All-too-Human*. In order to disclose Being as such (*Sein als solches*), Heidegger first analyzes Dasein (human existence), because it is precisely Dasein as the ecstatic openness of Being that can enable Being to reveal itself. He thus opens up the transcendental horizon that is the temporality of Dasein. This transcendental horizon is, however, essentially different from the transcendental subjectivity of speculative idealism, because the former is realized through anxiety in the face of death, which characterizes Dasein as "being-in-the-world" (*In-der-Welt-sein*). The transcendental subjectivity of speculative idealism, on the contrary, stands somewhat outside the world without confronting the problem of death.

Here we can see the uniqueness of Heidegger's philosophy in opening up a transanthropocentric horizon in which subjectivism is transcended to some extent by situating Dasein immediately in the world. For Heidegger, the experience of anxiety in the face of death entails the experience of Being as such, an experience that is—in a way that is essentially different from the experience of beings—the disclosure of the truth (*Wahrheit*) of Being. In Heidegger, however, the transanthropocentric horizon of Being as such is opened up through the phenomenological analysis of Dasein (human existence); hence, the problems of death, nothing, horizon, and the world are grasped from the side of Dasein as being-unto-death. Here we clearly see that the anthropocentric and subjectivistic approach is not completely overcome in Heidegger in his early period.

In marked contrast, Dōgen's standpoint is entirely transanthropocentric and completely beyond subjectivism. For Dōgen as well, the human being, or the self, is the key through which openness or transcendence is possible. But the Self that is free from the ego-self (*goga*), the Self realized through emancipation (*tōdatsu*) or casting off of body-mind (*shinjin-datsuraku*), is entirely nondual with the world, as seen in the following:

> The whole universe throughout the ten directions (*jinjippōkai*) is in itself the Self; this Self is the whole universe throughout the ten directions.[62]

> The whole universe throughout the ten directions is the light (*kōmyō*) of the Self.[63]

> All the earth is in itself the Dharma Body (*hosshin*) of the Self.[64]

This nonduality of Self and world is not grasped without the realization of the particularity of individuality of the human self. On the contrary, it is precisely in Buddhist awakening that the particularity of the human self, which, unlike nonhuman beings, *knows* the inescapability of death, is clearly and fully realized. While in Heidegger the human self (Dasein) is understood as being-unto-death, or being-unto-end, and thereby life and death are realized dualistically, in Dōgen life and death are completely nondual, and the process of living-dying is understood to be without beginning and without end. With the clear, existential realization of the beginning*ness* and endless*ness* of human living-dying, the Self transcends anthropocentrism and comes to stand on the horizon of the entire universe. The problem of humans' death is thus realized as a part of the impermanency common to all beings. This means that without the existential realization of the impermanency common to all beings, the problem of the death of the Self cannot be resolved. The emancipation from or breaking through of (*tōdatsu*) life-and-death takes place only through the realization of the beginninglessness and endlessness of the process of living-dying. The complete deanthropocentrism and nonduality of the Self and the world is possible in Dōgen because, unlike for Heidegger, (1) death is not realized as a future possibility or the end of the Self, but as an actuality residing at the core of the present moment; (2) death is not a problem to be coped with by an anticipatory resoluteness (*vorlaufende Entschlossenheit*), but can be resolved only through the thoroughgoing negation—right here and now—of the dualities of life and death, past-present-future, anticipation and actualization, self and world; for Dōgen, therefore, death is a "situation" of (timeless-) time and a manifestation of the total dynamic functioning of the universe; and (3) an horizon opens up with the existential realization of death and Nothingness. Nothingness does not manifest itself *before* the Self. Rather death and Nothingness are realized thoroughly nonobjectively *as* the Self, which is attained through breaking through (*tōdatsu*) time and space and casting off body-mind (*shinjin-datsuraku*).

In the later Heidegger, however, the situation is considerably different. As already mentioned, a transition from Being and time to time and Being does not simply indicate a reversal of point of view. Indeed, as Heidegger emphasizes, "Reversal is in play within the matter itself."[65] What Heidegger means by "the matter" is neither Being nor time, but *Ereignis* (Appropriation), which "determines both, time and Being, in their own, that is, in their belonging together."[66] In this *Ereignis*, the expressions *It gives Being* and *It gives time* are more appropriate than the expressions *Being is* and *time is*, because "Being is not a thing, thus nothing temporal" and "time is not a thing, thus nothing which is."[67] And yet "it [Being] is determined by time as presence" and "it [time] remains constant in its passing away without being something temporal like the beings in time."[68] In this way, Being and time belong together and this belonging together of Being and time is nothing but *Ereignis*, or the "It gives."

Accordingly, unlike the thought of early Heidegger, in which Being is understood to reveal itself solely through the openness of Dasein as transcendental ecstasis, in the later Heidegger Being is not only realized in itself apart from Dasein, but it is also grasped from the side of *Ereignis*, which is the deeper root source of Being itself. Furthermore, as *Geviert* (fourfold) or *Gegnet* (region), *Ereignis* indicates the "world" in which each and every thing is properly itself and yet is gathered together and mirrors everything. Here we can see the deepening of the transanthropocentric approach in the later Heidegger. This deepening can be seen in Heidegger's understanding of time, as well. In *Sein und Zeit*, fundamental temporality is grasped in accordance with Dasein as the temporality of Dasein (*Zeitlichkeit des Daseins*), whereas in the later works time is primarily understood from the side of the world as a constituent of that world:

> Time *is* not. There is, It gives time. The giving that gives time is determined by denying and withholding nearness. It grants the openness of time-space and preserves what remains denied in what has-been, what is withheld in approach. We call the giving which gives true time [*die eigentliche Zeit*] an extending [*Reichen*] which opens and conceals. As extending is itself a giving, the giving of giving is concealed in true time [*in der eigentlichen Zeit*].[69]

At this juncture, we must ask ourselves, however, whether Heidegger's thought is *completely* transanthropocentric. Also, are Heidegger and Dōgen equally thoroughgoing in their deanthropocentric approach? To elucidate these questions we must examine the remaining three points:

2. Do Being and time *completely* "belong together" in Heidegger's thought?

3. Is time (past, present, and future) understood as *completely* reversible in Heidegger's thought?

4. When he speaks of *Ereignis*, where does Heidegger himself stand? Is Heidegger identical with *Ereignis* itself or not? What is the relationship between *Ereignis* and the Self?

2. Do Being and Time Completely "Belong Together" in Heidegger's Thought?

In his lecture "Zeit und Sein," Heidegger remarks:

> What prompts us to name time and Being together? From the dawn of Western-European thinking until today, Being means the same as presencing [*Anwesen*]. Presencing, presence speaks of the present [*Aus Anwesen, Anwesenheit spricht Gengenwart*]. According to current representations, the present, together with past and future, forms the character of time. Being is determined as presence by time.[70]

Nowhere among things do we find Being. Every thing has its time. But Being is not a thing, is not in time. Yet Being as presencing remains determined as presence by time, by what is temporal.[71]

The proposition "Being is determined as presence by time" is a key point in Heidegger's thought concerning the relation of Being and time. In *Sein und Zeit* this indicates "temporal determinateness" (*temporale Bestimmtheit*), which implies "the way" in which Being and its modes and characteristics have their meaning determined primordially in terms of time.[72] In his lecture "Zeit und Sein," Heidegger states:

Being and time determine each other reciprocally, but in such a manner that neither can the former—Being—be addressed as something temporal nor can the latter—time—be addressed as a being.[73]

Being *and* time, time *and* Being, name the relation of both issues, the matter at stake (*Sacherverhalt*) which *holds* both issues toward each other and endures their relation.[74]

Accordingly, this "matter at stake" (*Sachverhalt*) does not indicate a relation between Being and time in which each first exists in itself independently, but one in which Being and time originally belong together (*Zusammengehören*) even while they are properly themselves. It is precisely this *Sachverhalt* that is used to indicate *Ereignis* as the "It gives," as in the expressions *It gives Being* and *It gives time.*[75]

If, however, we carefully scrutinize Heidegger's notion of *Ereignis*, we will realize that the realization of the belonging together (*Zusammengehörigheit*) of Being and time is not carried out thoroughgoingly, and that time has priority over Being. In his lecture "Zeit und Sein," emphasizing that the expressions *It gives Being* and *It gives time* are not statements about beings, Heidegger states:

Contrary to all appearances, in saying "It gives Being," "It gives time," we are not dealing with statements that are always fixed in the sentence structure of the subject-predicate relation. And yet, how else are we to bring the "It" into view which we say when we say "It gives Being," "It gives time?" Simply by thinking the "It" in the light of the kind of giving [*aus der Art des Gebens*] that belongs to it; giving as destiny [*das Geben als Geschick*], giving as an opening up which reaches out [*das Geben als lichtendes Reichen*]. Both belong together, inasmuch as the former, destiny, lies in the latter, extending opening up.

Thus true time [*die eigentliche Zeit*] appears as the "It" of which we speak when we say: It gives Being. The destiny in which It gives Being lies in the extending of time.[76]

In these two quotations, Heidegger clearly states that the destiny (*Geschick*) in which It gives Being *lies in* the extending of time. Here we see that while Being and time belong together, "extending opening up" (*das lichtende Reichen*) has priority over destiny (*Geschick*) or presence (*Anwesenheit*): in other words, time has priority over Being. That is because, for Heidegger, the giving in "It gives time" proves to be an extending or opening up of the realm, whereas the giving in "It gives Being" means to give Being as destiny or presence. What does this priority of time over Being mean? The fact that time and Being do not completely belong together seems to me to indicate the incompleteness of the transanthropocentric approach in Heidegger's thought. For openness (*Lichtung*), which is understood to be prior to presence (*Anwesenheit*), is not possible without human existence. Although Heidegger clearly states in his lecture "Zeit und Sein" that "time is not the product of man, man is not the product of time,"[77] this statement refers to the notion of production, not the notion of giving. Insofar as the notion of "giving" is concerned, man receives time, and

> true time is the nearness of presencing out of present, past and future—the nearness that unifies time's threefold opening extending. It has already reached man as such so that he can be man only by standing within the threefold extending, perduring the denying, and withholding nearness which determines that extending.[78]

In this special sense though, time and its "extending opening up" concerns human beings. Accordingly, the priority of openness over presence, that is, the priority of time over Being, shows a trace of anthropocentrism. This is perhaps the reason why, despite his statement that "everything has time," Heidegger, unlike Dōgen, does not say "rats are time. So are tigers,"[79] and "mountains are time and seas are time."[80] It is even far less possible for him to regard "entire time as entire being,"[81] as will be explained.

Because of the incompleteness of his transanthropocentric approach and the priority of time over Being in his thought, although we can say with Heidegger—with some reservation— that Being is time, we cannot say with the same justification that time is Being. On this point, we see an essential difference between Heidegger and Dōgen in their understanding of the identity between Being and time.

In Dōgen's notion of *uji* (being-time), time is being as much as being is time, as can be seen in the previously quoted statement, "'*Uji*' means [that] time, just as it is, is being, and being is all time."[82] Although being is thoroughly being and time is thoroughly time, being and time interpenetrate one another without hindrance. Dōgen also states:

> You must see all the various things of the whole world as so many times. These things do not get in each other's way any more than various times get in the way of each other.[83]

> Entirely worlding the entire world with the whole world is called *penetrating exhaustively*. To immediately *present* the body of the sixteen-foot golden body with the sixteen-foot golden body, as the arising of the mind, as practice, as enlightenment, as nirvāna—that is being; that is time. One does nothing but penetrate exhaustively *entire time as entire being*.[84] [Italics added]

For Dōgen, in speaking of being, all things interpenetrate each other without hindrance (*muge*). In speaking of time, all moments of time interpenetrate each other without hindrance. It is, however, not that that there are two kinds of "without hindrance," or no-hindrance. No-hindrance is single and encompasses all things and all moments of time. For the Self that has broken through time and space and cast off body-mind, the interpenetration of things without hindrance and the interpenetration of times without hindrance are nondual.

To understand more clearly Dōgen's notions of *uji* and the complete interpenetration of being and time, we must clarify that each and every moment of time encompasses all time, and that it is in the true Self that the interpenetration of being and time as thus characterized is realized.

First, each and every being, and each and every moment of time, has an irreplaceable particularity. Dōgen calls it "dwelling in a Dharma-situation,"[85] or a "situation of (timeless-) time."[86] As already quoted, in the "Genjōkōan" fascicle Dōgen states:

> You should realize that although firewood is at the dharma-situation of firewood, and that this is possessed of before and after, the firewood is beyond before and after. Ashes are at the dharma-situation of ashes, and possess before and after.... Life is a situation of [timeless-] time and death is a situation of [timeless-] time...[87]

Each thing dwells in a particular dharma-situation, yet in *each* dharma-situation, which is beyond before and after, the *whole* universe is preserved. It is precisely for this reason that in speaking of life and death, while Dōgen says on the one hand that "life is a situation of [timeless-] time and death is a situation of [timeless-] time," he also says that "within life there are multitudinous things manifesting their total dynamic functioning, and within death there are multitudinous things manifesting their total dynamic functioning."[88] Dwelling at each dharma-situation and being a manifestation of the total dynamic function of multitudinous things are not contradictory but identical.

This is true not only with life and death, but with all things and all moments of time. Accordingly, firewood, while dwelling at the dharma-situation of firewood, is a manifestation of the total dynamic functioning of multitudinous things; ash, while dwelling at the dharma-situation of ash, is a manifestation of the total dynamic functioning of multitudinous things. Today, while dwelling at the dharma-situation of today, is a manifestation of the total dynamic functioning of multitudinous things; yesterday, while dwelling at the dharma-situation of yesterday, is a manifestation of the total dynamic functioning of multitudinous things. In this way each and every being and each and every moment of time, while dwelling at a particular dharma-situation, is *equally* a manifestation of the total dynamic functioning of multitudinous things. Accordingly, (a) each being does not impede any other, (b) each moment of time does not impede any other, (c) each being and each moment of time as well do not impede one another and are interpenetrating completely.

Second, such a dynamic relationship of nonhindrance concerning being and time cannot be properly realized apart from the true Self, or true Person, who, having emancipated himself or herself from life-and-death and broken through the ego-self, can now state:

> The whole universe throughout the ten directions is in itself the Self.[89]

At the time the mountain was being climbed and the river being crossed, I was there [in time]. The time has to be in me. Inasmuch as I am there, it cannot be that time passes away.[90]

The essential point is: every entire being in the entire world is, each time, an [independent] time, even while making a continuous series. In as much as they are being-time, they are *my* being-time.[91] [Italics added]

In contrast to Heidegger's thought, for Dōgen time does not have priority over Being, but Being and time are mutually and completely interpenetrating. This is called *uji*. In *uji* the transanthropocentric approach is fully achieved. This is because in Dōgen, on the basis of the Buddhist principle of the nonsubstantiality (no self-being) of everything, it is clearly realized that Being is not Being and time is not time, nor is there anything that "gives" Being and time in Heidegger's sense.

3. Is Time (Past, Present, and Future) Understood as Completely Reversible in Heidegger's Thought?

In his lecture "Zeit und Sein," Heidegger develops a very elaborate path of thinking with regard to past, present, and future. For Heidegger, "time is not a thing, thus nothing temporal, and yet it remains constant in its passing away without being something temporal like the beings in time."[92] Time is given in the sense that "It gives time." Time is presencing as present: "present" (*Gegenwart*) is nothing but presence (*Anwesenheit*), which cannot be determined in terms of the present as the now.

Presence [*Anwesenheit*] means: the constant abiding that approaches man, reaches him, is extended to him. True, man always remains approached by the presencing of something actually present without heeding presencing itself. But we have to do with absence [*Abwesen*] just as often, that is constantly.[93]

Thus it follows that not only in the "present" but also in both the "past" (*Gewesen*), that is, "what has been," and the "future" (*Zukunft*), that is, "what is to come," presencing is extended. This is why Heidegger states:

We shall find in absence—be it what has been or what is to come—a manner of presencing and approaching which by no means coincides with presencing in the sense of the immediate present. Accordingly, we must note: Not every presencing is necessarily the present. A curious matter. But we find such presencing, the approaching that reaches us, in the present, too. In the present, too, presencing is extended.[94]

Approaching, being not yet present, at the same time gives and brings about what is no longer present, the past, and conversely what has been offers future to itself. The reciprocal relation of both at the same time gives and brings about the present. We say "at the same time," and thus ascribe a time character to the mutual giving to one another of future, past and present, that is, to their own unity.[95]

This unity, or the simultaneity of future, past, and present, cannot be objectified before us. Thus Heidegger calls "the openness which opens up in the mutual self-extending of futural approach, past and present" the "time-space" (Zeit-Raum).[96] And it is in this mutual self-extending and opening up of future, past, and present that "what is germane to the time-space of true time" (das Eigene des Zeit-Raumes der eigentlichen Zeit)[97] consists. Further, Heidegger characterizes this true time by three dimensions:

Dimensionality consists in the reaching out that opens up, in which futural approaching brings about what has been, what has been brings about futural approaching, and the reciprocal relation of both brings about the opening up of the openness. Thought in terms of this threefold giving, true time proves to be three-dimensional.[98]

If the above summary of Heidegger's understanding of time, especially of the dynamic relationship of past, present, and future is not mistaken, we see a striking similarity between Heidegger and Dōgen in this regard, although Heidegger's discussion is conceptually more elaborate than that of Dōgen.

In the "Uji" fascicle, Dōgen states:

You should not come to understand that time is only flying past. You should not learn that flying away is the property inherent in time. If time were to give itself to merely flying past, it would have to have gaps. You fail to experience the passage of being-time and hear the utterance of its truth, because you are learning only that time is something that goes past.

The essential point is: every entire being in the entire world is, each time, an [independent] time, even while making a continuous series. Inasmuch as they are being-time, they are my being-time.

Being-time has the virtue of passageless-passage (*kyōryaku*): there is passageless-passage from today to tomorrow, from today to yesterday, from yesterday to today, from today to today, from tomorrow to tomorrow. This is because the passageless-passage is a virtue of time. Past time and present time do not overlap one another, or pile up in a row, yet Ching-Yüan is time, Huang-po is time. Matsu and Shih-t'ou are times too [Chinese Zen masters of T'ang dynasty]. As self and other are both times, practice and realization are times: entering the mud, entering the water [entering the world of defilements to lead the unenlightened to awakening] is equally time.[99]

When Dōgen states, "You should not come to understand that time is only flying past. You should not only learn that flying past is the property inherent in time," he may seem to be indicating the same idea as Heidegger's notion that "time is not something temporal which passes away in the course of time."[100]

And when Dōgen speaks of a passageless-passage (*kyōryaku*), one might take this for Heidegger's idea that by passing away constantly, time remains as time, and yet past, present, and future belong together in the way they offer themselves to one another. If we heed more carefully what Dōgen says, however, we will find a significant difference between Heidegger and Dōgen in their understanding of the dynamic relation of past, present, and future.

Referring to his notion of passageless-passage, Dōgen states:

There is passageless-passage from today to tomorrow, from today to yesterday, from yesterday to today, from today to today, from tomorrow to tomorrow.[101]

Exactly the same idea is stated in a more elaborate manner in the "Den'e" fascicle, which discusses the meaning of the transmission of a robe as a symbol of the Buddhist Dharma:

The robe of the right transmission of the buddhas and patriarchs is not arbitrarily transmitted from buddha to buddha. It is the robe transmitted from the former buddha to the later buddha, and from the ancient buddha to the contemporaneous buddha. In order to transform the Way, to transform the buddha, and to transform the past, present, and future, there is a right transmission from past to present, from present to future, from present to past, from past to past, from present to present, from future to future, from future to present, and from future to past. It is the right transmission only between a buddha and a buddha.[102]

In the above two quotations, Dōgen speaks not only of a reciprocal passage or transmission between past (yesterday), present (today), and future (tomorrow), but also of a passage or transmission within each specific mode of past, present, and future. I will call the reciprocal passage or transmission between past, present, and future a passage "on the horizontal dimension," and a passage or transmission within each mode of past, present, and future, a passage "on the vertical dimension." In Dōgen, a reciprocal passage or transmission on the horizontal dimension is inconceivable without a passage or transmission on the vertical dimension. For each passage or transmission within the mode of past, present, and future extends infinitely downward along the vertical dimension to reach the bottomless depth of absolute nothingness that indicates passagelessness or nontransmission. A passage from today to today is passageless, and a transmission from future to future is a nontransmission. This passagelessness or nontransmission on the vertical dimension makes a *reciprocal* passage or transmission on the horizontal dimension possible. A right transmission between a buddha and a buddha is a transmission of nontransmission. A true passage between past (yesterday), present (today), and future (tomorrow) is a passageless-passage. A reciprocal relationship between past, present, and future is possible only by virtue of this passageless-passage or transmission of nontransmission (*fuden no den*). This is the reason Dōgen states that "*uji* (being-time) has the virtue of passageless-passage." For Dōgen this passageless-passage is realized by the true Self who has broken through time and space and has cast off body-mind.

In Heidegger, we can see a reciprocal relationship between past, present, and future on the horizontal dimension, but we do not see an equivalent to Dōgen's notion of a passage—for example, from past to past—within each specific mode of past, present, and future along the vertical dimension. We are told that "true time is four-dimensional"[103] and that true time itself is the prespatial region (*die vorräumliche Ortschaft*)[104] that first gives any possible "where." These notions, however, do not imply the idea of passagelessness or nontransmission that is realized only in the bottomless depth of the vertical dimension or in absolute nothingness. Instead, for Heidegger, true time, which is four-dimensional and in the prespatial region, is none other than *Ereignis* (Appropriation), which is the "It" in "It gives Being" and "It gives time."

Furthermore, this entails another difference in their understanding of time. Dōgen's notion of passageless-passage does not necessarily exclude flying past or passing away. It does not simply negate but rather includes the irreversibility of time. Passageless-passage embraces both the flying away and the tracing back to the origin of time. Furthermore, on the basis of passageless-passage, which entails the passing-without-passage from today to today, the modes of time are realized not only as reciprocal but also as reversible. This reversibility of time is realized to include the irreversibility of time fully from the bottomless depth of the vertical dimension. In Dōgen's notion of *uji* (being-time), this complete interpenetration of each moment of *time* without hindrance is just another aspect of the complete interpenetration of each *being* without hindrance.

On the other hand, in Heidegger's notion of *Ereignis* (Appropriation), past, present, and future belong together by "the three interplaying ways of giving,"[105] and thus reciprocity of time is fully realized, but reversibility of time is not clearly grasped. This is partly because of the lack of the realization of absolute nothingness at the bottomless depth in the vertical dimension, and partly because of the absence of the clear realization of beginninglessness and endlessness of time. In Dōgen, however, these two realizations are fully actualized: hence being-time (*uji*), passageless-passage, and the complete interpenetration of each and every time and the mutual penetration between being and time without hindrance.

4. When He Speaks of Ereignis, Where Does Heidegger Himself Stand?

Is Heidegger identical with *Ereignis* itself or not? What is the relationship between *Ereignis* and the self? Before examining these questions we must clarify Heidegger's notion of *Ereignis* through the following six points.

1. *Ereignis* cannot be represented by means of the current meaning of the words *occurrence* (*Vorkommis*) or *happen-*

ing (Geschehnis).[106] The "It gives" stands for *Ereignis,* and
when Heidegger says "It gives Being" and "It gives
time," he is not making statements *(Aussagen)* about
beings that are fixed within the sentence structure of
the subject-predicate relation.[107]

2. *Ereignis* sends the destiny of Being and extends time as
   the region. It determines both Being and time into their
   own, that is, in their belonging together.

3. This should not, however, be taken to mean that *Ereignis* is the encompassing general concept under which
   Being and time could be subsumed. Rather, it means
   that "time and Being [are] appropriated in Appropriation" *(Zeit und Sein ereignet im Ereignis).*[108]

4. *Ereignis* withdraws from boundless unconcealment what
   is most fully its own.[109] Expropriation *(Enteignis)*
   belongs to *Ereignis* as such. By this expropriation, *Ereignis* does not abandon itself—rather, it preserves what is
   its own.[110] Inasmuch as the modes of giving, that is,
   sending and extending, lie in *Ereignis,* withdrawal
   (Entzug)[111] must belong to what is peculiar to *Ereignis.*

5. As Heidegger writes, "Because Being and time are there
   only in Appropriating [*Ereignis*], Appropriating has the
   peculiar property of bringing man into his own [*in sein
   Eigenes*] as the being who perceives by standing within
   true time. Thus Appropriated *(geeignet),* man belongs to
   Ereignis."[112]

6. We can never place *Ereignis* in front of us. Time, as well
   as Being, can only be thought from *Ereignis* as the gift of
   Ereignis. As we look through Being itself, through time
   itself, we must say *Ereignis* neither *is* nor *is Ereignis there,*
   rather "*Ereignis* (Appropriation) appropriates" *(Das Ereignis ereignet).*[113] "At this juncture, thinking that explicitly
   enters *Ereignis* in order to say It in terms of It about It is
   necessary" *(dasjenige Denken das sich eignes in das Ereignis
   einlasst, um Es aus ihm her auf Es zu—zu sagen).*[114]

From the above examination of Heidegger's notion of
Ereignis, it is clear that in Heidegger's thought *Ereignis* is understood to be the ultimate Reality that is entirely unobjectifiable,
unconceptualizable, unnameable, undefinable, and yet the
root source of Being and time, world and history. Here it must
be asked: Where does Heidegger stand when he talks about
Ereignis? Is he identical with *Ereignis,* or does he stand some-

what outside of *Ereignis*? How are *Ereignis* and the Self related to one another? When Heidegger says, as cited above, "Appropriating has the peculiar property of bringing man into his own" (*in sein Eigenes*), does he indicate that through Appropriating (*Ereignen*), man awakens to the true Self, and that *Ereignis* is understood to be the true Self? Despite his careful and elaborate discussion of *Ereignis*, it is not clear how *Ereignis* is related to the Self and whether Being and time are identical with the Self.

When we compare Heidegger with Dōgen, we must raise these questions, because for Dōgen it is clear that Being is the Self and time is the Self. Further, since Being and time are completely interpenetrating without hindrance and are grasped in terms of being-time, there is no exact equivalent to Heidegger's notion of *Ereignis* in Dōgen's thought. In other words, in Dōgen's thought there is nothing that "gives" Being and time— or that "sends" Being as destiny and "extends" time as the region. This is because for Dōgen, Being is Being precisely because Being is *not* Being, and time is time precisely because time is *not* time. Heidegger says as well, it must be acknowledged: "Being—a matter, but *not* a being. Time—a matter, but *nothing* temporal."[115] We should not, however, overlook that the meaning or degree of *negation* involved in the respective understandings of Being and time in Heidegger and Dōgen are different. When Dōgen understands that Being is Being precisely because Being is *not* Being and that time is time precisely because time is *not* time, he so understands through his existential realization of breaking through or emancipation from life-and-death and casting off of body-mind. This entails an holistic, total realization of the complete (or great) Death of the ego-self, which is immediately the great affirmation of true Life, the great affirmation of life-and-death, body and mind. On the other hand, when Heidegger states, "Being—a matter, but *not* a being. Time—a matter, but *nothing* temporal," he does so through his "thinking of Being" (*Denken des Seins,*) which is completely nonobjective and nonmetaphysical and which "remains intent on persisting in its matter."[116] Although his "thinking of Being" is an entirely new way of thinking that is characterized by "the step back" (*Schrittzürick*) into the ground of metaphysics or even by "the step back from philosophy,"[117] it lacks a holistic and total realization of great Death that is paradoxically identical with great Life. This is perhaps the reason Heidegger states:

> Being is not a thing, thus nothing temporal, *and yet* it is determined by time as presence.
>
> Time is not a thing, thus nothing which is, *and yet* it remains constant in its passing away without being something temporal like the beings in time.[118] [Italics added]

Dōgen would reformulate this idea in the following way:

> Being is not a thing, thus nothing temporal, *precisely because so* [that is, precisely because Being is nothing temporal] it is determined by time as presence. Time is not a thing, thus nothing which is, *precisely because so* [that is, precisely because time is nothing which is] it remains constant in its passing away without being something temporal like the beings in time.

In Heidegger's understanding, "not" and "nothing" in the sentences "Being is not a thing, thus nothing temporal" and "Time is not a thing, thus nothing which is" have only a negative connotation; they indicate a *relative negation*. Therefore, when Heidegger wants, in this context, to make an affirmative statement such as "It [Being] is determined by time as presence" and "It [time] remains constant in its passing away," he finds it necessary to use the phrase *and yet* (*gleichwohl* and *aber*) to connect the first (negative) and the second (affirmative) statements. On the other hand, in Dōgen's view, "not" and "nothing" in "Being is not a thing, thus nothing temporal" and "Time is not a thing, thus nothing which is" indicate an *absolute negation* that is at once an *absolute affirmation:* "not" and "nothing" are therefore beyond the duality of positivity and negativity and hence have ultimately a *positive* connotation. Accordingly, in order to connect the first and second statements, instead of the phrase *and yet,* the phrase *precisely because so* would be substituted.

This difference between Heidegger and Dōgen in their understandings of the *negation* involved in their notions of Being and time entails a significant difference in their understandings of the identity of Being and time, although both of them equally emphasize that identity. For in Heidegger's thought, the identity of Being and time is grasped as the "belonging together" of Being and time and "bringing the two [Being and time] in their own,"[119] which is in turn called *Ereignis,* or the "It gives." Thus Being and time are "gifts" of *Ereignis.* And this is, for Heidegger, nothing other than "the matter of thinking" (*Sache des Denkens*).

On the contrary, in Dōgen's thought the identity of Being and time is realized as the complete interpenetration of Being and time without hindrance, while Being is thoroughly Being and time is thoroughly time. This is possible because Being is *not* Being—due to its nonsubstantiality—and time is *not* time—due to its nonsubstantiality. Accordingly, Being and time are not "gifts" but indicate "thusness" or "suchness." This is not a "matter of thinking" but a "matter of life" (*Sache des Lebens*).

THE UNTHINKABLE IN HEIDEGGER AND NONTHINKING IN DŌGEN

This difference entails the following three considerations.

1. For Dōgen, true thinking is "nonthinking" (*hishiryō*),[120] or, more precisely speaking, "thinking of nonthinking" (*hishiryōtei no shiryō*), which is beyond the duality of thinking (*shiryō*) and not-thinking (*fushiryō*) yet includes both of them. Thinking of nonthinking is fully realized in the great Life that is attained in and through the great Death that obtains with the breaking through of life-and-death and the casting off of body-mind. On the other hand, for Heidegger true thinking is a "recollection of another origin" (*Andenken an den anderen Anfang*)[121] and as such fundamentally differs from traditional Western metaphysical thinking. This thinking is generated by the fact that in Heidegger's attempt to approach this origin, he finds it "unthinkable" (*das Unvordenkliche*). Accordingly, Heidegger's thinking is an essentially new way of thinking that is beyond "metaphysical" thinking, and is a thinking of this other origin (*der andere Anfang*),[122] that is, the ground of Metaphysics. In Heidegger, however, this other origin of thinking is encountered as the unthinkable *from the side of thinking*.[123] This unthinkable as the source of thinking is listened to by Heidegger and heeded with strict obedience. The unthinkable is realized to some extent "over there." Consequently, despite their close resemblance, Heidegger's thinking is categorically different from Dōgen's notion of thinking of nonthinking, because the former does not reach the unthinkable as the true origin of thinking, whereas the latter is a thinking that is a self-realization of the unthinkable origin of thinking itself. Further, for Dōgen this unthinkable origin of thinking is the very Self that is realized through life-and-death.

2. As mentioned before, for Heidegger, that "Being is determined as presence by time" is a key point to his thinking concerning the problem of Being/time. Even in his notion of *Ereignis*, in which Being and time are said to belong together, time has priority over Being. In his lecture "Zeit und Sein" Heidegger states, "The gift of presence is the property of Appropriating. Being vanishes in Appropriation [*Ereignis*]."[124] Furthermore, in the "Summary of a Seminar on the Lecture 'Zeit und Sein,'" it is stated that "it is precisely a matter of seeing that Being, by coming to view as Appropriation [*Ereignis*], disappears as Being."[125] The same thing, however, is not stated concerning time. That only Being and not time disappears in *Ereignis* is further evidence of the priority of time over Being. This priority of time over Being, as I pointed out earlier, indicates that in Heidegger's thought anthropocentrism is not completely overcome. For whereas Being can be thought without beings, time cannot be thought apart from the human self. At this juncture, we see that Heidegger's understanding of the identity of Being and time is not universally applied to all beings—trees, animals, mountains included—of the universe.

In Dōgen's thought, on the contrary, all beings are time, and all moments of time are being. This can be seen in his notion of "impermanence-Buddha-nature" (*mujō-busshō*).[126] For Buddhism in general, and for Dōgen in particular, the notion of Buddha-nature indicates not a special supernatural divine reality but the original nature of everything, or the thusness (as-it-is-ness) of everything, human and nonhuman.

Against the traditional Mahayana Buddhist understanding that all sentient beings *have* Buddha-nature, Dōgen strongly emphasizes that all beings *are* Buddha-nature. For the traditional understanding takes Buddha-nature as an object of possession and a future possbility to be attained by sentient beings, an understanding that Dōgen rejects as dualistic. By overcoming all dualistic views, Dōgen emphasizes the identity of *all beings* (instead of all sentient beings) and Buddha-nature. Furthermore, Dōgen stresses the notion of impermanence-Buddha-nature, indicating that the impermanence common to all beings is itself the Buddha-nature. This is a revolutionary understanding of Buddha-nature, which before Dōgen had been understood to be unchangeable. For Dōgen, however, only this unusual interpretation is the correct one, and it is only on its basis that one can attain the unobjectifiable ultimate Reality. Herein, we see another example of Dōgen's

unique way of identifying Being and time. Without any conceptualization and metaphysical speculation he takes the
impermanence or mutability characteristic of time and all
beings as Buddha-nature, because for Dōgen Buddha-nature is
neither being nor nonbeing but thusness, or as-it-is-ness, of any
and every thing, human and nonhuman.

3. For Heidegger *Ereignis* may be said to stand for ultimate
Reality, because time and Being are appropriated in Appropriation (*Zeit und Sein ereignet im Ereignis*).[127] Therefore, referring to
Ereignis, we can only say: "Appropriation appropriates" (*Das
Ereignis ereignet*).[128] Where, however, does Heidegger stand when
he talks about *Ereignis* in this way? It seems to me that when he
talks about *Ereignis* Heidegger stands somewhat outside of *Ereignis* and looks at *Ereignis* to some extent objectively. Of course,
this is not an objectification in the ordinary sense or the "metaphysical sense." Strongly rejecting "metaphysical" thinking and
transcendental subjectivism, Heidegger strictly tries to reflect on
the true origin (*Andenken an den Anfang*) and obediently receive
its gift. Yet, *in the final analysis*—before the *Kehre,* or turn—he
looks at death as an impenetrable wall and Being primarily
through the phenomenological analysis of Dasein. Further—
even after the *Kehre*—he grasps the unthinkable, which is the
true origin of thinking, from the side of thinking and *Ereignis*
without identifying it with himself. The incompleteness of his
transanthropocentric approach, as evidenced by his understanding of the priority of time over Being, implies a trace of objectification. This may be a consequence of the fact that while Heidegger overturns the Western way of thinking since Aristotle and
opens up an entirely new, nonmetaphysical thinking from the
true origin, he does not break through "thinking" itself. Heidegger stands at the extreme limit of thinking but does not jump
into the nonthinking that is beyond the duality of thinking and
not-thinking. Although Heidegger's persistent adherence to
thinking constitutes a great and revolutionary achievement as a
philosopher in the history of Western philosophy, it prevents
him from "advancing," as is said in Zen, "a step further from the
top of a hundred-foot pole, thereby presenting the entire body
in the universe throughout the ten directions."[129] Without this
step, awakening to the true Self is impossible.

Dōgen's notions of breaking through life-and-death and
casting off body-mind are nothing but this one step further
from the top of a hundred-foot pole. Dōgen expresses this final
step essential to awakening in his own unique fashion:

You should...learn the backward step that turns your light inwardly to illuminate your self. Body and mind of themselves will naturally drop away, and your original face will be manifest.[130]

This "backward step," at once the casting off of body-mind and presencing of the original face, is fundamentally the same as advancing a step further from the top of a hundred-foot pole. When one takes one more step from the top of a hundred-foot pole and jumps into empty space, one immediately realizes that the boundless empty space is oneself, one's true Self that is nondual with others. It is precisely "the Self prior to the universe's sprouting any sign of itself" (chinchō mibō no jiko).[131]

From Dōgen's standpoint, there is absolutely nothing behind or beyond Being, time, and thinking—even a so-called Buddha-nature or Ereignis. It is, however, in the very actualization of this absolute nothingness that all Being, time, and thinking, while distinct from one another, are interpenetrating completely without hindrance. This absolute nothingness is not apart from Dōgen's Self. Rather, for Dōgen, this absolute nothingness is the true Self, and the true Self is this absolute nothingness.

It is on the basis of this realization of the Self prior to time and space, self and world, being and nothingness, that Dōgen states "The Self is being" and "The Self is time." It is precisely in the true Self that the identity of Being and time, the interpenetration of Being and time without hindrance, is fully realized.

Thus, to conclude,[132] in Dōgen's view the root source of Being and time is not "It," but the Self that is emancipated from body and mind, time and space, self and others. Again, the true origin of thinking is not the unthinkable, to be approached from the side of thinking, but is the original face of oneself and indeed of the whole universe—or nonthinking (hishiryō)—in which Being, time, and thinking are inseparable and dynamically one.

I have tried in the above to elucidate several differences between Heidegger and Dōgen. All of them, however, finally emerge from the lack, on Heidegger's part, of a thoroughgoing realization of absolute nothingness that is beyond the duality of being and nothingess, yet includes both of them.*

V

The Problem of Death in Dōgen and Shinran, Part I

THE BUDDHIST APPROACH TO DEATH

Buddhism interprets human existence as "something that undergoes birth-and-death" (*shōji suru mono*) rather than merely as "something that must die" (*shi subeki mono*). The interpretation of human existence as something that must die sees *life* in its present state in opposition to dying and seeks the conquest of death; immortality, or eternal life, is sought as the overcoming of death. In contrast to this, the interpretation of human existence as something that undergoes birth-and-death does not view life and death as objects in mutual opposition but as the twofold aspects of an indivisible reality. Life in the present is understood as *life that undergoes birth-and-death*. Therefore, Buddhism, which is based on such a realization, seeks liberation from birth-and-death (*shōji*) rather than the mere conquest of death. Its aim is not immortality and eternal life through a resurrection that conquers death, but the unborn and undying (*fushō-fumetsu*) state of nirvāna realized directly in and through birth-and-death by liberation from birth-and-death itself. This is the fundamental standpoint of Buddhism.

The interpretation of human existence as something that must die implies the beginning and the end of human existence. This means that it grasps human existence as human, or as distinct from other animals. The fact that a human is something that must die suggests that there is a beginning and an end *as definitive of human existence*. In contrast to this view, the interpretation of human existence as something that undergoes birth-and-death does not give special consideration to the beginning or end of human existence. Human existence is seen as an infinite process of birth-and-death that in itself is beginningless and endless. Thus, Buddhism, in interpreting human existence as something that undergoes birth-and-death, or "something that undergoes arising-desistance" (*shōmetsu suru mono*), does not necessarily view humans as distinct from other animals. Rather, it sees humans as part of impermanent existence undergoing the vicissitudes of arising-desistance, or as living creatures experiencing arising-desistance; that is, as part of the dimension of "sentient beings" (*shujō*). Human existence is grasped in the dimension transcending the limits of "human" defined as a being that has a beginning and an end. That is the reason Buddhism discusses the vicissitudes of birth-and-death that humans experience in terms of samsara, or transmigration through the six realms of hell, hungry ghosts, animals, fighting spirits, humans, and gods. It is also understood that karma, as the root of transmigration, penetrates the six realms covering the "triple world." Therefore, Buddhism transcends humanism and anthropocentrism; it can be referred to as "beyond humanism." Buddhism, which interprets human existence as something that undergoes birth-and-death rather than merely as something that must die, sees humans in terms of the dimension of sentient beings originally transcending anthropocentrism. And it also discloses the way to a fundamental emancipation of human existence based upon this dimension. The standpoint of what is called the "Dharma" (*hō*) of Buddhism is grounded on this "way."

Dōgen's view of "whole-being Buddha-nature" (*shitsuubusshō*) represents the purest and most complete realization of the standpoint of fundamental Buddhism liberated from anthropocentrism. This view regards sentient beings as "one integral entity of whole-being" and maintains that "both within and without sentient beings is in itself the *whole-being* of the Buddha-nature."[1] Since Shinran is also part of the current of Buddhist thought, naturally he fundamentally expresses a view transcending anthropocentrism in the manner indicated above. But for Shinran, birth-and-death is realized in terms of "sinful birth-and-death" (*zaiaku shōji*) or the "sins of birth-and-death" (*shōji no tsumi*), as expressed by the phrase "karmic evil that would involve one in eight billion *kalpas* of birth-and-death."[2] Karma is understood as "sinful karma" (*zaigō*) rather than merely as "karma" (*gō*). This doctrine differs markedly from traditional Buddhism, including Dōgen. For while expressing the standpoint of sentient beings transcending anthropocentrism, Shinran emphasizes and seeks a resolution to the problem of sin that is peculiar to human existence and is not seen in other living creatures. In that way, for Shinran, human existence becomes problematic in its uniqueness differing from other living creatures of any form. In short, while Shinran's view represents fundamental Buddhism that is "beyond humanism," it also displays a humanistic standpoint in the pursuit and emancipation of human nature seen as differing from other living creatures through the realization of and deliverance from sin. To determine how Shinran's doctrine contrasts with Dōgen's, we must consider this point more fully.

Although Dōgen's approach represents the purest and most complete realization of the Buddhist transcendence of anthropocentrism, it still never implies that human existence is not to be grasped as problematic in a unique way differing from other living creatures. Rather, the reverse is true. (This is, of course, also the case with Buddhism in general and not only with Dōgen). The very fact that human existence is *grasped* in terms of the transanthropocentric dimension of sentient beings is peculiar to the realization of a particular human being who is distinct from other living creatures. In turn, because of this realization, humans can consciously take a standpoint on the basis of the dimension of sentient beings liberated from anthropocentrism. Dōgen's notion of whole-being Buddha-nature does not indicate an objective fact somehow separate from the human realization—indeed, from one's own realization—that whole-being is Buddha-nature. In the experience of whole-being Buddha-nature, the occurrence or dimension of our realization is thoroughly deepened in terms of the occurrence or dimension of whole-being transcending egocentrism and anthropocentrism, so that one becomes the true Person awakened to the Buddha-nature only on this basis. Therefore, when one attains a standpoint "beyond humanism" in terms of "whole-being is Buddha-nature," the awakening of the true Person, or the original Self that is itself the realization of genuine humanism, is realized. The approach of Dōgen in particular, as reflective of Buddhism in general, does not merely contain a dimension transcending anthropocentrism. For while attaining such a dimension, it grasps human existence, by virtue of self-realization in terms of its uniqueness differing from other living creatures. This is the reason Dōgen writes in *Fukanzazengi*, "You have gained the pivotal opportunity of human form. Do not use your time in vain."[3] However, it is an issue for Shinran even more than it is for Dōgen that human existence becomes especially problematic in its uniqueness differing from other living creatures, even though his doctrine still occupies the fundamental standpoint of Buddhism transcending anthropocentrism. That is, although in both thinkers human existence is equally realized in its particularity at the same time as the transcendence of anthropocentrism is maintained, the *content* or the *direction* of realization is a matter of difference. To contrast the two thinkers, for Dōgen the uniqueness of human existence, or the foundationally problematic aspect of human nature seen as differing from other living creatures, is disclosed through the realization that one's own personal transmigration is none other than the "*coming and going of birth-and-death*" (*shōjikorai*). For Shinran, this is disclosed through the realization of the "*sinfulness of birth-and-death*" (*zaiaku shōji*), or the "sins of birth-and-death." In other words, whether the form of the transmigration undergone by human existence—a form that is common to other living creatures—is grasped in terms of the coming and going of birth-and-death or in terms of the sinfulness of birth-and-death, this awakening experience for both Buddhist thinkers is peculiar to human existence. In this awakening, the transmigration process permeating other living creatures as well becomes problematic for human existence, and emancipation from samsara is genuinely pursued. But the key issue lies in the difference in the content or direction of the coming and going of birth-and-death, either as permeating other living creatures or as the sinfulness of birth-and-death peculiar to human existence.

TRANSANTHROPOCENTRIC AND ANTHROPOCENTRIC DIMENSIONS

The issue of the difference in the content and direction of awakening is twofold in nature because it involves divergent ways of interpreting the transanthropocentric and anthropocentric dimensions of life and death. Both Dōgen and Shinran grasp human existence from the fundamental Buddhist standpoint of sentient beings liberated from anthropocentrism. The realm of sentient beings is temporally beginningless and endless as the occurrence of the unceasing vicissitudes of the arising-desistance of sentient beings. Spatially it is the boundless horizon of the world itself as the triple world in which the transmigration of the six realms unfolds. Therefore, to truly occupy the standpoint of sentient beings is to realize the very realm of sentient beings (the beginningless and endless world) in terms of its boundary situation. To grasp human existence from the standpoint of sentient beings is to see it in terms of the dimension of sentient beings, which is liberated from and thus broader and more basic than the limitations of what is human; that is, to see human existence in terms of the fundamental reality of the unceasing arising-desistant world. If the view stops here, however, although it means that human existence is certainly liberated from the limitations of what is human, there is as yet no emancipation from the realm of arising-desistance. The aim of Buddhism is to attain the realm of nirvāna, which is characterized by nonproduction and nonextinction that is of course liberated from the very realm of arising-desistance—and yet does not stand apart from this realm. Liberation not only from the limitations of what is human, but also from the limitations of what is sentient—that is, from arising-desistance—is the manifestation of the Dharma, which is emancipated from all temporal-spatial limitations. This Dharma is realized in and through one's own subjectivity. The person who embodies the realization of the Dharma in and through one's personal subjectivity is the original Person (*honrai no ningen*) proposed and sought in Buddhism, or the Awakened One who is a buddha. This results in a standpoint of a genuine humanism that is also thoroughly beyond humanism; it is the standpoint of the so-called true Person (*shinnin*).

The subjective realization of the Dharma in Dōgen's view is known as the casting off of body-mind (*shinjin-datsuraku*). That is, in the experience of the casting off of body-mind, the Dharma is realized. This is why the casting off of body-mind is at the same time the body-mind that has been cast off (*datsuraku-shinjin*). But considered in light of Dōgen's clear affirmation that whole-being is Buddha-nature, the casting off of body-mind as the subjective realization of the Dharma does not stop at a liberation only from human limitations or even from sentient limitations. Rather, it culminates in a liberation from the *limitations of being and nothingness* (*umuteki gentei*) encompassing all beings. In the casting off of body-mind, which surpasses the limitations of being and nothingness encompassing all beings, whole-being Buddha-nature is authentically realized for the first time. In the just-sitting experience of the casting off of body-mind, one must not "think of good or evil" or "administer pros and cons," but "cease all movements of the conscious mind, the gauging of all thoughts and views."[4]

This experience constitutes a profound and complete liberation from all of what is human, sentient, and existent. When emancipation from the body-mind is experienced directly in a dimension liberated from everything existent—the dimension that Dōgen refers to as "whole-being"—the Self of the casting off of body-mind is realized. This is reflected in the realization that is expressed as "Whole-being is Buddha-nature," "The entire great earth is the Dharmakaya of the self,"[5] or "The entire realm of ten directions itself is the illumination of the self."[6] The Self of the casting off of body-mind is manifested in such a complete realization of self-extrication (datsu). Similarly, what Dōgen calls the "true Person undergoing the coming and going of life-and-death" does not merely represent self-extrication from birth-and-death (shōji) or from generation-extinction (shōmetsu). It is truly the standpoint of self-extrication from being and nothingness, that is, the standpoint of whole-being. For that reason, we consider Dōgen's view the purest and most complete realization of Buddhism transcending anthropocentrism.

Dōgen's view offers the clearest understanding of fundamental Buddhism in a way that surpasses conventional Buddhist approaches that interpret the coming and going of the birth-and-death of the self merely in terms of the vicissitudes of the generation-extinction of sentient beings. He deeply and thoroughly realizes the dimension of the being and nothingness and the appearance-disappearance (kimetsu) of all beings and, thereby, self-extricates the birth-and-death of the self as a matter of being and nothingness. Right here, according to this view, "the Self prior to the great void"[7] realizes that "to turn the mountains, rivers, and the great earth is to return them to the Self."[8] In these expressions, Dōgen represents the standpoint of fundamental Buddhism and, therefore, of the authentic Person sought in Buddhist practice.

Dōgen's self-extrication from human limitations—that is, from the egotism of the self—is attained in and through the *realization of his own birth-and-death* encompassing the polarities of pro and con, and good and evil. The realization of his own birth-and-death is attained not merely in terms of human birth-and-death or sentient generation-extinction, but in terms of the *problem of being and nothingness* in the dimension of all beings. The resolution of the polarities of pro and con, and good and evil, as well as the problem of sinful karma, is ultimately grasped in terms of the *problem of birth-and-death as being and nothingness*, or as a matter of the appearance-disappearance of thought or the being and nothingness of thought (*nen*, Skt. *smrti*). That is, for Dōgen, birth-and-death as the fundamental problem of human existence encompassing the polarities of pro and con, and good and evil is deeply and thoroughly resolved in terms of the dimension of all beings that is furthest removed from what is human. Thus, our birth-and-death—and therefore, human egotism—is truly self-extricated by realizing this dimension, and the standpoint of the true Person who knows that the entire great earth is the Dharmakaya of the Self is fully attained. Therefore, for Dōgen, on the one hand, the original nature of humans as seen from the standpoint of fundamental Buddhism is thoroughly realized through the attainment of self-extrication. On the other hand, the problem of sinful karma peculiar to humans, including the polarities of pro and con and good and evil, is grasped and resolved as a matter of the appearance-disappearance of being and nothingness in the most radically trans-human dimension of all beings.

In contrast to this, Shinran, who is just as much in the current of Buddhist thought, did not grasp his own birth-and-death as a matter of being and nothingness in the dimension of all beings. Or rather, he *could not have* grasped it in this way. Shinran also understands that the standpoint of fundamental Buddhism, or the true Dharma, is reflected in the realization that the entire world of ten directions is the illumination of the Self—a view that grasps birth-and-death as a matter of being and nothingness and resolves birth-and-death by detachment from being and nothingness. However, Shinran laments:

> One may seek to pacify the waters of meditative awareness, yet the waves of mental activity will still arise; one may contemplate the moon of Mind, yet the clouds of delusion will still envelop it.[9]

Thus, he could not grasp the problem of his own personal birth-and-death in terms of the dimension of all beings, or attain self-extrication from it as a matter of being and nothingness. Nor could he even grasp his own birth-and-death in terms of the dimension of all sentient beings, or attain self-extrication from it as a matter of their generation-extinction. That is, Shinran did not expect to attain by any means whatsoever a subjective self-extrication from human limitations in dealing with the problem of his own birth-and-death. Rather, in coming to grips with this issue, he could not help but realize how firmly human limitations are rooted in his own being. But since in Shinran's view there cannot be a liberation from human limitations in terms of the problem of *his own birth-and-death,* doesn't this lead to the conclusion that there also cannot be a liberation from the *limitations of the self?* That seems to be exactly the case in Shinran's thought.

That is, Shinran painfully felt how difficult it is to be liberated from human limitations in the problem of his own birth-and-death, and precisely because of this feeling he could not help but realize—in the midst of despair without possibility for release—the deep-rootedness of his own ego as an obstacle to attaining liberation. When he says that "the self is currently a foolish being of karmic evil caught in birth-and-death," he expresses the deep belief that in his own existence there is "never a condition that would lead to emancipation"[10] from ever-changing transmigration. For Shinran, in contrast to Dōgen, there is no self-extrication even from what is human or egotistical, let alone from everything existent or sentient in the problem of his own birth-and-death. In fact, no attainment of self-extrication can be expected. To Shinran, who could not attain a self-extricating liberation even from his own birth and death, the *problem of his own birth-and-death* is not a matter of generation-extinction, much less of being and nothingness, but a realization of the problem of sinful karma for which there can be no resolution. In the *realization of the self that cannot extricate itself* by any means, the problem of his own birth-and-death is understood as the "sins of eight billion *kalpas* of birth-and-death." The realization of birth-and-death as sin is based exclusively on the discovery by Shinran of the root of his own fundamentally corrupt nature in trying to penetrate his own birth-and-death. This notion of corrupt nature seems opposed to the standpoint of the Dharma of fundamental Buddhism, which teaches the possibility of resolving birth-and-death.

Therefore, in the realization of sinful karma that recognizes birth-and-death as sin, the totality of the self that cannot liberate or extricate itself is radically grasped in terms of its fundamentally corrupt nature. Shinran's transcendence of egocentrism, and thereby of human limitations—which occurs by virtue of "being transformed by Amida's chosen vow"—is based on grasping fundamentally the totality of self-existence in terms of its essentially corrupt nature. Thus, his notion of being transformed by the Tathāgata's vow to save all sentient beings, which releases human limitations, does not occur in and through a realization of self-extrication emancipated from birth-and-death by attaining a person's original nature in light of the Dharma. Rather, it occurs in and through a realization of "transformation" (*ten*); that is, the corrupt karma-strickenness of the self is realized by the illumination of the Dharma and is transformed by the vow through the merit-transference of the Tathāgata. Shinran realizes sin in his own birth-and-death and pervading other sentient beings in terms of generation-extinction. This indicates that in transcending human limitations through such an understanding, Shinran grasps the limits of his own existence, and therefore of human existence—involving the matter of the appearance-disappearance of the thought of the polarities of pro and con, and good and evil, that is, the matter of being and nothingness—in a way that is fundamentally opposite to Dōgen's view and thus most distant from the realm of all beings, or whole-being. In other words, he grasps the limits of his own existence in terms of its most distinctively human significance, or most corrupted karma-strickenness, so that it differs and is set apart from all other sentient beings. Therefore, on the one hand, Shinran's view of the corrupt nature of humans, which is quite unusual and rather conspicuous when seen from the standpoint of fundamental Buddhism, is most deeply grasped through the realization of a transcendental transformation based on Amida's vow. On the other hand, the problem of the appearance-disappearance of being and nothingness permeating all beings is grasped and resolved by Shinran through a realization of this in terms of the problem of sinful karma that is most peculiar to human existence.

In the fundamental resolution of human nature (or egotism of the self) discussed above, the respective standpoints of Dōgen and Shinran, which seem to go in two opposite directions—one based on a subjective attainment of transanthropocentrism and the other based on an awareness of sin by Amida's vow—cross each other in the horizon of human "realization." This presents us with the following issue in comparing the thinkers. That is, in Dōgen's *attainment of self-extrication*, the egotism of the self is emancipated through a transanthropocentric realization of the problem of birth-and-death in terms of the dimension of being and nothingness, and original human nature is manifested as the Buddha-nature. But does this view thoroughly confront and transcend Shinran's realization of the corrupt nature of human existence as sinful in its particularity? Conversely, in Shinran's *attainment of transformation*, the inauthenticity of the egotism of the self, thoroughly examined in terms of the realization of human sin, cannot accede to the original Buddha-nature through the emancipation of birth-and-death, and is transformed only by the Tathāgata's vow mediated by that very realization of sin. But does Shinran's emphasis on sinfulness as the corrupt nature of the self penetrate into and confront the dimension of Dōgen's subjective realization of the original nature of humans as being in itself the Buddha-nature? In the remaining sections, we will consider the philosophical encounter between Dōgen and Shinran concerning these issues by discussing the role of the realization of death and the understanding of naturalness (*jinen*) in the two Buddhist thinkers. [See also the section entitled "Shinran's View of Death and 'Rebirth'" in chapter 6—Ed.]

DŌGEN'S VIEW OF DEATH

Dōgen's approach to death as well as his resolution of the problem of birth-and-death are expressed in the "Shōji" fascicle:

> Just understand that life-and-death itself is nirvāna, and you will neither hate one as being life-and-death, nor cherish the other as being nirvāna. Only then can you be free of life-and-death.[11]

He also states:

> This present birth-and-death itself is the life of Buddha. If you attempt to reject it with distaste, you are losing thereby the life of Buddha. If you abide in it, attaching to birth-and-death, you also lose the life of Buddha, and leave yourself with [only] the appearance of Buddha. You only attain the mind of Buddha when there is no hating [of life and death] and no desiring [of nirvāna]. But do not try to gauge it with your mind or speak it with words.[12]

The view that "birth-and-death itself is nirvāna" is also expressed by Dōgen as "The coming and going of birth-and-death is the coming and going of illumination" and "The coming and going of birth-and-death is the true Person." This experience, however, does not terminate with the attainment of a static state of being a buddha while liberated from birth-and-death. Rather, it discloses the nonobstructive freedom of "the great Way of the fulfillment of life-and-death,"[13] which is to be unhindered by birth-and-death while returning to birth-and-death. In "the great Way of the fulfillment of life-and-death," because life does not obstruct death and death does not obstruct life, the standpoint of the "manifestation of total dynamism" (*zenkigen*) is realized, such that "life is the manifestation of total dynamism, and death is the manifestation of total dynamism."[14]

The standpoint of the clear manifestation of total dynamism, in which there is a fundamental breaking through of birth-and-death and yet life is life and death is death, is none other than the realization Dōgen calls "This very mind itself is buddha" (*sokushin-zebutsu*). Although the doctrine is referred to as "This very mind itself is buddha," the term *mind* signifies neither the rational mind that somehow transcends the corporeal mind nor the ordinary physical mind. As Dōgen writes in the "Sokushin-zebutsu" fascicle, "The mind correctly transmitted means that one mind is all dharmas and all dharmas are one mind. That is why a former master said, 'When you attain the mind, the heavens come crashing down and the earth is torn asunder.'"[15] This "mind" is not the mind relative to all dharmas, either conceptually or phenomenally. In this sense it is *no-mind* (*mushin*). Rather, precisely because it is no-mind, it is as it is *all dharmas*. Since it is the mind that has broken through all minds and is detached from all perspectives of being and nothingness, it is the mind that is whole-being or whole-being Buddha-nature. Therefore, mind is nothing other than all dharmas. Mind is all dharmas in themselves, including the body-mind of the self. That is why Dōgen writes, "It is clear that the mind is the mountains, rivers, and the great earth, or the sun, moon, and stars." But he immediately states, "In this realization, however, if you add to it, it is insufficient, and if you subtract from it, it is too great."[16] This indicates that although the mind is all dharmas, it is mistaken to thereby understand that any one of of all the dharmas can somehow increase or reduce the mind. That all dharmas precisely are all dharmas in themselves indicates mind, and there is not one iota of increase or decrease of all dharmas in relation to the mind.

Dōgen maintains that "the mind of the mountains, rivers, and the great earth is only the mountains, rivers, and the great earth, and not waves or mist." This means that when the mind is the mountains, rivers, and the great earth, the mountains, rivers, and the great earth are clearly and distinctively revealed just *as* the mountains, rivers, and the great earth without one iota of increase or decrease or without "waves or mist." The same, of course, must be said of the coming and going of birth-and-death. The mind is not sought outside of the coming and going of birth-and-death, and the coming and going of birth-and-death in itself is the mind. When the coming and going of birth-and-death is truly the coming and going of birth-and-death in the mind, the coming and going of birth-and-death is clearly and distinctively revealed as the coming and going of birth-and-death without one iota of increase or decrease. This is expressed by "The mind of the coming and going of birth-and-death is *only* the coming and going of birth-and-death, and not delusion or enlightenment."[17] *The mind of the coming and going of birth-and-death is only the coming and going of birth-and-death—*this is Dōgen's standpoint of "This very mind itself is buddha."

However, it must be pointed out that the doubt young Dōgen experienced during his early training on Mt. Hiei originated precisely in his struggle to come to terms with this view of the mind. Also, the so-called naturalist heresy (*jinen-gedō*) that he consistently and severely criticized in his later years seems to be implicit in this view. According to the traditional biography, *Kenzeiki*, the doubt Dōgen encountered was the following:

> Both exoteric and esoteric Buddhism teach the primal Buddha-nature [or Dharma-nature] and the original self-awakening of all sentient beings. If this is the case, why then have the buddhas of all ages had to awaken the longing for and seek enlightenment by engaging in ascetic practice?[18]

This is the question people cannot help but confront in regard to the standpoint of "This very mind itself is buddha." But this question itself reflects an attitude that tends to conceptualize the Dharma-nature (*hosshō*) as something separate from the real suffering of birth-and-death. There remains in this query a sense of "gauging [the Dharma] with the mind...or speaking it with words." That is, "This very mind itself is buddha" is conceived of as an ideal outside of the lived subjectivity of Dōgen, and realization is seen as something beyond practice. However, when this question is more strictly confronted by Dōgen in terms of his own existential problem of birth-and-death, and when the practice of seeking emancipation is further deepened in terms of the oneness of practice and attainment, the conceptualization inherent in the question dissolves. There is then the realization of a decisive self-extrication through the casting off of body-mind, which is a release from the ego by neither "gauging with the mind" nor "speaking with words." Through this Dōgen comes to know that "when buddhas are genuinely buddhas there is no need for them to be conscious that they are buddhas. Yet they are realized buddhas, and they continue to realize buddha."[19]

In the primal Dharma-nature the self is not conscious of its being the Dharma-nature. In realization, there is no trace of realization and therefore of practice. But at the same time, if the primal Dharma-nature is not negotiated by the practice of the casting off of body-mind—that is, without "continuing to realize buddha"—it is not awakened. In order to attain realization, practice is indispensable. This certainly seems to be a contradiction. However, to see this as contradictory is based on standing outside the primal Dharma-nature. "Not gauging with the mind" implies a liberation from the kind of discrimination that sees the indispensability of practice as contradictory. In the original Dharma-nature liberated from such discrimination there is no contradiction. In *Fukanzazengi*, Dōgen asks on the one hand, "The Way is basically perfect and all-pervading. How could it be contingent upon practice and realization?"[20] On the other hand, he argues, "If you want to attain suchness, you should practice suchness without delay," thereby stressing "simple devotion to sitting" and "total engagement in immobile sitting."[21] In the "Bendōwa" fascicle Dōgen describes the relation between practice and attainment as "This Dharma is amply present in every person, but unless one practices, it is not manifested, unless there is realization, it is not attained."[22] All these statements reflect that there is no contradiction between practice and realization. *This very mind itself is buddha*—which was still interpreted conceptually by young Dōgen, as the *Kenzeiki* passage on his doubt indicates, "[With] the primal Buddha-nature and the original self-awakening of all sentient beings... why then have the buddhas of all ages had to awaken the longing for and seek awakening by engaging in ascetic practices?"—is liberated from conceptualization only through an absolute negation of the fabricated ego by the casting off of body-mind.

"This very mind itself is buddha" is experientially awakened directly in the subjectivity of the true Self, rather than an hypostatized ego, as expressed in the "Sokushin-zebutsu" fascicle, "'This very mind itself is buddha' is aspiration, practice, *bodhi*, and nirvāna; if there is no aspiration, practice, *bodhi*, and nirvāna, there is no 'this very mind itself is buddha.'"[23]

In his later years Dōgen often severely criticized the Senika heresy (*sennigedō*),[24] which is the erroneous view that the mind abides while the form perishes. According to this view, there is a bright spiritual intelligence contained in our body that is the source of self-understanding. When the body dies, the spiritual intelligence alone does not perish but abides immutably. This view, Dōgen argues, when "hearing of the doctrine of this very mind [itself is buddha], takes it to mean that the discriminating knowledge of sentient beings is itself the buddha."[25] In hearing of the doctrine of the Buddha-nature, it "regards the movement or stillness of wind and fire as the enlightenment of the Buddha-nature." The Senika heresy considers "This very mind itself is buddha," or whole-being Buddha-nature, to represent an immutable Buddha-nature directly experienced in our innate mind. But this indicates a dualistic standpoint that distinguishes body and mind, as well as form and nature, and regards the former terms perishable and the latter ones immutable. It represents a kind of discriminative immanentism that, without going through any experiential negation, takes the Buddha-nature to be directly immanent in the mind—the empirical mind—on the basis of the actual empirical distinction of body and mind. The Senika heresy violates Buddhism in a double sense: it does not understand the oneness of body and mind, and furthermore it falsely projects an immutable nirvāna (mind) outside of generation-extinction (the body). Therefore, Dōgen strongly admonishes that "to learn this view and try to set it up as the Buddha Dharma is more foolish than picking up a roof tile or pebble and supposing it to be a golden jewel. The deplorability of such a foolish illusion is without parallel."[26]

DŌGEN'S VIEW OF NATURALNESS

Dōgen's standpoint of "This very mind itself is buddha," referred to above as the notion that the mind of the coming and going of birth-and-death is only the coming and going of birth-and-death—that is, the doctrine that birth-and-death itself is nirvāna—constitutes neither a conceptual nor an empirical immediacy. In Dōgen's doctrines of "This very mind itself is buddha" or "Birth-and-death itself is nirvāna," Dharma-nature and nirvāna are not idealized as *a priori*, and resolve and practice are not seen as mere activities that come before the awakening of the Dharma-nature. To Dōgen there is also no immediate Buddha-nature in the body-mind undergoing birth-and-death, and nirvāna is not found in an immutable mental nature. For in such views, Dōgen emphasizes, there is no realization that "this very mind itself is buddha," and "you must realize that birth-and-death itself is nirvāna."[27]

Therefore, in Dōgen's approach, the Dharma-nature completely transcends the empirical self and yet is never conceptual. Rather, it is precisely the original face of the Self. The subjective realization transcending the empirical ego takes place by virtue of the manifestation of the Dharma-nature as the original face. Right here we see Dōgen's view of *naturalness (jinen)*, which is expressed as follows:

> You should therefore cease from practice based on intellectual understanding, pursuing words, and following after speech, and learn the backward step that turns your light inwardly to illuminate your self. Body and mind of themselves will naturally drop away, and your original face will be manifest.[28]

Therefore, what Dōgen calls the "natural" is not the notion of an empirically immanentist spiritual intelligence identified with the Dharma-nature, which is the approach of the Senika heresy. On the one hand, Dōgen suggests an absolute negation of immanentist subjectivity by advising, "Learn the backward step that turns your light inwardly to illuminate your self," and "We must detach from our body and mind." On the other hand, by "natural" he suggests that the natural manifestation of "expressing the Way" (*dōtoku*) in and of itself transcends the capacity of our body and mind, as in the following: "Expressing the Way occurs in and of itself and not through our body or mind. Expressing the Way is not something unusual or mysterious."[29] Precisely because the manifestation of expressing the Way transcending the capacity of our body and mind is not "unusual or mysterious," it occurs "in and of itself," that is, "naturally."

Therefore, what Dōgen calls "naturalness" is completely different from what the Senika heresy means by "natural." Dōgen's view does not refer to what is empirical or immediate, but to expressing the Way in and of itself, which represents an absolute negation of immanentism. In fact, what Dōgen calls "naturalness" is more than this, for he cautions against a naive understanding of negation. For example, he argues in the passage immediately following the previously cited one from the "Dōtoku" fascicle:

> But when expressing the Way is expressed, non-expressing the Way is not expressed. If you recognize expressing the Way as expressing the Way but do not realize non-expressing the Way as non-expressing the Way, you will not attain the original face or core of the buddhas and patriarchs.[30]

According to this, the true meaning of naturalness is not conveyed by a view that equates transcendental subjectivity realized simply through an absolute negation of immanentism with expressing the Way. That is because such a view reinforces the tendency to conceptualize expressing the Way, and thus "does not inquire into non-expressing the Way as non-expressing the Way." In order to understand the true meaning of "expressing the Way in and of itself," the absolute negation of expressing the Way as a transcendental subjectivity (non-expressing the Way) must be realized to be always identical with expressing the Way itself—as suggested by "Not expressing is the true head and true tail of expressing the Way."[31] This constitutes the thoroughgoing negation of the tendency to conceptualize expressing the Way.

For Dōgen, *expressing the Way as naturalness* is realized through the complete negation of what is both empirically and conceptually immediate. Therefore, naturalness in this sense is the *effortlessly (or nonactively) natural (mui-jinen)* rather than the conditioned (or actively) natural (*ui-jinen*), as expressed in the "Immo" fascicle: "The supreme wisdom of Shōbōgenzō is quiescent and effortless."[32] Expressing the Way as effortless naturalness is not the standpoint of causation or noncausation, but of *not-obscuring causation (fumai-inga)* or "natural becoming" (*jinenjō*).[33] The standpoint of causation reflects the world of inevitable causation, or karmic influence and retribution, that is, the view of conditioned or karmic naturalness (*gōdo-jinen*). The standpoint of noncausation is the direct negation of inevitable causation and retribution for good and evil. It is the view of not-falling into causation (*furaku-inga*), which includes the Senika heresy, as described in the "Jinshininga" fascicle: "When someone dies, he inevitably returns to the sea of original nature. Since one naturally returns to the sea of awakening even without the practice of the Buddha Dharma, there is no transmigration through birth-and-death."[34]

In contrast to this, expressing the Way as effortless naturalness represents not-obscuring causation and "natural becoming." This view does not deny causation by emphasizing not falling into causation. But beyond that, it is neither conditioned naturalness as karmic naturalness nor the Senika heresy's approach to effortless naturalness. Dōgen's view represents a liberation from causation in itself without regard to the issue of falling or not-falling into causation, as suggested in the "Ikka myōju" fascicle, "You must not worry about falling or not-falling into the causation of the six realms."[35] Rather, natural becoming is the standpoint of deep belief in the *principle of selfless causation,* as expressed by "The law of causation is clear and selfless."[36] It is none other than the standpoint of natural becoming as "practicing the causation of the public realm and feeling the causation of the public realm."[37] "Self-extrication" is an awakening in which the standpoint of natural becoming, or of expressing the Way as effortless naturalness, is disclosed or manifested.

An explanation of the significance of expressing the Way as effortless naturalness for the problem of birth-and-death is clearly shown in the "Gyōbutsuigi" fascicle: "The great sage entrusts birth-and-death to the mind, to the body, to the Way, and to birth-and-death."[38] Even if Dōgen talks about "entrusting birth-and-death to birth-and-death," he does not indicate the vicissitudes of birth-and-death led by or at the mercy of karma, nor entrusting to birth-and-death based on a belief in an immanent bright spiritual intelligence. Rather, this entrusting represents the manifestation of the total dynamism of birth-and-death transcending a view of the being and nothingness of Buddha-nature in relation to birth-and-death, as expressed by the following: "When there is birth, there is being-Buddha-nature and no-Buddha-nature, and when there is death, there is being-Buddha-nature and no-Buddha-nature."[39] Therefore, "entrusting birth-and-death to birth-and-death" means that we utilize birth-and-death freely and without hindrance from birth-and-death, as in: "Completely utilizing life, we cannot be held back by life. Completely utilizing death, we cannot be bothered by death.... They are where the Buddha-nature is. Clinging in attachment to life, shrinking in abhorrence from death, is not Buddhist."[40]

Dōgen's view is neither the standpoint of karmic naturalness attached to birth-and-death nor the Senika heresy that
abhors birth-and-death. Rather, it is the standpoint of the clear
and distinct process of undergoing birth-and-death according
to the principle of selfless causation. The total dynamic working of life is manifested, and the total dynamic working of
death is manifested. The total dynamic working of coming is
manifested, and the total dynamic working of going is manifested. But birth does not obstruct death, and death does not
obstruct birth. Coming does not obstruct going, and going does
not obstruct coming. Further, in the total dynamic working of
birth, the whole universe throughout the ten directions is manifested, and in the total dynamic working of death, the whole
universe throughout the ten directions is manifested. In the
total dynamic working of birth, the whole universe throughout
the ten directions does not obstruct birth or death. In the total
dynamic working of death, the whole universe throughout the
ten directions does not obstruct death or birth. For the whole
universe throughout the ten directions as well undergoes the
clear and distinct process of coming and going and birth-and-
death according to the principle of selfless causation. This is the
standpoint of natural becoming, or the manifestation of total
dynamism. That is why Dōgen writes:

> Although the principle of 'life is the manifestation of the
> total dynamism' covers all the world and all space, without
> concern for beginnings or endings, not only does it not
> even hinder [any] 'life as the manifestation of the total
> dynamism,' it does not even hinder [any] 'death as the
> manifestation of the total dynamism.' Although when
> 'death is the manifestation of the total dynamism,' it covers
> all the world and all space, not only does it not impede
> [any] 'death as the manifestation of the total dynamism,' it
> does not even impede [any] 'life as the manifestation of the
> total dynamism.' Therefore, life does not impede death;
> death does not impede life. All the world and all space exist
> equally within life and within death.[41]

However, this passage does not indicate that one and the
same whole universe throughout the ten directions dynamically
exists in life as well as in death. The whole universe throughout
the ten directions manifesting total dynamism in life and in
death is neither uniformity nor diversity. What totally manifests
dynamically is the whole universe throughout the ten directions

in life and the whole universe throughout the ten directions in death. Indeed, the manifestation of total dynamism is neither life nor death. The manifestation of total dynamism is manifesting total dynamism. Natural becoming is becoming naturally. When the manifestation of total dynamism is manifesting total dynamism, birth-and-death undergoes birth-and-death, and coming and going undergoes coming and going. When natural becoming is becoming naturally, life does not hinder death, and death does not hinder life. It is also the case that in life the whole universe throughout the ten directions is manifested, and in death the whole universe throughout the ten directions is manifested. Dōgen further writes:

> This does not mean, however, that one single world, or one single space, is totally dynamically worked within life and within death. Though this is not oneness, it is not difference, though it is not difference, it is not sameness; though it is not sameness, this is not multifariousness. Therefore, within life there are multitudinous dharmas manifesting their total dynamic working, and within death there are multitudinous dharmas manifesting their total dynamic working. And the manifestation of their total dynamic working exists within what is neither life nor death. In the manifestation of the total dynamic working, there is life, and there is death.[42]

This passage explains what was just discussed as the manifestation of total dynamism manifesting total dynamism. Isn't this Dōgen's standpoint of naturalness, or of expressing the Way as effortless naturalness? Of course, it also reflects his standpoint of "This very mind itself is buddha." As he says, "The true Dharmakaya of the Buddha is like the vast, empty sky but, just as the moon reflects itself on the water, it manifests forms in response to the object";[43] thus the true Dharmakaya of the Buddha is none other than the manifestation of total dynamism.

SHINRAN'S VIEW OF NATURALNESS

It is well known that Shinran also discusses the "principle of naturalness" (*jinen no kotowari*). For Shinran, the Pure Land is the world of *effortless naturalness,* and the person who attains the Pure Land is interpreted in a way that "their features, subtle and delicate, are not those of human beings or devas; all receive the body of naturalness (*jinen*) or of emptiness, the body of boundlessness."⁴⁴ That is, when Shinran speaks of the "necessary attainment of nirvāna," that "nirvāna" is supreme nirvāna, or the effortless Dharmakaya. In "Jinenhōnishō" (the passage on spontaneous naturalness), he writes, "The supreme Buddha is formless, and because of being formless is called *jinen*, that is, naturalness."⁴⁵ On the arrival of Amida, he writes in *Yuishinshō mon'i*:

"Come" also means "to return." To return is to attain the supreme nirvāna without fail because one has already entered the ocean of the vow; this is called "returning to the city of Dharma-nature." The city of Dharma-nature" is none other than the enlightenment of Tathāgata, called Dharmakaya, unfolded naturally. When a person becomes enlightened we say he "returns to the city of Dharma-nature." It is also called "realizing true reality of suchness," "realizing the uncreated Dharmakaya," "attaining emancipation," "realizing the eternal bliss of Dharma-nature," and "attaining the supreme enlightenment."⁴⁶

The Pure Land of Amida is the Pure Land of the Dharma-nature of naturalness, and being reborn in the Pure Land is a return to the city of Dharma-nature.

For Shinran, being reborn is ultimately a "return to the city of Dharma-nature," and the city of Dharma-nature is the world of effortless naturalness. In this sense Shinran's standpoint seems to greatly approximate Dōgen's view of self-extrication. Shinran also maintains that "as for *jinen* (naturalness) *ji* means 'of itself'— it is not through the practitioner's calculation."⁴⁷ This view of Shinran is also found in Dōgen, who severely rejects "practicing and confirming all things by conveying one's self to them" in regard to the casting off of body-mind. For both thinkers, whether they criticize the "effort by the practitioner" or "practicing and confirming…by conveying one's self," the attainment of effortless naturalness is possible only through a complete detachment from the actions of the self. To put it another way, unless there is freedom from conditioned, or karmic, naturalness regulated by the causation of pro and con and good and evil, the attainment of effortless naturalness cannot occur. For Dōgen, however, freedom from conditioned naturalness is referred to as "self-extrication" or "the casting off of body-mind."

In contrast, according to Shinran, extrication from conditioned naturalness can never be expected. Conditioned natural-

ness is grasped as the bondage of iron chains to karmic naturalness that cannot be removed or severed, or as a dark path of
sinful karma without release. This is why, for Shinran, naturalness in the genuine sense that "is not through the practitioner's
calculation" at the same time implies that "from the very
beginning one is made to become so," and that "it is through
the working of the vow of the Tathāgata."[48] Thus, naturalness
simultaneously indicates the absence of the practitioner's conscious effort and dependence on the power of the Tathāgata's
vow. In *Songō shinzō meimon* Shinran comments on the passage
from the *Larger Sukhāvatīvyūha Sūtra*, "This land is not discor-
dant with the vow; one is drawn there by its spontaneous working of naturalness." He writes:

> Through the karmic power of the great vow, the person
> who has realized true and real *shinjin* (faith) naturally is in
> accord with the cause of birth in the Pure Land and is
> drawn by the Buddha's karmic power; hence the going is
> easy, and ascending to and attaining the supreme great
> nirvāna is without limit. Thus the words, *one is drawn there*
> *by the working of jinen.* One is drawn there naturally by the
> cause of birth, the entrusting with sincere mind that is
> other-power.[49]

Naturalness based on this great vow—if we call this "naturalness through the power of the vow" (*ganriki-jinen*)—means that
for Shinran there is detachment from karmic naturalness and
the attainment of effortless naturalness only by virtue of naturalness through this power of the vow.

According to Dōgen, conditioned naturalness and effortless
naturalness are nondualistically realized in the complete subjective fulfillment of liberation. This realization does not imply
attaining effortless naturalness by breaking through conditioned
naturalness. Rather, it is a realization that in the experience of
expressing the Way as effortless naturalness, conditioned naturalness is expressed by the Way as truly conditioned naturalness
while it is at the same time extricated from conditioned naturalness. This is the self-extrication referred to as the "casting off of
body-mind" and "body-mind that has been cast off." Conditioned and effortless naturalness are mediated by an absolute
negation, but they are originally interdependent by means of a
correspondence, in that they are complementary aspects of the
Dharma. As the converse of this standpoint, for Shinran, conditioned and effortless naturalness are in a mutual and infinite sep-

aration. However, it is the naturalness of the power of Amida's vow that synthesizes the mutual separation of conditioned (or karmic) naturalness and effortless naturalness. This is what the principle of naturalness means for Shinran. In "Jinenhōnishō," on the one hand he says of effortless naturalness:

> The supreme Buddha is formless, and because of being form-less is called *jinen*. When this Buddha is shown as being with form, it is not called the supreme nirvāna (Buddha).[50]

At the same time he continues:

> In order to make us realize that the true Buddha is formless, it is expressly called Amida Buddha; so have I been taught. *Amida Buddha* is the *medium* through which we are made to realize *the way of naturalness*.[51]

These statements express the standpoint of the naturalness of the power of Amida's vow, which implies that it is Amida Buddha as "the medium through which we are made to realize" the formless supreme Buddha that transforms karmic natural-ness (sentient beings of sinful karma) into effortless naturalness (supreme Buddha). Causing conditioned naturalness to be com-patible with effortless naturalness by transforming it at the extreme point of the realization of their infinite separation is made possible only by the exertion of the naturalness of the power of Amida's vow. The formless supreme Buddha (or effort-less naturalness) developed this process in terms of an inverse correspondence to the Dharma in order to make karmic natural-ness know its own way of naturalness. The realization of the transformation referred to above—the process by which sentient beings of sinful karma bound to karmic naturalness are trans-formed into the Pure Land of effortless naturalness—is based on the exertion of the naturalness of the power of Amida's vow.

Philosophical Encounter

The differences between Dōgen and Shinran, who are both trying to attain effortless naturalness that is detached from con-ditioned naturalness, cannot be overlooked. These differences are basically the same as the issues summed up in the final para-graph of the earlier section on "Transanthropocentric and Anthropocentric Dimensions." We should restate the matter concerning naturalness. Dōgen's view of expressing the Way as effortless naturalness is highlighted by the sayings "Expressing the Way in and of itself" or "The casting off of body-mind occurs naturally and the original face is manifested." The question is, in Dōgen's view, does our conditioned naturalness of inevitable causation—although it originally includes the polarities of pro and con, and good and evil, as well as the problem of sinful karma—thoroughly and consciously confront and overcome the realization of sinful karma as in Shinran's view? According to Shinran, sinful karma cannot help but be aware of itself as a "corpse of the acts of those who commit the five grave offenses and those who slander the Dharma" in a way that is far removed from the true Dharma. But for Shinran, precisely because conditioned naturalness is realized as such—that is, as sinful karma far removed from the true Dharma—the attainment of effortless naturalness occurs not through a self-extrication that subjectively casts off one's bondage, but through a transformation that only occurs by the naturalness of the power of Amida's vow. Does Dōgen's standpoint of effortless naturalness consciously transcend the realization of sinful karma in Shinran's sense?

On the other hand, in Shinran's view of the naturalness of the power of Amida's vow, referred to by saying "Supreme nirvāna occurs naturally by the power of the great vow," his own sinful karma "with never a condition that would lead to emancipation" is radically realized. Is this realization of the supreme Buddha without form (or by effortless naturalness), however, realized as deeply as Dōgen's view of the formless true Buddha, especially given that Dōgen cites the sayings of Lin-chi (J. Rinzai): "The corporeal body is not enlightened, the shapeless one is the true form" or "The true Buddha has no form, the true Dharma is formless"?[52] In Shinran's standpoint of the naturalness of the power of Amida's vow, or of Amida Buddha making known the way of naturalness, there is a relation in regard to the "supreme Buddha without form" that is characterized by neither identity nor difference. But doesn't this fall somewhat short of Dōgen's view of the formless true Buddha, or subjective awakening?

We have attempted to clarify some of the differences in the religious realizations of Dōgen and Shinran by examining their respective approaches to the problems of death and naturalism. Yet we cannot help but confront the issues just discussed when we subjectively inquire into the religious attainment of the two thinkers in terms of our own existential realization rather than objectively compare them by putting ourselves outside of their experiences. A fuller explanation of this matter is undertaken in the following essay, "The Unborn and Rebirth."

The Unborn and Rebirth

The Problem of Death in Dōgen and Shinran, Part II

DŌGEN'S VIEW OF DEATH AND THE "UNBORN"

Dōgen writes that "it is a mistake to understand that you pass from birth to death."[1] This means that it is mistaken to interpret the relation of birth and death in terms of the passing away from the former to the latter. In this understanding, the person who thus "understands" not only sees death as an object over there while standing on the side of life, but by interpreting the relation of birth and death in terms of passing away, looks upon not only death but the present life of the self *from outside* of it. The person who understands in this way grasps the relation of birth-and-death while standing outside it and thereby lapses into a standpoint that is severed from the existential reality of the birth-and-death of the self. In that case, anxiety about death is not understood experientially, and the meaning and reality of life is not investigated truly. One should not regard the relation of birth-and-death objectively from outside of it but existentially awaken to it *from within*. When one existentially awakens from within, the relation of birth-and-death is not seen as a sequential change from the former to the latter. Rather, living as it is, is no more than dying, and at the same time there is no living separate from dying. This means that life itself is death and death itself is life. That is, we do not shift sequentially from birth to death, but undergo living-dying in each and every moment. That is why Dōgen writes that "in inquiry all aspects are birth-and-death," and that "birth is not one single thing, and death is not a separable thing, birth is not opposed to death, and death is not opposed to birth."2

The interpretation of human existence as something constantly undergoing birth-and-death is the fundamental standpoint not only of Dōgen but of Buddhism in general. The Buddhist view can be clarified by contrasting it with Christianity, which sees human existence not as "something that undergoes birth-and-death" but as "something that must die." In the Christian interpretation of human existence as something that must die, dying, and the conquest of death, are regarded as a serious issue for which life is presupposed. At least, it appears that in Christianity the ultimate root of human life as part of creation is understood to be clear. The view that life is presupposed indicates that belief in God the creator is also presupposed. Our human lives originate and develop by virtue of God the creator who dwells eternally. But even in Christianity, life is never simply presupposed. Christianity fundamentally holds that because Adam, the primordial person, committed the sin of disobeying the word of God, humans in punishment for this sin became something that must die, cut off from a connection of life to the original existence of God the creator. In Christianity, for humans to try to establish themselves as separate from God and therefore be autonomous *humans* in itself is regarded as sin in defiance of God. For this reason, humans, while originally deriving from the eternal life of God, become something that must die. Thus humans are seen in Christianity as something that must die not simply as a matter of natural necessity but as a consequence of sin.

Underlying the view that death is humans' "wages of sin" (*Romans* 6: 2–3) is the belief in God who rules over birth-and-death and His creation. Therefore, interpreting human existence as something that must die reflects on the *beginning* of human existence. At the same time it reflects on the *end* of human existence. Humans began history as something that must die alienated from the existence of God because of the sin of disobeying Him. But even those humans, by believing in the resurrection from death of Jesus Christ, the son of God, are resurrected at the end of history and attain eternal life as a basic presupposition. In Christianity, the beginning and end of the world and history is determined by the will of the one and only God of love and justice who rules over life and death.

Although one may speak of a beginning or end of history and human existence, this does not simply mean that there is a temporal beginning or a temporal end. In Christianity, as indicated above, the realization of human existence as human, that is, the realization of being an autonomous existence independent from God, is the sin of disobeying God, and through this the history of humans as something that must die begins. This realization is based on the essence of being human, which transcends time, and in the same way the beginning of history and of human existence is seen as an eternal origin surpassing time. But the understanding that there is an eternal beginning, which is simultaneously the beginning of history and of human *existence,* is derived from the interpretation in which this "beginning"—that is, humans' realization of themselves as an autonomous existence—is grasped in contrast to God, particularly the will of God, who is the creator of all and dwells eternally. The same can be said for the end of human existence and the end of history. The resurrection at the end of history is for one to be justified by God and to be made to conquer death. This occurs at the time of the last judgment for those who repent for the sin of trying to be human as autonomously independent from God and who stake the self on the belief in absolute obedience to the will of God. Therefore, the possibility that a human who casts aside the body that must die will dwell in an eternal resurrection is based on the will of God transcending time. For that reason, the end of human existence and the end of history—while ending within time—have the character of an eternal end transcending time. This "end," which has thus a twofold meaning, is based on the fact that resurrection transcending the death of a human who must die is originated in the will of God who dwells eternally without beginning or end. In Christianity, everything derives from and returns to the will of God. Its understanding of the beginning and end of human existence and history in this sense, as just indicated, fundamentally rests on the absolute will of God transcending and ruling over humans.

In contrast to this, the Buddhist interpretation of human existence as something that undergoes birth-and-death rather than merely as something that must die maintains that all existence, including the human, is without beginning or end. This is referred to as "beginninglessness and endlessness." There is no presupposition of belief in a creator, and no anticipation of the end. There is also no presupposition of a transcendental principle that gives rise to the beginning or end of humans and history. The view that there is nothing transcendent in relation to human existence is none other than the thoroughly existential realization of human existence from within it. In the event of the crucifixion that marked the death of Jesus Christ, the Incarnation, God in Christianity is profoundly immanent in human existence, and the transcendence of God is profoundly manifested in the immanence of the world. Yet insofar as the will of God commands every phase of humans, human existence is still interpreted *from outside* in its absolute sense. The Christian interpretation of human existence as having a beginning and end rather than as beginningless and endless is related to the fact that human existence, as indicated above, is grasped from the outside though in its absolute meaning. (At the same time, however, one must not overlook the fact that the above makes a unique feature of Christianity possible, which is that an ultimate purpose is given to human history on which is based a transcendental morality demanding that humans be vigilantly righteous in light of God's will.)

On the other hand, in the Buddhist interpretation of human existence thoroughly from within rather than from outside of it, everything is beginningless and endless. Thus, there is no duality of birth and death, and human existence is understood as undergoing the beginningless and endless moment-to-moment vicissitudes of birth-and-death. In this realization of the momentary vicissitudes of birth-and-death, humans return to the root of birth-and-death and thereby try to transcend it. If we refer to what is presupposed, we can say that undergoing birth-and-death presupposes undergoing birth-and-death. Undergoing beginningless and endless vicissitudes, or undergoing birth-and-death moment-to-moment precisely because of the beginningless and endless vicissitudes of birth-and-death, is the form of the *actual reality* of human existence existentially realized in Buddhism.

Therefore, our life is not simply life that must die, but life that undergoes life-and-death, or life that is itself life-and-death. The Buddhist doctrine that human existence is impermanent derives not because humans are something that must die, but because they are perpetually undergoing the beginningless and endless vicissitudes of birth-and-death. Therefore, the goal in Buddhism is not to conquer death but to liberate birth-and-death. One does not seek the attainment of eternal life through a resurrection that conquers death, but the realization of no-birth-and-death directly through birth-and-death by releasing birth-and-death. In order to accomplish this, the principle of birth-and-death must be clarified. That is why Dōgen writes that "the clarification of birth and death is the most important thing in Buddhist teaching."³ Dōgen is the thinker who accomplished the clarification of birth-and-death to the fullest extent.

The view that sees the relation between birth and death in terms of the passing away from the former to the latter is, as previously indicated, a standpoint that is severed from existence and looks upon birth-and-death from outside of it, as if from a third-person perspective. This is a mistaken view that fails to realize the existential standpoint. In contrast, the interpretation of human life in terms of beginninglessness and endlessness in which life itself is life-and-death is a view completely liberated from the notion of things passing away; it can be said to overcome any objectification that sees birth-and-death from outside of it. But Buddhism does not stop here. Although with this view one may recognize the actual reality of human existence, one cannot yet be said to realize its true form. The realization of the true form of human existence is to have an awakening that human existence that undergoes birth-and-death is originally no-birth-and-death. This is the standpoint of liberation from birth-and-death that is sought in Buddhism. But, to interpret human existence just as existence that undergoes birth-and-death cannot yet be said to existentially and directly attain liberation from birth-and-death. For it may still lapse into some kind of objectification of birth-and-death.

How does this happen? It is due to the fact that in this interpretation birth-and-death is not yet *truly* existentially realized as originally moment-to-moment birth-and-death. In this way, the vicissitudes of birth-and-death, or, rather, that which undergoes the vicissitudes of birth-and-death, is interpreted in terms of being a continuous and therefore substantive being. At the same time, the subject that engages in this interpretation is seen as something other than that which undergoes vicissitudes during birth-and-death. This view lapses into seeing that which undergoes birth-and-death as something outside of the self.

To see the oneness of life and death in terms of that which continuously *undergoes life-and-death,* rather than to see it as the passing *from life to death,* is certainly a sort of liberation from objectification through interpreting life-and-death from within the process. But if this interpretation regards the under-going of life-and-death itself as something continuous and sub-stantive, then it again lapses into the kind of objectification discussed above. That is not all. This interpretation represents a more deeply-rooted objectification of life-and-death, that is, a double objectification by refracting inwardly the first level of objectification. This is because in spite of having previously realized the root of life-and-death by overcoming objectifica-tion of life-and-death from outside, it again objectifies life-and-death at the very root of life-and-death. This objectification of life-and-death is, to put it more concretely and existentially, none other than turning life-and-death itself into an object of attachment. Thus, when life-and-death is not sufficiently real-ized in terms of the original moment-to-moment experience of life-and-death, and is substantialized by being seen as some-thing continuous, there is a latent attachment to life-and-death on a deeper level than the previously discussed attachment in the perspective that sees the passing away from life to death. This constitutes not an attachment to life viewed as changing into death, but an attachment to life that undergoes life-and-death—that is, to life that is itself life-and-death—that suppos-edly transcends the aforementioned attachment.

How then does the truly subjective and existential realiza-tion of life-and-death as the original experience of "moment-to-moment life-and-death" take place? The first thing is to real-ize that life that is itself life-and-death is none other than noth-ingness, or to put it another way, that life that is itself life-and-death is fundamentally none other than death in its essence. In the mode of attachment described above, life that is itself life-and-death is grasped as being. But when life-and-death is real-ized in terms of the original moment-to-moment life-and-death, there cannot be substantialization or objectification. That is because moment-to-moment life-and-death is the life-and-death directly realized right here and now in subjectivity. Therefore, our life-and-death is "nothingness" in that it cannot be substantialized by any means. Further, this is the *nothingness of subjectivity itself realized at the root of the subject* in that it is nonobjectifiable by any means—that is, it is death. In the real-ization of moment-to-moment life-and-death, our life that undergoes life-and-death is indeed realized as death.

This is the realization of the "great death" rather than a simplistic view of death. In thoroughly realizing the death of life that is itself life-and-death in the realization of the great death, the root of life-and-death of the self is attained. The great death is to die a death in the authentic sense by realizing from the *origin* or *basis* that the root of life-and-death is none other than death in its authentic sense. But to undergo death by realizing the root of life-and-death as death is none other than to be liberated from life-and-death in the root and precisely thereby to live life in its authentic sense. Therefore, in the realization of the great death, when we thoroughly die the death of life that is itself life-and-death, the realization of *life that is itself no-life-and-death* is manifested. The realization of life that is itself no-life-and-death, that is, the realization of nirvāna, is inseparable from the realization of the great death. Indeed, it is precisely the realization of the great death. This is the principle that life-and-death itself is nirvāna.

The second implication of a truly existential realization that life-and-death is originally moment-to-moment life-and-death is the insight that life is life and death is death. In the existential realization of moment-to-moment life-and-death, the oneness of life-and-death never means that life and death are seen in an im-mediate identity. When our life that is itself life-and-death is realized as nothingness originally without substance, one realizes that life is bottomlessly life and death is bottomlessly death. Life does not change into death, and death does not take away life. That is why Dōgen writes that "life does not obstruct death, and death does not obstruct life."[4] In the existential realization that transcends life-and-death by thoroughly dying a death in life-and-death, right-now life is absolute and *at the same time* death is absolute. But of course, although life is absolute, this does not mean that life should be interpreted only as a substantive being. Rather, to realize life as absolute is to be existentially emancipated from life itself in that very realization, which understands that life is not life. The same applies to death. That is why Dōgen writes:

> Being a situation of [timeless-] time (*hitotoki no kurai*), birth is already possessed of before and after. For this reason, in the Buddha Dharma it is said that birth itself is no-birth. Being a situation of [timeless-] time as well, cessation of life also is possessed of before and after. Thus it is said, extinction itself is nonextinction. When one speaks of birth, there is nothing at all apart from birth. When one speaks of death, there is nothing at all apart from death.[5]

And in the "Zenki" fascicle he writes:

In the culmination of its quest, the great Way of all buddhas is emancipation and realization. "Emancipation" means that life emancipates life, and that death emancipates death. For this reason, there is deliverance from birth and death, and immersion in birth and death. Both are the great Way totally culminated. There is discarding of birth and death, and there is crossing of birth and death. Both are the great Way totally culminated.[6]

Therefore, to realize existentially birth-and-death truly as birth-and-death liberated from any trace of objectification is none other than an awakening to the unborn and undying realm. This indicates that birth itself is no-birth and cessation itself is no-death simply because "life is a stage of total time, and cessation is a stage of total time." But the realization of no-birth and no-cessation is the realization of no-birth and no-cessation inseparable from birth and inseparable from cessation. In the same manner, only when liberation from birth-and-death occurs as "life emancipates life, and death emancipates death" is the great Way of all buddhas manifested. This is stated above as "Deliverance from birth and death, and immersion in birth and death...are the great Way totally culminated." Nirvāna in Buddhism, and in Dōgen in particular, is never the attainment of eternal life as a conquest of death, or the mere transition to a world without birth and death as the overcoming of birth-and-death. Rather, nirvāna is none other than a liberation in terms of the "root" of birth-and-death, or the return to birth-and-death absolutely in the realization of no-birth and no-death.

Therefore, if nirvāna, no-birth-and-death, or the world of no-birth and no-death, is understood as lying outside of the world of birth-and-death, then that view has lapsed into the standpoint of one who externalizes reality as something outside of the self. In a truly existential realization, nirvāna is not outside birth-and-death. This should be clear from the above discussion. Without thoroughly penetrating into the reality of birth-and-death, there can be no liberation from birth-and-death or entrance into nirvāna. Conversely, the only way of entering nirvāna is the thorough penetration into and return to the bottom of birth-and-death by undergoing birth-and-death in terms of birth-and-death. (This is really possible only upon the realization of moment-to-moment birth-and-death.) In the realization of the great death, our life that is itself life-and-death is understood as "death," and life-and-death is liberated. At the same time, life is grasped as "a stage of total time" and death as "a stage of total time." In this way, life is clearly realized as absolute life, and death is clearly realized as absolute death. That is, in the realization of emancipated life and emancipated death that penetrates the holistic nature of life-and-death, in a seemingly contradictory way life is clearly realized as absolute life and death as absolute death. That is, the emancipation from life-and-death is as it is the manifestation of absolute life-and-death. This is none other than nirvāna. Thus, "the great Way is totally culminated" in the "discarding of birth and death" and the "crossing of birth and death." True nirvāna is completely separate and yet inseparable from birth-and-death and thus is not sought outside of *real birth-and-death*. That is why Dōgen writes, "This present birth and death itself is the life of Buddha. If you attempt to reject it with distaste, you are losing thereby the life of Buddha."[7] He also maintains, "Buddhism never speaks of nirvāna apart from birth-and-death."[8]

The view that "this present birth and death itself is the life of Buddha" represents the realization of the "unborn" (*fushō*) in Dōgen. Therefore, it is mistaken both to detest birth-and-death as something separate from nirvāna and to seek nirvāna as something different from birth-and-death. Since, as Dōgen writes, birth-and-death is the "practice of the Buddha Way"[9] or the "place of the Buddha Dharma,"[10] "to think that birth-and-death is something to be eliminated is a sin of hating the Buddha Dharma."[11] At the same time, if one only stops at nirvāna while seeking nirvāna, that is not genuine nirvāna. Genuine nirvāna is realized in entering into nirvāna yet not abiding in nirvāna; being liberated from birth and death, yet playing in the garden of birth-and-death. That is also genuine birth-and-death. It is the meaning of Dōgen's expressions "Just understand that birth-and-death itself is nirvāna"[12] and "The coming and going of birth-and-death is the true Person."[13] It is also the principle of birth-and-death in the true sense. Dōgen writes, "Although birth-and-death is the vicissitudes of the average person, it is the liberated place of the great sage";[14] this explains that "the coming and going of birth-and-death is the true Person." That is, we may vacillate lost in the delusion of everyday birth-and-death, but if we penetrate the principle of birth-and-death abandoning all illusory views, there is a detachment from birth-and-death while undergoing birth-and-death.

For Dōgen the notion that "birth-and-death itself is nirvāna" does not apply only to the subjectivity of *individuals* iso-
lated from others and the world. Dōgen writes, "The practice of
the Buddha is exerted together with all sentient beings
throughout the entire great earth";[15] that is, "Birth-and-death
itself is nirvāna" is also the casting off of *world itself*, in that
"birth-and-death itself is nirvāna" covers and applies to all sentient beings. To clarify this point, it is necessary to consider
Dōgen's thought concerning whole-being Buddha-nature. It is
well known that Dōgen gives the saying from the *Nirvāna Sūtra*,
"All sentient beings have the Buddha-nature," a new reading as
"Whole-being is the Buddha-nature." [See chapter 2, "Dōgen
on Buddha-nature."—Ed.] Whole-being refers to sentient
beings, buddhas, and mountains, rivers and the great earth.
Whole-being in this sense is identified with the Buddha-nature.
That is why, for Dōgen, the Buddha-nature does not exist as a
potentiality within sentient beings; the converse is rather the
case, that sentient beings exist within the Buddha-nature.
Since, as Dōgen writes, "the entire world is completely free of
all dusts as objects to the self. Right here there is no second person!",[16] there is nothing outside the Buddha-nature. Therefore,
it is not that *I* awaken to the Buddha-nature, but that the *Buddha-nature* awakens to the Buddha-nature. And that this is manifested *in me* is the true meaning of *my* awakening to the Buddha-nature. Thus, Dōgen writes the following: "You must know
with certainty that it is impossible to encounter sentient beings
within *whole*-being no matter how swift you are. Understood in
this way, *whole-being* is in itself completely and totally emancipated suchness."[17]

Therefore, true realization of the principle of birth and
death, that is, of "Birth-and-death itself is nirvāna" and "The
coming and going of birth-and-death is the true Person," is
made not by a single subject known as "I" but by the awakening of that whole-being that is originally Buddha-nature.
Whole-being, and therefore all sentient beings transcending the
individual *I* realize the principle of birth-and-death. As Dōgen
writes, "The entire world in the ten directions itself is the true
Person,"[18] the world itself is the true Person. This is an absolutely objective reality transcending the existence of a particular subject. But at the same time, "Whole-being is the Buddha-
nature" does not mean that Buddha-nature exists generally or
objectively outside of the individual *I*. The notion that "Whole-
being is Buddha-nature" is not separable from *my own realiza-*

tion that "whole-being is Buddha-nature." That is why Dōgen writes:

> As for the truth of the Buddha-nature: the Buddha-nature is not incorporated prior to attaining Buddhahood; it is incorporated upon the attainment of Buddhahood. The Buddha-nature is always manifested simultaneously with the attainment of Buddhahood. This truth should be deeply, deeply penetrated in concentrated practice. There has to be twenty or even thirty years of diligent Zen practice.[19]

The Buddha-nature is necessarily manifested simultaneously with my own attainment of Buddhahood. It does not exist objectively by itself prior to my attainment of Buddhahood. Seen in this light, it is an absolutely subjective matter. The "practice of the Buddha," which is "exerted together with all sentient beings throughout the entire great earth," must be my own personal practice. Therefore, "The coming and going of birth-and-death is the true Person" is absolutely objective and at the same time absolutely subjective. The true Buddha Dharma lies in understanding that "birth-and-death itself is nirvāna" at the point of such a fundamental interpenetration of self and world. Dōgen regards this view as the right Dharma and takes it as his own standpoint.

FAITH IN DŌGEN AND SHINRAN

It seems that Shinran also did not doubt that such a view is the "right Dharma" realized by Śākyamuni himself. Indeed, his basic presupposition is that this standpoint is the right Dharma. This is expressed in the opening passage of the "Attainment" ("Shō") chapter of *Kyōgyōshinshō*. But Shinran could not help but realize that he himself could not live up to the standpoint of the right Dharma. He recites:

> Though we may believe this age and ourselves to be of the
> Right Dharma-age
> We are fools bottom-deep in afflicting passions,
> And utterly without a mind of purity or truth,
> How can we awaken the aspiration for enlightenment?[20]

For Shinran, the notion of a person receiving the illumination of the right Dharma does not indicate, as it does for Dōgen, that the realization of the birth-and-death of the person in

itself is this illumination, which Dōgen expresses as "The coming and going of birth-and-death is the coming and going of
illumination."[21] Rather, for Shinran this implies that the person
who has been clearly thrown a light of the right Dharma is led
to deeply believe that he is a fool, insincere, and karma-strick-
en, without a chance for release. This is just like someone in
the midst of illumination who is aware of the thick darkness
cast by his own shadow. Thus, salvation is based on *faith and
attainment,* in which the illumination that shines constantly on
one's own sinfulness becomes ever clearer through the very
darkness of sin. Shinran expresses this in the following verse:

> Although my eyes, blinded by passions,
> Do not see the brilliant light which embraces me,
> The great compassion never tires,
> Always casting light upon me.[22]

On the one hand, there is always a realization of the "darkness of the long night of ignorance," or of the beginninglessness
of sinful karma. But this realization itself is evidence of an "illumination of salvation."[23] In Shinran's view of sinful karma from
the beginningless beginning, this world is understood not merely as "this-shore" but as the "land of defilement," and not merely as the "present world" but as the "world of the five corruptions." *Now* is the time of the final Dharma far removed from
the time of the right Dharma, and the self is the occasion of profound sinfulness and corruption thoroughly unsuited to the
right Dharma. Such a realization of "time and occasion" is rooted in the realization of being divorced from and antithetical to
the right Dharma. It is a realization of a bottomlessly deep darkness that is opened at the base of the subjectivity of the self. The
recognition of this darkness comes through a realization that
the sinfulness of birth-and-death unsuited to the right Dharma
is without a chance for release, rather than through a realization
of the unceasing vicissitudes of birth-and-death.

   Shinran deeply believes that deliverance of the sinful self
living in this corrupt world comes not through the teachings of
the holy path (of self-power) but only through the true teaching of the Pure Land. He writes:

> Truly we know that the teachings of the path of sages were
> intended for the period when the Buddha was in the world
> and for the Right Dharma-age; they are altogether inappro-
> priate for the times and beings of the Semblance and Last

Dharma-ages and the age when the Dharma is extinct. Already their time has passed: they are no longer in accord with beings.

The true essence of the Pure Land way compassionately draws all of the innumerable evil, defiled beings to enlightenment without discrimination, whether they be of the period when the Buddha was in the world, of the right, semblance, or last Dharma-ages, or of the time when the Dharma became extinct.[24]

The Jōdo-shin teaching is necessarily considered by Shinran to be ideally suited to his time and occasion. Furthermore, as seen in the passage from the "Keshindo" chapter of *Kyōgyōshinshō* quoted above, the Jōdo-shin teaching is recognized as having salvific value not only for the age of the final Dharma, but *equally* for the "innumerable evil, defiled beings" permeating all three ages of the right, semblance, and final Dharma. Therefore, the Jōdo-shin teaching has a twofold nature. On the one hand, it is first revealed in the age of the final Dharma. But at the same time, it also has always been functioning behind the teachings of the holy path as the genuine and appropriate teaching for the decadence of sinfulness—though not for the wise and sagely—permeating the three ages of the right, semblance, and final Dharma subsequent to the era of Śākyamuni. Shinran never negated the right Dharma as such. But since the right Dharma in his day missed the time and occasion, it had to be superseded by the Jōdo-shin teaching, which had been latent in the background of the right Dharma until then as an undercurrent teaching to save evil and sinful beings. The right Dharma was thus regarded by Shinran as something to recede from the plane of the final Dharma, thereby revealing the final Dharma inversely from its background.

Dōgen, however, completely refuted the notion of the final Dharma. This is quite natural, because Dōgen maintained the standpoint of whole-being Buddha-nature. As he writes in the fifteenth dialogue of the "Bendōwa" fascicle:

While doctrinal schools of Buddhism make much of names and forms, authentic Mahayana teaching does not differentiate right, semblance, and final Dharma. It preaches that those who practice all attain the Way. Indeed, in this unvaryingly transmitted right Dharma, you receive and make use of your own treasured possession equally in entering and in transcending realization. Those who practice are

themselves aware of their attainment or non-attainment, as
one who uses water clearly knows himself whether it is
warm or cold.[25]

This passage negates the division of history into the three peri-
ods of right, semblance, and final Dharma. Dōgen maintains
that "in the standpoint of the right Dharma practitioners simply use their own treasured possession" in the transition from
initial aspiration to attaining the Buddha. He emphasizes that
"those who practice know this naturally." That is, for Dōgen,
all sentient beings are originally corresponding to the right
Dharma, or are truly in accord with the right Dharma without
regard to time or place and one's inborn capacity. This is none
other than the standpoint of whole-being Buddha-nature, or
the oneness of practice and attainment.

In contrast, Shinran's emphasis on the time and occasion of
the final Dharma realizes the bottomless sinful karma that cannot by itself correspond to the right Dharma, however much
one practices. The realization of sinful karma in the self is close-
ly connected with the realization that in the historical reality of
the three ages, the current time is the era of the final Dharma
without the Buddha. In Shinran's view, practice and attainment are not one and inseparable but are infinitely and mutually separated and opposed. His words in *Tannishō*, "Since I am
absolutely incapable of any religious practice, hell is my only
home,"[26] clearly express this. He also maintains:

> My evilness is truly difficult to renounce;
> The mind is like serpents and scorpions.
> Even doing virtuous deeds is tainted with poison,
> And so it is called false practice.[27]

What is the reason Shinran says that "my evilness is *truly* difficult
to renounce" rather than "my evilness is difficult to renounce"?
It must show how diligently he tried to practice to renounce the
sinful nature. At the conclusion of his performance of good
deeds, he realized that the transformation of the awareness of
"false practice" occurs only through pure faith in merit-transference by the power of Amida's primal vow. He writes:

> When beings of this evil world of the five defilements
> Have faith in the selected primal vow,
> Immeasurable, inexplicable, and inconceivable
> Virtue fills the entire existence of these practicers.[28]

That is, for Shinran, practice and realization, which are infinitely and mutually separated and opposed, are realized in terms of their inseparable unity through his own subjectivity only by "faith in the transformative power of the vow." Therefore, it is quite natural that both practice and realization for Shinran have decidedly different meanings than in Dōgen's case.

Dōgen asserts that "even while one is directed to practice, he is told not to anticipate realization apart from practice."[29] Thus, for Dōgen practice is never a means to attain realization as an end, and practice and realization are not at all mutually opposed. As long as one practices, this "practice" is already *practice in realization.* "One's initial negotiation of the Way" is "the whole of original realization."[30] Whether there is an initial aspiration or complete realization, the "beginning, middle, and end are all the Buddha Way."[31] But for practice to be originally practice in realization, it must involve forgetting the self.[32] There also "must not arise a single thought." The fundamental transformation of the subject requires "all things to advance forward and practice and confirm the self" rather than "to practice and confirm all things by conveying one's self to them;"[33] that is, "the backward step that turns your light inwardly to illuminate your self" is required. But learning the backward step that turns your light inwardly and illuminates your self never implies that practice is a means to attain realization. The true meaning of "learning the backward step that turns your light inwardly to illuminate your self" is immediately none other than realizing that "body and mind of themselves will naturally drop away, and your original face will be manifest."[34] Indeed, "Your original face will be manifest" in itself is "Learning the backward step that turns your light inwardly to illuminate your self," or "Body and mind of themselves will naturally drop away." This is the manifestation of realization.

True "practice" in itself is the manifestation of realization. "Practice in realization" is originally "realization," or more precisely "original realization." That is why Dōgen writes, "To forget one's self is to be confirmed by all dharmas." "To forget one's self" is not merely practice but is already realization, and "to be confirmed by all dharmas" is not merely realization but the true form of practice.

Therefore, realization must not be sought as mere realization outside of practice. Because realization as "being confirmed by all dharmas" is none other than "pointing directly to original realization," it is not found beyond but is realized directly through forgetting one's self. The immediacy of the experience of the casting off of body-mind that forgets the self is the immediacy of pointing directly to original realization that attains the body-mind being cast off. Original realization is not separable from practice. Thus, because true realization is not realization that can be distinguished from practice, "as it is already realization in practice, realization is endless."[35] Although there is a oneness of practice and realization, it is not a direct identity on the dimension of the relative distinction of practice and realization in terms of means and end, and cause and effect. It is oneness realized by transcending or negating this relative distinction on the basis of subjectivity. Again, it is oneness realized at the root and source of subjectivity by casting aside both the instrumental nature of practice, seen as a conventional means to reach realization, and the teleological nature of realization seen as a goal of practice.

The "root and source of subjectivity," in which practice and realization are one, refers to mind, Dharma, Buddha-nature, or nondiscriminative wisdom as the ground for transcending particularistic individuality by realizing its basis. Indeed, the oneness of practice and realization in Dōgen originates only when the standpoint of mind or Buddha-nature is maintained. The oneness in which practice and realization are liberated from their relativity is truly a subjectivity realized by overcoming all relative distinctions within itself, as in the notions of "This very mind itself is buddha" or "Whole-being is Buddha-nature."

For Shinran, as already indicated, practice and realization are infinitely opposed to one another and can never become one. This view of the separation and opposition of practice and realization is none other than an understanding of the inevitability of hell. It accompanies the recognition of the sinfulness of birth-and-death without a chance for release. This is the so-called deep faith concerning the inborn capacity. This deep faith concerns the inborn capacity without a chance for release; that is, the realization of sinfulness is the realization that sinfulness is currently the nature of *one's own self*. However, the realization of the sinfulness of one's own self does not mean that sinfulness is realized in the self, but that the self is realized in sinfulness. In the understanding that sinfulness is in the self, sinfulness is objectively grasped as something contained in the self, and the self that thinks in such a way is concealed behind this conventional view. This view therefore portrays neither *sinfulness* nor the *self* in the true sense. But if the very fact that the self's sinfulness is thus seen objectively by the self even within the self that is realized as utmost sinfulness, then the realization of sinfulness and of our self in the true sense is attained. In that case, sinfulness is not realized outside of the self, but the self realizes the *complete body* of the self as sinful, and sinfulness is subjectively seen in accord with the complete existence of the self. Furthermore, this is because the self in this subjective realization of sinfulness understands the *complete body* of the self in terms of the self. This is why I have just stated that it is not a matter of realizing sinfulness in the self but of realizing the self in sinfulness—it is the true form of the realization of the sinfulness of our own self.

When the self is realized as within sinfulness, rather than sinfulness realized in the self, this realization of sinfulness transcends the self. It is, on the one hand, the realization of sinfulness in accord with the present reality of *our own self,* and at the same time the realization of the sinfulness of the *whole of humankind* transcending the self. The sinfulness of the whole of humankind is realized at the root of the sinfulness of the self, and the sinfulness of our own selves is seen in the sinfulness of the whole of humankind, that is, in the sinfulness of human existence as such. The deep faith in the inborn capacity that "for aeons there has been no chance for release from everyday decadence and vicissitudes" is not merely the subjective feeling of a particular person. It is none other than the realization that the vicissitudes of the sinfulness of all sentient beings from time immemorial constitute reality in accord with our own self. It is a limitlessly deep realization of the sinfulness of *our own self* based on and including the sinfulness of the whole of humankind.

But deep faith in this despondent capacity without a chance for release is founded on the earnest religious desire to fully attain release. Apart from the fervent desire to attain release, there can be no despondent realization that there is no chance for release. Therefore, deep faith in this profoundly despondent inborn capacity is grounded on the equally profound desire to attain release. This desire to attain release, which is of course the desire of an individual self, is the desire for the release of the whole of humankind, or human existence as such transcending the individual. For in that case, when the self's desire to attain release is deepened within oneself, it transcends the framework of the self, and the desire for release of human existence as such is consciously realized.

But what is *the very desire to attain release,* which is deeply rooted in the whole of humankind, transcending and yet remaining as the self? Isn't it the function of the Dharma or Dharma-nature itself? If we put it in Shinran's terms, isn't it none other than the vow of the Dharma to not take final enlightenment unless all sentient beings have been saved, or the so-called primal vow of the Tathāgata? At the basis of the limitlessly deep desire to attain release in the "inborn capacity" of sentient beings, the vow of the Dharma is already functioning. But for the time being this is not self-awakened in the existence of sentient beings. When the existence of sentient beings is illuminated in the self by the light of its own earnest desire to attain release, there is a realization of the self as the sinfulness of birth-and-death without a chance for release from ever-changing transmigration. But when this realization is deepened to realize the sinfulness rooted in all humankind beyond the framework of the self, a *deep faith in the Dharma* is manifested as the vow of the eternal Dharma transcending such sinfulness that has already been functioning in the background of the desire for release of the self. Deep faith in the Dharma is none other than deep faith in release based on faith in the power of the *vow* functioning in the limitlessly deep darkness of despondent existence without a chance for release. This faith in the power of the vow is expressed by the reminder "To believe deeply and decidedly that allowing yourself to be carried by the power of the vow without any doubt or apprehension, you will attain birth."[36] Further, this faith in the power of the vow itself is also based on the function of the power of the vow. The way to realize nirvāna is disclosed right here through the transformation of the self of sinful birth-and-death.

This does not mean, however, that the Dharma is realized on the basis of the realization of sinfulness without a chance for release. Rather, it means that in the manifestation of the Dharma, the realization of sinfulness without a chance for release is truly grasped by the light of the Dharma. The Dharma discovered in the realization of sinfulness—however deep the realization—is not the true Dharma that can transform sinfulness. The realization of sinfulness without a chance for release, as stated above, recognizes that there are no means for release in spite of the earnest desire to attain release, and at its bottom the earnest desire for release is already functioning. The desire for release, or the wish to realize the Dharma, illuminates by its light the whole existence of the "inborn capacity," that is, the whole existence of the inborn capacity of the self that cannot attain release by any means. At the same time, through the illumination it returns to the very realization of the Dharma. That is, when the Dharma confronts and realizes itself with existence as a momentum, the existence realizes the true form of its own sinful birth-and-death in the light of the absolute Dharma. At the same time, through this realization, existence is made to transcend its own sinful birth-and-death. Thus, the way of true realization is attained.

This is what is called "twofold deep faith in existence and Dharma." Although it is twofold, there is only one faith. It is faith in the vow, or the "primal vow," which leads precisely the sinful person with no chance for release however much he practices to attain realization and entrance into nirvāna. But for Shinran, this faith is the vow, that is, the functioning of the vow as the realization of Dharma, as indicated by the sayings, "Faith as the gift of the Tathāgata" or "Faith in the transformative power of the vow." Faith in the vow is really faith by the vow or through the vow. Therefore, twofold deep faith in existence and Dharma is the self-development of the vow; it is consistently the power of the vow of the Dharma that leaves nothing outside of it. When this faith, penetrated by the power of the vow, is transferred to the subject, the mutually opposing factors of existence and Dharma become unified even as they remain in opposition. Therefore, practice and realization that oppose one another also become nondual while remaining separate. Thus, the oneness of practice and realization in Shinran's view is manifested. Manifesting the oneness of practice and realization in our subjectivity is possible only by faith in, and by the power of, the primal vow. This is why Shinran especially emphasizes faith over and against practice and realization, as expressed by "You must know faith alone is essential."

Even for Dōgen, faith is stressed to some extent. He writes in *Gakudōyōjinshū*, for example, "Those who practice the Buddha Way must believe in the Buddha Way."[37] And in the "Bendōwa" fascicle he comments, "Only a person of great capacity based on right faith is able to enter the domain of all buddhas."[38] Faith is necessary and is regarded by Dōgen as the basis even of practice. In short, for Dōgen, "to believe in the Buddha Way" is the foundation of Buddhist practice. What, then, does it mean to believe in the Buddha Way? Dōgen further explains:

Those who believe in the Buddha Way should believe that they have existed in the Way from the beginning, without delusion, illusory thoughts, and confused ideas or increase, decrease, and misguided understanding. Raise such faith, clarify the Way in this manner, and practice appropriately. That is the foundation of learning the Way.[39]

That is, to believe in the Buddha Way is to believe that the self is in the midst of the Way and is originally pure in the Way; and to practice is to practice the Way clarified by such faith. Therefore, "practice" in this sense is not practice in pursuit of the Way without already having faith in or attaining realization. It is *practice in realization*, as in "What is to be understood is that one must practice in realization."[40]

Practice in attaining the Way is, of course, no different than the oneness of practice and attainment. Therefore, unifying practice and realization is based on faith, referred to as "faith in the Buddha Way." As stated before, the unification of practice and realization is based on self-awakening to "This very mind itself is buddha" and whole-being Buddha-nature. To make the appropriate connection, we can say that "faith in the Buddha Way" is faith in "This very mind itself is buddha" and whole-being Buddha-nature. Indeed, in the case of Dōgen as well as Shinran, the oneness of practice and realization is manifested based on faith in the Buddha Way. Insofar as the matter of faith is concerned, Dōgen's standpoint seems to have a subjective structure that is the same as Shinran's view of practice, faith, and realization.

It must be pointed out, however, that although practice and realization are seen by both thinkers as unified and inseparable, based on faith, for Dōgen in contrast to Shinran, the separation and opposition between practice and realization is fundamentally not an issue, and therefore there is no realization of their opposition. For Shinran, as indicated above, practice and realization are in infinite and mutual separation and opposition in the subjectivity of the self; the two become one based on subjectivity only by absolute faith in the power of the vow encountered at the ultimate point of awareness of this separation and opposition. But for Dōgen, to begin with practice and realization in mutual separation and opposition is not true practice and realization; true practice and realization arise from faith in the Buddha Way as expressed in "The self exists in the Way from the beginning." As long as one's approach is based on faith, as expressed in "Believe in the Buddha Way," practice and realization naturally accompany each other. This is clearly conveyed by Dōgen's words in the "Bendōwa" fascicle, "If people just practice in right faith, regardless of whether they are keen-witted or not, they equally attain the Way."[41] That is, for Dōgen, faith is practice and practice is realization; thus faith is realization. The triad of faith, practice, and realization are completely reciprocal and originally one rather than in mutual separation and opposition. Therefore, practice and realization are unified on the basis of faith in different senses for Shinran and Dōgen. For Shinran practice and realization, which are infinitely separated, are unified through faith while remaining separate; this represents his standpoint of "practice, faith, and realization." In contrast, for Dōgen the oneness of practice and realization represents the standpoint of "faith, practice, and realization" by being directly manifested on the basis of faith in the Buddha Way.

What does it mean that for Dōgen the triad of faith, practice, and realization is completely reciprocal and originally one rather than in mutual separation and oppostion? This means that it is essential to experience "the right way of directly pointing" and to realize that "this very mind itself is buddha" because, as Dōgen emphasizes, "if you wish to transcend even complete enlightenment you must only understand" that direct awakening is none other than "direct awakening."[42] For Dōgen, it is imperative to understand *directly right now* that the "mind of aspiration itself is already buddha," and not to seek the buddha beyond practice by adding up the merits of practice and realization. This indicates looking for the buddha not outside of the self but deeper and deeper within the self and thus breaking through the self. The "mind" not relative to inside or outside that is directly manifested by this breaking through— this is the original Self—is the buddha. *Direct awakening* is to thoroughly *break through* everything relative in the foundations of the self. It is not found beyond the self "over there." Rather, Dōgen consistently remains in the standpoint that "this very mind itself is buddha," which is attained by absolutely returning to this side of the self. For Dōgen, the separation and opposition of practice and realization is not a fundamental problem, and therefore there is no recognition of it on any level. This is because he returns to the mind that is the basis of the relativity of practice and realization instead of transcending their opposition. According to Dōgen, although there is a provisional distinction of faith and realization, both can be said to rest on "This very mind itself is buddha." That is why he writes:

> To aspire, practice and realize even for a single moment is a manifestation of this very mind itself being buddha; to aspire, practice and realize even in an atom is a manifestation of this very mind itself being buddha.[43]

For Dōgen, "This very mind itself is buddha" is at once the point of departure and the point of return, and therefore it is everything. Whatever stands at this point is completely true and the experience of enlightenment, but if there is the slightest divergence from this point, all will degenerate into deception and delusion. Dōgen asks:

> The Way is basically perfect and all-pervading. How could it be contingent upon practice and realization? The Dharma-vehicle is free and untrammelled. What need is there for human's concentrated effort?[44]

At the same time he writes:

> And yet, if there is the slightest discrepancy, the Way is as distant as heaven from earth. If the least like or dislike arises, the Mind is lost in confusion.[45]

Shinran laments that "my evilness is truly difficult to renounce," and he confesses, "I am so falsehearted and untrue that there cannot be any mind of purity."[46] "Emancipation" or "direct awakening" is not achieved in his own self by any amount of practice. In contrast, for Dōgen "awakening" means "to realize the buddha directly in this body-mind." For Shinran, it is not possible to attain direct awakening by breaking through in the sense that to aspire, practice, and realize even for a single moment is a manifestation of this very mind itself being buddha. Rather, isn't it the case that Shinran's introspective eye sharply grasps even "the slightest discrepancy" and arrives at the realization of the separation and opposition of practice and realization, which are "as distant as heaven from earth?" Shinran turns aside adroitly, returns to, and faithfully accepts the transformative power of the Tathāgata's vow at the extreme point of the realization of the separation and opposition of practice and realization:

> With my mind as deceitful as serpents and scorpions, I am incapable of accomplishing virtuous deeds of self-power.

Unless I rely on Tathāgata's merit-transference, I will end without shame or repentance.[47]

Therefore, for Shinran, the *illumination* (or realization) of the Dharma does not directly liberate the root of the separation and opposition of practice and realization through the emancipation of the body and mind. There is also no *realization* of an original face as it is in the body-mind right here and now. Rather, in complete contrast to Dōgen, there is a subjective realization of the separation and opposition of practice and realization as long as we cannot emancipate or awaken ourselves directly in the body and mind no matter how much we practice, or an awareness of sinfulness without a chance for release. This becomes the fulcrum for a transformation in which one encounters the name of the Tathāgata as a call of the Dharma and lets his body and mind be completely carried off. This, in turn, leads to a direct experience of faith and realization of the Dharma in everyday life as the "power of the vow." For both Dōgen and Shinran, the ultimate end is the illumination of the Dharma, or self-realization of the Dharma within one's own existence, that is, the attainment of Buddhahood. True, there are striking differences between the two thinkers on a number of points. In fact, the only reason we can say that they equally represent Buddhist doctrine or the Buddha Way in its foundations is their common concern with attaining Buddhahood. Although they are equally concerned with the illumination of the Dharma, the major difference, as indicated above, is in the *direction of the illumination*. Therefore, the religious meaning of the realization that is illuminative is not completely the same. In order to clarify this point, we must now examine the significance of practice in Dōgen and Shinran.

THE ROLE OF PRACTICE

It is well known that for Shinran all practice involving self-power is refuted, while absolute other-power is established as the foundation. "When [a person] abandons his attachment to self-power and entrusts himself totally to other-power, he will realize birth in the Pure Land."[48] What is referred to as the "practice of self-power" indicates not only the practice of the so-called holy path of salvation other than the *nembutsu* (recitation of the name of Amida). For even if the *nembutsu* within the gate of the Pure Land is practiced, if the slightest thought of

self-power operates at its root, then it is severely rejected as a
self-power-oriented recitation. Therefore, for Shinran, the practice of self-power means any practice based on the ego, or not
liberated from self-centeredness regardless of its form, throughout the gates of the holy path or of the Pure Land. What, in
contrast to this, is other-power? Shinran explains:

> Other-power means that no self-working is true working.
> 'Self-working' is the practicer's calculating and designing.[49]

Also, "Tathāgata's primal vow surpasses conceptual understanding: it is a design of the wisdom of buddhas. It is not the design
of foolish beings."[50] Thus, to be liberated from all self-centeredness, and to be completely free from a sense of calculation by
the practitioner or the thought of self-power, is called "other-
power." But this is still a negative understanding of other-
power. What is the positive significance of other-power for
Shinran? He writes, "Other-power is none other than the power
of Tathāgata's primal vow."[51] Also, "Other-power means that
when you experience the Buddha's marvelous wisdom, if there
is a supreme awakening of the average person who is thoroughly passion-ridden, it is determined only between a buddha and
a buddha. It is not determined by the practitioner."[52] Furthermore, according to Shinran, "Since this is the vow of Tathāgata,
Hōnen said, 'In other-power, no self-working is true working.'... Other-power is entrusting ourselves to the primal vow
and our birth becoming firmly settled; hence it is altogether
without self-working."[53] For Shinran, other-power is the "power
of Tathāgata's primal vow" that is "determined only between a
buddha and a buddha." When we are liberated from self-centeredness and have abandoned all self-working, this is none
other than the function of the Dharma that is manifest based
on our subjectivity. Or it is the function of the Dharma
received existentially as the "power of Tathāgata's primal vow,"
or the "determination only between a buddha and a buddha."

Therefore, for Shinran, *true practice* is by no means the practice of self-power but the practice of other-power in the manner
just indicated, that is, the practice of the power of the primal
vow as the function of the Dharma or of the name as the calling of the Tathāgata. As already suggested, although the *nembutsu* praises the name of the Tathāgata, if there is only the
slightest thought of self-power at its root or the smallest degree
of self-working by the practitioner, it must be severely refuted
as not representing true practice, or the practice of other-power.

Yet although true practice is the practice of other-power, this is not something that exists objectively. This does not exist outside our subjectivity as an "other." It is the function of the Dharma that is manifested—as the power of the Tathāgata's primal vow—based on our subjectivity when, as discussed above, we are liberated from self-centeredness and have cast off all self-working. Of course, it transcends our subjective "self" as the function of the Dharma or the call of the Tathāgata. But it functions based on the subject as the function of the Dharma or the call of the Tathāgata only when we return to it by renouncing all self-power. That is why Shinran writes, "*Kimyō* (taking refuge) is the command of the primal vow calling to and summoning us."[54] The selfless recitation of Amida's name truly detached from all calculation by sentient beings is as it is the recitation of the name of the Tathāgata himself. Calling "Namu Amida Butsu," in which the Tathāgata and sentient beings are identical, and which is manifest based on our subjectivity, is *true practice* as transformative other-power, and that is why it is called "great practice" by Shinran.

It is clear that for Dōgen, the practice of zazen-only (*shikantaza*) is the "true gate of the Buddha Dharma." He quotes his teacher Ju-ching: "Studying Zen is the casting off of body-mind. It can be obtained only from single-minded seated meditation, not incense-offerings, homage-paying, *nembutsu*, penance disciplines, or sūtra-readings."[55] Thus, all practice except zazen is refuted, and zazen-only is the true Way of the directly transmitted Buddha Dharma. Further, zazen practice is always understood as "practice in realization." Dōgen also writes, "Because one's present practice is practice in realization, one's initial negotiation of the Way in itself is the whole of original realization."[56] Practice separate from realization is severely refuted. Practice separate from realization is aimed at a realization for the sake of the self and is entangled in egotism. That is why Dōgen states, "Buddhist Dharma should not be practiced for the sake of oneself; how could it be practiced for the sake of fame and fortune? You should practice it for the sake of Buddha Dharma alone."[57] Also, "You must not practice the Buddha Dharma for your own benefit.... Simply to practice the Buddha Dharma for the sake of the Buddha Dharma is the Way."[58] "To practice the Buddha Dharma for the sake of the Buddha Dharma" is "practice in realization." Therefore, in practicing in order to seek the Buddha Dharma rather than to seek fame and fortune, if there is the slightest sense of doing it "for one's own sake," it is not the Way to enlightenment. Even when the Buddha Dharma is sought, insofar as the seeking mind is there, it is done for the sake of the self and not for the sake of the Buddha Dharma. That is why Dōgen writes, "To practice and confirm all things by conveying one's self to them, is illusion."[59] Also, "To forget one's self is to be confirmed by all dharmas." Practice that completely forgets the self is practice in realization; indeed, such practice is as it is the manifestation of realization.

Unless there is a grave error in the above considerations, practice refuted by Shinran as "self-power," and practice refuted by Dōgen as *not* "practice in realization," must represent fundamentally the same practice. That is, both thinkers refute practice based on the calculation of the practitioner, or practice that is self-centered. For Dōgen as well as Shinran, self-centered practice for the sake of the self is thoroughly refuted as inauthentic practice. To attain true practice, the notions of "abandoning the thought of self-power," for Shinran, and of "forgetting the self," for Dōgen, are indispensable. Therefore, Shinran's view of true practice as great practice and Dōgen's view of it as practice in realization show a sort of equivalence. That is, for both thinkers the Dharma is manifested or actualized when the practitioner transcends all self-centeredness. Further, the manifestation or actualization of the Dharma is based *on the subjectivity* of the practitioner.

Yet the manifestation of the Dharma through the absolute negation of self-centered practice is referred to by Shinran as "other-power" or "the power of Tathāgata's primal vow," and by Dōgen as "Buddha-nature," or "original face." While true practice for both thinkers is equally the existential manifestation of the Dharma transcending all self-centeredness, it is realized as *other-power,* or the power of the Tathagatha's vow, in Shinran, but as the Buddha-nature, mind-nature, or original face of the self in Dōgen. This is an important difference that cannot be overlooked. What is the basis of the difference between Shinran and Dōgen on the self-realization of the Dharma (or Buddha-nature) transcending our self-centeredness (or egotism)? It seems based on discrepancies between the thinkers in *understanding the nature of the ego-self* as a paradoxical (or affirmation-in-negation) condition for the realization of Dharma-nature. To put it more precisely, this refers to a question of how Shinran and Dōgen understand *practice based on self-centeredness,* which is equally refuted by them as inauthentic practice. It is a question of how to understand the present existence of the self, or the body and mind of the self.

For Dōgen, in order for practice to be originally practice in realization, one must forget the self, or "turn your light inwardly to illuminate your self." That demands "abandoning our body-mind." In this way, one "awakens directly," and "body and mind of themselves will naturally drop away, and your original face will be manifest." Therefore, for Dōgen, in forgetting the self, or "abandoning our body-mind," liberation from self-centeredness or emancipation from egotism is manifested. Emancipation from egotism is as it is the manifestation of the Dharma-nature. Indeed, egotism is emancipated primarily upon the manifestation of the Dharma-nature. For Dōgen, the body-mind of "abandoning our body-mind" or "the casting off of body-mind" is the body-mind that undergoes the coming and going of birth-and-death, or the vicissitudes of arising-desistance. Body and mind are not realized, unlike in Shinran, in terms of the body and mind of sinful birth-and-death without a chance for release, or the sin-ridden body-mind that is likened to a "corpse of the acts of those who commit the five grave offenses and those who slander the Dharma." Also, for Dōgen, as already indicated, practice separate from realization is thoroughly refuted as self-centered practice that seeks the Buddha Dharma for the sake of the practitioner rather than the Dharma. This type of practice is not criticized, as it is by Shinran, as "corrupt practice" or "futile and fictitious practice." Thus Dōgen does not come to the realization of a separation between practice and attainment as expressed in Shinran's words, "Since I am absolutely incapable of any religious practice, hell is my only home."[60]

For Dōgen, it is completely misguided and wrong to believe that body and mind are full of sinfulness and without a chance for release, or to grasp self-centered practice as "futile and ficti-tious practice," or to lament that "I am absolutely incapable of any religious practice." That is why Dōgen warns, "You must know that infinite transmigration will result from a single dis-criminative thought, and worldly delusions will recur through incessant calculation." And he also emphasizes enlightenment *directly within* one's own self by continuing, "If you wish to transcend even complete enlightenment, you must understand it is directly in you."[61] The realization of the sinfulness and fic-titious nature of practice as discussed above is only a delusion, according to Dōgen, that does not understand what is directly within you.

Of course, Dōgen clearly realizes that the egotism of the body-mind that undergoes birth-and-death lies at the root of self-centered practice. But Dōgen fundamentally believes that direct realization of the Dharma-nature as true self-nature is possible by continuing to penetrate into the inner self in order finally to gain emancipation from the ego at its root. He writes, "You must believe...that no delusory feeling exists within the original Way of the self." Complete accordance with the Dharma directly in you is none other than "entering directly into the transcendental realm of Tathāgata." At this point of emancipation, the body-mind of the coming and going of birth-and-death is grasped as the body-mind of the coming and going of the ultimate illumination of liberation:

> To realize the Buddha directly in this body-mind is complete accordance with the Dharma directly in you. There is no revolution in our existing body-mind, for what is called complete accordance with the Dharma directly in you is to follow up the realization of the other."[62]

According to Dōgen, there is no need to *revolutionize* "the existing body-mind" in order to realize the Buddha, for when the self has been cast aside, liberation and emancipation are naturally manifested. The existential manifestation of the Dharma, which for Dōgen is the realization of the original face rather than the other-power of the primal vow, is inseparably connected with the above understanding of the existing body-mind and therefore with *self-nature.* The passage just cited from *Gakudōyōjinshū* says that what is called complete accordance with the Dharma directly in you is to follow up the realization of the other. The "other" in "the realization of the other" indicates something experienced as other to the existing body-mind and therefore to the egotistical self. In reality this other is none other than the true Self to be realized, that is, the original face. Dōgen continues the passage, "Following up the other is not bound to old views. To be in complete accordance with the Dharma is not bound to new ones." With this statement Dōgen shows that the other that is followed up is the true Self.

In contrast to this, Shinran could not help but realize in the midst of his despair that in seriously seeking the Way, he could not emancipate self-centeredness, and the body-mind of the self could not be cast off naturally, no matter how much he practiced. He gazed at the existential actuality of self-centeredness without even slightly glossing over it, and he tried to penetrate into that actuality. He thereby attained the realization of sinful karma without a chance for release, or of the judgment that hell is his only home because "I am absolutely incapable of any religious practice." This is the extreme opposite of Dōgen's view concerning complete accordance with the Dharma directly in you. For Shinran, this is the realization of self-nature as a paradoxical condition for realizing the Dharma-nature. That is why Shinran's taking part in true practice that refutes self-centered practice is expressed as "turning aside the thought of self-power" rather than as "forgetting the self." To him, self-nature cannot be *emancipated,* which is to say that it is *transformed* only by the power of the Dharma. This is the reason the existential manifestation of the Dharma that negates self-centeredness is, for Shinran, thoroughly realized as the power of the Tathāgata's primal vow—that is, by other-power—rather than as the original face.

Practice negated as inauthentic by both Shinran and Dōgen is egotistical practice based on self-centeredness. However, the existential manifestation of the Dharma as the absolute negation of egotistical practice is understood by Shinran as the transformative power of the Tathāgata's vow, and as the manifestation of the original face by Dōgen. These approaches represent different ways of understanding the body-mind, or the egotism of the self; that is, they are different views that stand on opposite extremes.

According to Dōgen's doctrines of whole-being Buddha-nature and the oneness of practice and realization, all beings are originally appropriate to the right Dharma, that is, they are truly in accord with the right Dharma without regard to time or place and one's inborn capacity. The standpoint of complete accordance with the Dharma directly in you indicates such true accord with the right Dharma. Therefore, in Dōgen's view, "This very mind itself is buddha" is at once the point of departure and the goal of everything. By contrast, for Shinran, who stands in extreme opposition to Dōgen on the matter of egotism, "This very mind itself is buddha" cannot be the point of departure. Rather, the realization of the sinfulness of birth-and-death without a chance for release is the point of departure. That is why Shinran discusses the aspects of going forth to the Pure Land and returning to this world with the standpoint of sentient beings taken as the standard. Of course, as long as salvation for Shinran is simply based on the primal vow of Amida as the manifestation of Dharma, it is clear that the *ultimate* point of departure and goal of the self lie in the primal vow and therefore the Dharma-nature itself. This is well portrayed in the following expressions: "Because faith arises from the vow, becoming a buddha through the *nembutsu* is natural";[63] and "Return to the city of the Dharma-nature,"[64] which indicates Amida's "coming to welcome [believers]." Also, *merit-transference* for Shinran always occurs from the side of the Tathāgata and never from the side of sentient beings; this is none other than saying that everything originates and culminates in the Tathāgata. But when the coming and going of the aspect of the merit-transference by the Tathāgata is discussed, sentient beings are cited as the standard. Why is it that for Shinran merit-transference is based on the Tathāgata and directed at sentient beings, when for Buddhism in general it is based on sentient beings? And why, despite this, is the aspect of the coming and going of merit-transference discussed with sentient beings as the standard?

There is only one answer to these two apparently contradictory questions concerning Shinran's view of merit-transference. That is, for Shinran, the person and therefore sentient beings are understood in terms of the sinful, unenlightened self that lacks a purity of mind. In fact, Shinran asks, where are the good deeds in the self to transfer merit for others? With the discovery that apart from the sages of the world or the saints of the holy path there is only passion-ridden and sinful evil in our body of ignorance and insincerity, how is it possible to discuss our own merit-transference? In the midst of the realization of his own bottomless sinful karma, Shinran accepted with pure trust the manifestation of the Dharma as merit-transference by the Tathāgata. "Whether with regard to the cause or to the fruition, there is nothing whatever that has not been fulfilled through Amida Tathāgata's directing of virtue to beings out of his pure vow-mind."[65] This is Shinran's spontaneous cry of joy in the encounter with the light of the Tathāgata, which overcomes and illuminates the darkness of sinful karma. Without his understanding of sinful karma—such that the self cannot perform good deeds to achieve a merit-transference—as a paradoxical condition, Shinran could not believe that all merit-transference is based on the practice of the Tathāgata. Also, he could not talk about the aspect of going forth to the Pure Land unless even sentient beings who are unable to transfer merit come to be reborn only by the merit-transference of the Tathāgata.

For Shinran, who could not help but have a deep faith that there is no chance for release because of the realization of his own sinful karma, the self cannot be considered in true accord with the Dharma. Rather, at the ultimate point of his realization that the despondent sinful karma of the self is far removed from the right Dharma, he believed in and realized in his own exisential subjectivity the manifestation of the Dharma as the merit-transference of the Tathāgata's power of the vow. Therefore, the manifestation of the Dharma in his case is not the realization of what is truly corresponding to or truly in accord with the Dharma, as expressed by Dōgen in terms of "complete accordance with the Dharma directly in you" or "This very mind itself is buddha." Rather, the manifestation of the Dharma as the vow, that is, the Tathāgata's primal vow, which saves those whose sinful karma has no chance for release, is a matter of "inverse correspondence." This is well explained in *Tannishō* by "The evil person who entrusts himself to other-power is truly the one who attains birth in the Pure Land."[66] The Dharma that manifests itself as inversely corresponding is Amida Buddha, or the primal vow as the Reward Body "manifesting a form by virtue of a oneness which is without form and color." That Dharma beyond all limitations is encountered as the vow in its existential manifestation in a way that is inseparably connected with the realization of egotism as sinful karma in its subjectivity that can never be emancipated.

Remarks on Terminology

The term *inverse correspondence* (*gyakutaiōtēkī*) is derived from Nishida Kitarō's philosophy. But here it is used in a somewhat different meaning from that in Nishida's philosophy. According to Nishida, "The relation between God and the human self is the inverse dialectical correspondence."[67] Also, "Our selves encounter God in inverse dialectical correspondence only through death."[68] As we see in these passages, the term *inverse correspondence* is used to characterize a religious quality as distinct from a moral quality. That is, morality, which takes values as its problem, does not necessarily realize the fundamental self-contradiction (death) of our existence. In contrast, the world of religion, which realizes this fundamental self-contradiction and tries to solve it, is referred to by Nishida as "the world of the self-identity of absolute contradiction in which negation itself is affirmation," and the "world of completely inverse dialectical correspondence."[69]

In this essay, however, the issue is not to characterize the world of religion as distinguishable from the standpoints of morality and knowledge, but to clarify the differences between Dōgen and Shinran within the world of religion. Here, the terms *true correspondence (seitaiōteki)* and *inverse correspondence (gyaku-taiōteki)* are used to characterize the standpoints of Dōgen and Shinran, respectively, within the world of religion, which has been called by Nishida the "world of inverse dialectical correspondence." The following are the reasons for using these terms:

1. In Dōgen's notions of whole-being Buddha-nature and "complete accordance with the Dharma directly in you," all sentient beings as sentient beings are original-ly *in accord* with, that is, are *truly corresponding* to, the right Dharma. If we speak from the side of the Dharma, because the way of sentient beings is understood as a development truly corresponding to the Dharma in the sense that the practice of sentient beings is originally "practice in realization," Dōgen's standpoint is called "true correspondence."

2. Of course, in this case originally it is not necessary to add the qualifier that *if we speak from the side of the Dharma* then "the way of sentient beings is a develop-ment truly corresponding to the Dharma." Sentient beings are originally corresponding to the Dharma as whole-being Buddha-nature or complete accordance with the Dharma directly in you. But if we do not expe-rience the realization of absolute negation known as the casting off of body-mind or the realization of death, as discussed by Nishida, there cannot be an existential realization of whole-being Buddha-nature. Therefore, this experience is here called "truly corresponding" because it includes the realization of death mentioned above. That is, the notion of inverse dialectical corre-spondence (*gyakutaiōteki*) of the religious world in Nishida's philosophy is here expressed by the single term *tai*, "correspondence."

3. But *if we speak from the side of the Dharma*, the develop-ment of the Dharma is understood *consistently* in terms of *true* correspondence. Why do we nevertheless use, especially in Dōgen's case, the term *true correspondence* as distinguishable from *inverse correspondence?* Right here the comparison with Shinran comes into play. As already indicated, for Shinran, sentient beings (the karma-stricken self) are understood as not correspond-

ing to the right Dharma and as without a chance for release no matter how much one practices. In this understanding the self is seen in terms of its being ultimately evil, or profoundly sinful, because Shinran realizes that sentient beings not only are not corresponding to the right Dharma but are *violating* or *contradicting* the right Dharma. This is the realization of the complete falling away from true correspondence to the right Dharma, and it means that "hell is my only home." With this profound sense of sinfulness Shinran encountered the transformative power of Amida's primal vow "for the sake of Shinran alone." In this essay, I will call the Dharma manifest as the transformative power of the primal vow the development of "inverse correspondence" of the Dharma. Therefore, to make the contrast with Shinran's view, Dōgen's whole-being Buddha-nature is called "true correspondence."

4. For Dōgen, the self of the casting off of body-mind, or the body-mind that has been cast off, is the development of what is truly corresponding to the Dharma. In contrast, for Shinran, Amida Buddha as the Reward Body (*Sambhogakaya*) is none other than the Dharma that has developed in inverse correspondence. The self of the casting off of body-mind in Dōgen's case cannot be discovered anywhere in Shinran's approach to the development of what is inversely corresponding to the Dharma. Shinran's view of Amida Buddha as the Reward Body is not seen anywhere in Dōgen's approach to the development of what is truly corresponding to the Dharma. Amida Buddha is the Dharma that is trying to adapt even to those selves among sentient beings who realize they are antithetical to and cut off from the development of what is truly corresponding to the Dharma. But it is received as the embodiment (or development) of the Dharma that functions as a response to sentient beings (who are antithetical to the Dharma) that is inversely corresponding in the sense of inverse dialectical correspondence. It functions as the formed Reward Body, rather than the formless Cosmic Body (*Dharmakaya*), which develops itself in a direction that is the inverse of the direction of what is truly corresponding to the Dharma. Therefore, the word *correspondence* is used here as in the Nishida passage, "The religious world is the world of

inverse dialectical correspondence." In other words, to clarify the differences between Dōgen and Shinran, "true correspondence" is used for the former and "inverse correspondence" for the latter. The differences and philosophical encounter between the standpoints of true and inverse correspondence will be discussed further in the "Conclusions" section, below.

SHINRAN'S VIEW OF DEATH AND "REBIRTH"

How is death understood by Shinran? Shinran is grounded in the fundamental Buddhist standpoint that interprets human existence as something that undergoes birth-and-death rather than merely as something that must die. But for Shinran, undergoing birth-and-death is always seen as undergoing sinful birth-and-death. The vicissitudes of birth-and-death are understood in terms of not merely karma but sinful karma (*zaigō*). That is because the beginningless vicissitudes of birth-and-death in the present existence of the self are deeply colored by a realization of beginningless defilement antithetical to the right Dharma. The defilement antithetical to the right Dharma is not merely an ignorance concerning the right Dharma but a slanderous attitude that doubts its existence, or an awareness of the so-called ten evil deeds and five corruptions.[70] Shinran states reminiscently:

> *When I consider deeply* the vow of Amida, which arose from five *kalpas* of profound thought, I realize that it was entirely for the sake of myself alone! Then how I am filled with gratitude for the primal vow, in which Amida settled on saving me, though *I am burdened thus greatly with karma.*[71]

Isn't this because he realized that he himself is none other than the five corruptions and the slander of the right Dharma, which are far removed even from that great vow of Amida's to not claim enlightenment until all sentient beings in the ten directions are saved? In short, for Shinran, it is through the realization of birth and death not merely as birth and death, but as "*karmic evil* that would involve one in eight billion *kalpas* of birth-and-death,"[72] that he attains the realization of despondent sinful evil "without a chance for release."

For Dōgen, our life is originally life that is itself life-and-death, but for Shinran life is originally life that is sinful karma.

Thus, in regard to death, in Dōgen, life that is itself life-and-death is none other than death in the authentic sense. Realizing the authentic meaning of death is liberation from life-and-death at its *root*. At the same time, the life of no-life-and-death, that is, life in the authentic sense, is realized. In this principle of "life-and-death itself is nirvāna," Dōgen finds the way of emancipation and deliverance. In contrast to this, for Shinran, authentic death is seen as the *root* of life-and-death in a such a way that life-and-death is the result of sinful karma that does not sanction living life-and-death any longer. In the "*sins* of eight billion *kalpas* of life-and-death" in the present existence of the self undergoing life-and-death, the absolute death of inevitable hell is experienced. Therefore, this form of realization of death, however deepened, cannot itself attain emancipation from life-and-death. Death that is not sanctioned to live anymore has no resolution other than being turned into a new and thoroughgoing realization of living by being given life. Living by being given life in this sense, that is, living by being given life through the thorough realization of the sins of life-and-death, is none other than rebirth by the power of the primal vow.

Prior to Shinran, rebirth was symbolized in the Pure Land tradition either spatially as going to a far Western direction, as in the expression "Abhor this defiled world, aspire for the Pure Land," or temporally as a rebirth at one's deathbed, as in the saying "It occurs at one's deathbed." At least such a tendency was not completely abandoned. Therefore, before Shinran, the Pure Land tended to be understood as something spatially and temporally outside of the subjectivity of the self. For that reason, rebirth, or being reborn from the land of defilement to the Pure Land, was perceived as a sequential process, that is, as something self-identical and without rupture. Actually, the externality of the Pure Land and the sequential yet self-identical nature of rebirth are the same.

But for Shinran, rebirth is realized as the "birth of no-birth" rather than as being reborn in a literal way. Shinran interprets T'an-luan's view of the "birth of no-birth" (*mushō no shō*) disclosed from the standpoint of San-lun teaching[73] by a deeply existential experience of an exhausted and despondent subjectivity "without a chance for release." The birth of no-birth, according to Shinran, means the negation of the Pure Land symbolized as existing spatially and temporally outside the subjectivity of the self; therefore, it refutes the notion of rebirth as something sequential yet self-identical by which dying into the Pure Land, is mediated. The complete negation of the externality of the Pure Land or the sequential character of rebirth as seen in previous Pure Land teachings, is realized without any deception concerning the depth of the sins of the self that cannot be liberated through self-power even in reciting the *nembutsu* as a prayer for rebirth; this is none other than a realization of the profundity of sinfulness. That is why Shinran shifted his position from making *nembutsu* fundamental to making faith fundamental and thus believing in *nembutsu* itself as the great practice of Amida— a radical shift within the Pure Land School. Therefore, Shinran's emphasis on fulfillment of rebirth in everyday life rather than on "It occurs at one's deathbed" did not indicate a mere change of the time of the determination of rebirth from the deathbed to everyday life. The realization of no-birth intervenes between the notions of "occurring at one's deathbed" and "fulfilling rebirth in everyday life." In the realization of *no-birth*, the standpoint of fulfilling rebirth directly in everyday life rather than at one's deathbed, as the end of life, is attained—this is the realization of the *birth* of no-birth. For Shinran, the Pure Land is discovered deeply within the subjectivity of the self rather than outside the self temporally or spatially, and rebirth is attained directly in everyday life without waiting for it to occur at one's deathbed. That is because, for Shinran, rebirth is also referred to as the "immediate attainment of rebirth" (*sokutokuōjō*). But in order to clarify this point we must reconsider the matter of the birth of no-birth.

As mentioned above, the birth of no-birth, on the one hand, indicates the negation both of other-shore-oriented rebirth to the Pure Land by reciting the *nembutsu* by itself, as well as of the manifestation of the Tathāgata appearing at one's deathbed at the end of life. But at the same time, true rebirth is the function of the Dharma as the vow, that is, a merit-transference by the Tathāgata. That means that one who experiences no-birth is reborn by faith in the Tathāgata's vow, which is manifested directly in this present existence rather than at the time of death, and on the basis of subjectivity rather than in a spatial dimension beyond the self. Thus, one aspect of the birth of no-birth is the negation of other-shore-oriented rebirth and the Tathāgata's appearance at one's deathbed. This negation means that we cannot recognize these possibilities in our own existence. But just as that negation is based on the complete realization of sinful karma, the other aspect of the birth of no-birth, that is, true rebirth occurring as a merit-transference by the Tathāgata, cannot be realized apart from a decisive correspondence through despair by which the subjectivity of sinful karma trusts Amida's merit-transference. Therefore, for Shinran, although the Pure Land is discovered deeply within the subjectivity of the self rather than externally, it is not to be sought in the direction of subjective selfsameness (or self-identity) from a dimension of objective selfsameness. The Pure Land is certainly sought in a subjective direction but beyond the dimension of *selfsameness*. For Shinran, the *depth within the self* in which the Pure Land is discovered is an empty abyss that no subjective selfsameness can reach, or, rather, an abyss of sinful karma. The Pure Land manifests itself through the bottomless abyss of sinful karma unfolding within the self. It is transferred by Amida's transcending the abyss of sinful karma just to save the sinful subject. Therefore, the Pure Land is manifest with the opportunity for the realization of sinful karma directly in everyday life rather than at one's deathbed. Thus, death refers to sinful karmic existence in everyday life rather than physical death occurring at one's deathbed. The manifestation of the Pure Land and transference by the Tathāgata take place in that they are mediated by a realization of sinful karma directly in ordinary life. Therefore, although Shinran speaks of the fulfillment of rebirth in everyday life and immediate attainment of rebirth (*sokutokuōjō*), this is different from other Buddhist teachings, such as "Attaining buddha in this very body" or "This very mind itself is buddha."

As stated in the *Yuishinshō mon'i* passage referring to the notion of *sokutokuōjō, soku* means "immediately," and "immediately" implies that "without any passage of time and without any passage of days"[74] rebirth is determined directly in everyday life. But, it is also stated:

> *Sokutokuōjō* means that when a person realizes *shinjin* (faith), he is born immediately. To be born immediately is to dwell in the stage of non-retrogression. To dwell in the stage of non-retrogression is to become established in the stage of the truly settled. This is also called the attainment of the *equal of perfect enlightenment.*[75]

One does not attain the "realization" of perfect enlightenment by becoming a buddha directly in ordinary life. Rather, it is based on faith that is determined to attain perfect enlightenment necessarily in the future without any more retrogression.

This is of course rebirth but not no-birth. Rebirth for Shinran is the birth of no-birth, but no-birth does not mean that the "Buddha-nature is no-birth/no-death." Shinran's view of the birth of no-birth does not indicate complete accord with the Buddha-nature of no-birth/no-death realized directly in you through the body-mind casting off, as in Dōgen. Instead, it signifies that the subjectivity of no-birth without a chance for release because of sinful karma cannot fail to be reborn by the power of the Tathāgata's vow. Then what is the meaning of the "equal of perfect enlightenment" that is attained through rebirth as the birth of no-birth? To ask this itself is to inquire about the relation of faith and realization in Shinran.

Shinran does not take the standpoint of realization, that is, "perfect enlightenment" that attains nirvāna presently in this world, but the standpoint of faith that the attainment of nirvāna necessarily in the future is determined in this present existence. The equal of perfect enlightenment is none other than speaking from within such a standpoint of faith. Faith in rebirth, for Shinran, does not imply moving sequentially at one's deathbed to a Pure Land external to the self. Faith in rebirth to the Pure Land as the *other-shore* occurring merely at death is not acceptable in terms of the *realization of sinful karma* in this *present life*. That is because rebirth for Shinran is the birth of no-birth. It is to be reborn by believing in the power of the Tathāgata's vow that causes all sentient beings to be reborn, that is, by believing that *nembutsu* itself is the Tathāgata's practice rather than an act performed by the self—that is what faith in rebirth means for Shinran. Therefore, the basis of rebirth is faith in the power of the Tathāgata's vow, and faith is to believe in the "arising of the cause and effect of the Buddha's vow." Shinran, who accepted rebirth as the birth of no-birth because of the realization of sinfulness, believed in the power of the Tathāgata's vow transcending the bottomless abyss of sinful karma unfolding at the basis of this present life, rather than in the power of the vow of an objective Tathāgata coming toward one from the other-shore of death.

The formless Dharma beyond all limitations is manifested as the original face in the subjectivity of the body-mind that has been cast off and therefore is emancipated from egotism. But in the subjectivity of sinful karma, which realizes that it does not accord with the Dharma and cannot be emancipated from egotism, the Dharma is encountered as the vow, that is, as the Tathāgata's primal vow. We call this "the development of inverse correspondence of the Dharma." Faith in the arising of the cause and effect of the Buddha's vow is none other than the realization, through an awareness of sinfulness, of the subjective necessity in which the formless Dharma is encountered as the Buddha's vow. What is called "the vow of Dharmakara Bodhisattva and its fulfillment as Amida Buddha" represents the development of inverse correspondence of the Dharma to the realization of sinful karma.

In speaking of the "arising of the cause and effect of the Buddha's vow," Shinran usually refers to Amida's eighteenth vow. The vow is expressed thusly:

> If, when I attain Buddhahood, the sentient beings of the ten quarters, with sincere mind entrusting themselves, aspiring to be born in my land, and saying my Name perhaps even ten times, should not be born there, may I not attain the supreme enlightenment.[76]

For Shinran, at the ultimate point of the realization of sinful karma "without a chance for release," egotism collapses. But through this event the Dharma is encountered as the voice of the primal vow—as expressed by "with sincere mind entrusting themselves, aspiring to be born in my land"—which calls from the abyss unfolding at the base of collapsed subjectivity. Shinran's religious demand of "aspiring to be born in the Pure Land" discovers its deepest basis in the primal vow as the manifestation of the Dharma through the realization of no-birth, and returns to its basis. His religious demand is thus fulfilled by this experience.

Let us pay attention to the phrases *with sincere mind entrusting themselves* and *should [they] not be born there, may I not attain the supreme enlightenment.* "With sincere mind entrusting themselves" indicates faith, in the sense as quoted above, that is "without a doubt in the arising of the cause and effect of the Buddha's vow." Aren't the last words of the vow, "[If the sentient beings] should not be born there, may I not attain the supreme enlightenment," the *basis of the Buddha's vow* implied in "the arising of the cause and effect of the Buddha's vow"? As indicated above, Shinran accepted Amida's vow to not attain true awakening until sentient beings in the ten quarters are reborn by saying, "When I consider deeply the vow of Amida, which arose from five *kalpas* of profound thought, I realize that it was entirely for my sake alone." But doesn't Shinran's "faith in its basis" deeply reach the world of supreme enlightenment by going through the world of the vow? That is because he recites in "Kōsō wasan":

Because faith arises from the vow,
Becoming a buddha through the *nembutsu* is natural.
And naturalness itself is the Land of the Fulfilled Vow—
The enlightenment of supreme nirvāna is certain.[77]

But this in no way means that Shinran attains the supreme enlightenment in this present life. Shinran attains in this present life to the end the standpoint of faith, not the standpoint of realization or supreme enlightenment. However, the standpoint of faith does not simply stop with faith, but unfolds the world of the vow within itself and is thus deeply rooted in the world of realization. In short, Shinran's faith is already based on the world of realization in the present, that is, supreme enlightenment in the present—although complete fulfillment is attained in the future after death. It seems that this is because Shinran calls the rank of the truly settled ones (*shōjōjū*) a "rank of the equal of perfect enlightenment" (*tōshōkaku*).

Why did Shinran stop at attaining the "equal" of perfect enlightenment and think himself unable to reach perfect enlightenment in this present existence? Why did he stop at the standpoint of rebirth even though he has immediate attainment of rebirth, and not reach the standpoint of no-birth, or of "This very mind itself is buddha?" Here is the reason. It is because Shinran realized with his entire self that he spent "a whole life creating evil" and could not accord with the right Dharma no matter what he did. It is not that Shinran stopped at the standpoint of the equal of pefect enlightenment, finally failing to reach perfect enlightenment while maintaining the same dimension of being truly in accord with the Dharma, as found in Dōgen's doctrine of whole-being Buddha-nature. If that were the case, then the incompleteness of Shinran would be too obvious, and the issue would be extremely simple. But in seeing the matter as that simple, the underlying reason that Shinran stops at the equal of perfect enlightenment itself—that is, the realization of sinful karma as "a life creating evil"—is overlooked. The realization of sinful karma in the standpoint of the equal of perfect enlightenment is the extreme opposite of Dōgen's view of emancipation in terms of "complete accordance with the Dharma directly in you." That is, it is none other than the realization of the complete separation of practice and realization without a chance for release that cannot attain true emancipation from egotism no matter how much one practices. The encounter with the Dharma occurs with the realization that there is no chance for release—the extreme opposite realization of the view of complete accordance with the Dharma directly in you—as a paradoxical opportunity. This form of encounter consists in the calling of the Dharma as the primal vow of Amida Buddha and one's response and entrusting oneself to it.

Therefore, the encounter with the Dharma discussed here is not an encounter in the dimension of right correspondence with the Dharma—or the manifestation of the Dharma in the sense that body-mind are cast off and the original face is naturally manifest. Rather, it is an encounter with the *Dharma developed in terms of inverse correspondence* as the vow, or Amida, that is, the merit-transference by the Dharma for the sinful subject who realizes that he fails to be truly corresponding to the Dharma and has no chance for release. What is called the "equal of perfect enlightenment" is emphasized not in the dimension of true correspondence to the Dharma as in Dōgen's case, but in the dimension of inverse correspondence of the Dharma, which is opened up with the realization of sinful karma as a paradoxical opportunity.

Shinran writes:

> The aspiration in the Path of Sages for enlightenment
>   through self-power
> Is beyond our mind and words.
> For us ignorant beings, ever spun in the rush of waves,
> How is it possible to waken such an aspiration?[78]

This is the confession that the self can never attain true accord with the Dharma. Such a realization of the ordinary vicissitudes of the fool, or of sinful karma without a chance for release, is not the realization that one *cannot attain* enlightenment, but that one *cannot be worthy of* enlightenment or *should not be* enlightened.

The mere realization that one cannot attain enlightenment is part of the standpoint of being in true correspondence to the Dharma. Even if those of us who cannot attain enlightenment are made to attain it, this does not exhaust the "intention of the primal vow of other-power," expressed by Shinran in saying that "the evil person who entrusts himself to other-power is truly the one who attains birth in the Pure Land."[79] The development of what is inversely corresponding to the Dharma is expressed in the view that the evil person who should not be enlightened, rather than merely cannot be enlightened, is the very one who possesses the true cause for rebirth. The equal of perfect enlightenment is none other than the view that the evil person is made inversely to correspond to the Dharma in the dimension of the development of inverse correspondence. Therefore, the equal to perfect enlightenment, on the one hand, is never perfect enlightenment or realization rightly in accord with the Dharma, but faith. On the other hand, this is not merely an objective faith that is not internalized, but a faith that internalizes perfect enlightenment, in that it is made inversely corresponding to the Dharma. The reason this is called "the equal of perfect enlightenment while internalizing perfect enlightenment" is that it does not indicate a truly corresponding realization that attains perfect enlightenment directly through the casting off of body-mind. Rather, it is none other than accord through faith with the Tathāgata's vow as the inverse correspondence of the Dharma, which takes the realization of sinful karma as a paradoxical opportunity for faith.

Shinran laments:

> Although I have taken refuge in the true teaching,
> The mind of truth hardly exists in me,
> Moreover, I am so falsehearted and untrue
> That there cannot be any mind of purity."[80]

This is because he sharply inquires into the self-identity of the self, that is, an attachment to egotism, in the kind of faith that tends naively to affirm as a matter of course the Jōdo-shin teaching that maintains that the evil person is the true cause of rebirth; he recognizes such a teaching as being necessarily in accord with the Dharma. In the above hymn, Shinran severely refutes such an attachment to egotism in faith. Shinran has a thoroughgoing realization of his own false and inauthentic nature that fully criticizes such "self-identity" in faith. However, it is just this realization of his own false and inauthentic nature that becomes the *proof of the certainty of faith* that he is made to accord with the Dharma in the dimension of the inversely corresponding development of the Dharma. According to Shinran, within the subjectivity of the intention of the primal vow of other-power, there is always an accord that is inversely corresponding. But to him such an inverse correspondence with the Dharma through faith is the only way of being in accord with the Dharma.

CONCLUSIONS: ENCOUNTER BETWEEN TRUE AND
INVERSE CORRESPONDENCE

To sum up briefly, in Dōgen's standpoint of whole-being Buddha-nature, sentient beings are truly corresponding to the Dharma. The way of sentient beings in practice is also understood as the truly corresponding development of the Dharma, in that practice is originally practice in realization. By contrast, according to Shinran's view of the evil person as the paradoxical opportunity, sentient beings cannot be truly corresponding to the Dharma. Sentient beings can be made inversely corresponding to the Dharma only by faith in the merit-transference of the primal vow as the inversely corresponding development of the Dharma that will grasp just those sentient beings who cannot be truly corresponding. But even in Shinran, in referring to the development of the Dharma as the merit-transference by the power of the primal vow adapted to evil persons, *if we speak from the perspective of the Dharma itself,* it does not seem necessary to characterize it as the development of the inversely corresponding Dharma. If anything, shouldn't it be called the *truly corresponding* development of the Dharma as well? Therefore, although we spoke above of "the inversely corresponding development of the Dharma" in regard to Shinran's view, if we speak from the perspective of the Dharma itself, this notion must also already be present in Dōgen's standpoint. For the Dharma itself originally holds no distinction of true or inverse; thus, despite the above-cited differences, being truly corresponding to the Dharma and being inversely corresponding to the Dharma are both none other than *self-development of the Dharma.*

Dōgen's notion of the unceasing circulation of continuous practice seems to be a clear realization that everything is the self-development of the Dharma. Dōgen writes:

The great Way of the buddhas and patriarchs is necessarily supreme continuous practice which circulates unceasingly and without interruption. Resolve, practice, *bodhi,* and nirvāna have no interval between them; that is the unceasing circulation of continuous practice.[81]

The great Way of buddhas and patriarchs never exists objectively. It is manifested only upon our continuous practice, or our supreme continuous practice. This really means that our resolve, practice, *bodhi,* and attainment of nirvāna are all none

other than the self-development of the great Way of the buddhas and patriarchs. Right there the unceasing circulation of
continuous practice is realized. Therefore, Dōgen's view is
opposed to the standpoint of the Senika heresy,[82] which maintains that there is a bright spiritual intelligence abiding eternally by naively affirming "The great Way is in the body right-
now." Dōgen strongly emphasizes the necessity of negotiating
the Way through practice in the great Way of the buddhas and
patriarchs and the transmission of the right Dharma. This is
expressed by "The Dharma is amply present in every person,
but unless one practices, it is not manifested, unless there is
realization, it is not attained."[83] But no matter how essential
negotiating the Way through practice may be, if practice and
realization are interpreted as *two different stages* (or dualistically)—as in "If practice and realization were two different stages
as ordinary people consider them to be, the one sitting in zazen
and things should perceive each other [as separate]"[84]—that
would be severely criticized as a discriminative standpoint lacking direct realization. While emphasizing the necessity of practice on the one hand, Dōgen maintains the need to realize that
the practice of sentient beings is originally practice inseparable
from realization, in saying that "what is to be understood is
that one must practice in realization."[85] Thus Dōgen stresses
the standpoints of the oneness of practice and realization and
the unceasing circulation of continuous practice. In the final
analysis, while stressing that the merit of unceasing circulation
is based on our continuous practice, as in "We have the merit
of unceasing circulation by our continuous practice,"[86] Dōgen
at the same time clarifies that this continuous practice occurs
"by neither our effort nor the effort of others." Rather, it is originally none other than the manifestation of the great Way of
the buddhas and patriarchs, or the self-development of the
Dharma as "the undefiled continuous practice."[87]

What is problematic here is as follows: Certainly the Dharma transcends all relative distinctions and naturally transcends
the distinction of true and inverse as well. The truly corresponding and inversely corresponding developments of the
Dharma are both the self-development of the Dharma. But
transcending the distinction of truly and inversely corresponding does not simply eliminate it. Rather, no matter how clearly
the distinction of the truly and inversely corresponding developments of the Dharma is realized, the Dharma itself is not
obstructed by this distinction; this represents an existential

meaning of the Dharma transcending the distinction. In fact, in the authentic standpoint of the Dharma, what is truly corresponding is clearly realized as truly corresponding, and what is inversely corresponding is clearly realized as inversely corresponding.

In looking back now on Dōgen and Shinran, if we speak from the perspective of the Dharma itself, that is, from the Dharma existentially realized, Dōgen's standpoint can be said to include not merely the development of what is truly corresponding to the Dharma, but, equally as the self-development of the Dharma, the development of what is inversely corresponding to the Dharma, as in Shinran's approach. But in Dōgen, although practice is always indispensable, fundamentally the doctrines of the unceasing circulation of continuous practice and whole-being Buddha-nature are emphasized, and sentient beings are grasped as "one whole" of whole-being. Does this standpoint of Dōgen fully and self-consciously realize the inversely corresponding development of the Dharma for sentient beings who deeply realize their own sinfulness without a chance for release, as seen in Shinran?

In Dōgen's view of the Dharma as well, the development of what is inversely corresponding to the Dharma should be said to be encompassed in terms of the dimension *it is in itself* or *in its immediacy,* because the Dharma transcends the distinction of what is truly and inversely corresponding and yet allows the distinction without obstruction within itself. But, in Dōgen, is the development of inverse correspondence fully and self-consciously realized to the same degree as the development of true correspondence?

To put this another way, in Dōgen's doctrine of the oneness of practice and realization, isn't there a thoroughgoing realization of a paradoxical contradiction that fundamentally accompanies our *practice,* that the more one concentrates on practice, one cannot help but increasingly see that the self is not in accord with the Dharma? The paradoxical contradiction inevitable to practice is understood, in that at its extreme point one cannot help but come to a realization of sinfulness in the separation and opposition of practice and realization. But for Dōgen, although the matter of the two different stages of practice and realization unfolding in practice is taken into question, isn't it the case that any realization of sinfulness in terms of the separation and opposition of practice and realization as the necessary conclusion of the dualistic view does not become problematic? The expression "If there is the slightest discrepancy, the gap will be as great as heaven and earth" may refer to an extreme view stemming from the notion of the two stages of practice and realization. However, this may not signify a realization of the *separation and opposition* of practice and realization, which would be an even further extreme in considering practice and realization to consist of two stages. Doesn't the above expression still reflect the dimension of true correspondence to the Dharma? In Dōgen, such an increasing realization of the self as not being in accord with the Dharma as one concentrates more and more in practice is strongly rejected as a dualistic view of practice and realization. He emphasizes the need to return to the basic standpoint of the oneness of practice and realization by overcoming the dualistic view at its root. Indeed, he stresses the necessity of realizing that the stages of practice and realization understood dualistically are encompassed originally in an undefiled practice-realization that is fundamentally nondual and inseparable. Therefore, in his standpoint of the oneness of practice and realization, we do not discover that Dōgen self-consciously questions and overcomes the separation and opposition realized by breaking through even the dualistic view of practice and realization. But the inversely corresponding development of the Dharma can be realized only through penetrating the standpoint of the separation and opposition of practice and realization. That is why we previously asked whether in Dōgen's views of the oneness of practice and realization and whole-being Buddha-nature, *the inversely corresponding development of the Dharma* is fully encountered in the same way as the truly corresponding development of the Dharma.

The same sort of issue must be raised in regard to Shinran's view, but in the opposite manner. For Shinran, it is believed that one attains supreme nirvāna without fail and returns to the city of the Dharma-nature by being grasped by the Dharma in the form of the power of Amida's primal vow. In so far as this is the case, the Dharma itself must include not merely the inversely corresponding development of the Dharma as the merit-transference by Amida in Shinran's sense. It must also equally encompass the truly corresponding development of the Dharma as seen in Dōgen. This is indicated by Shinran when he writes, "Rebirth is...for all to receive the body of naturalness or of emptiness, the body of boundlessness."[88] Shinran deeply believes in the Dharma precisely in terms of deep faith in the self as a sinful being as the decisive opportunity. But is the truly corresponding development of the Dharma fully and self-consciously encountered in its original meaning, whereby sentient beings are grasped as pure in their original nature and our practice is regarded as "undefiled practice?" We may say that in Shinran's view of the Dharma, as well in Dōgen's, the truly corresponding development of the Dharma is encompassed as *it is in itself* or *in its immediacy*. But is that development (or if we put it exactly, the Dharmakaya as the "body of emptiness") fully and self-consciously encountered in the same degree as the inversely corresponding development of the Dharma as the primal vow of Amida, who is the Sambhogakaya, or Reward Body?

In other words, when Shinran reached the deep realization of the separation and opposition of practice and realization in his own *practice* by saying, "Since I am absolutely incapable of any religious practice, hell is my only home," he refers to the extreme realization of practice and realization as two different stages such that he cannot in any way be emancipated from that dualistic view. So far as this is the case, without attaining the oneness of practice and realization reached by Dōgen, who was emancipated from the dualistic view at its root, Shinran attained the realization of the separation and opposition of practice and realization in a way that is the opposite of Dōgen's view of the oneness of practice and realization. Shinran did not only attain the realization of the self in two different stages of practice and realization in terms of what Dōgen calls "the slightest discrepancy." He further realized an absolute and antagonistic gap, as great as that between heaven and earth, in the opposition of practice and realization, transcending even the standpoint of there being two different stages. Thus he was made to move in the direction of faith in the primal vow rather than the direction of self-emancipation. From this view, didn't Shinran move farther and farther away from the standpoint of the oneness of practice and realization, or "This very mind itself is buddha," while retaining at least "the slightest discrepancy?" Therefore, although Shinran returned to the city of the Dharma-nature by attaining a realization in the inversely corresponding manner through the transformative power of Amida's vow, as in "The evil person entrusting the primal vow," didn't he still fail to overcome naiveté and overlook the standpoints of the oneness of practice and realization and whole-being Buddha-nature in Dōgen's sense? The truly corresponding development of the Dharma is clearly manifested in the standpoint of whole-being

Buddha-nature, which realizes this very mind itself is buddha as "practice-realization is undefiled."[89] That is why we raised the question of whether, in Shinran's notions of the evil person as the true opportunity and merit-transference through the power of the primal vow, *the truly corresponding development of the Dharma* is fully and self-consciously encountered in the same way as the inversely corresponding development?

If we consider only Dōgen's own view or only Shinran's own view, the issue discussed above cannot arise. But while standing in Dōgen's view of whole-being Buddha-nature, if we authentically encounter Shinran's view of the power of the primal vow on the basis of subjective experience encompassing this other view rather than merely looking at it from the outside, we will inevitably confront the following issue. That is, although Dōgen's view naively encompasses the inversely corresponding development of the Dharma (the development of the Dharma as the vow that redeems even evil persons), does it fully and self-consciously encounter this view? In the same way, while standing in Shinran's view of the transformative power of the primal vow, if we authentically confront Dōgen's view of the oneness of practice and realization on the basis of subjective experience encompassing it rather than merely looking at it from the outside, we will inevitably confront the following issue. That is, although Shinran's view naively encompasses the truly corresponding development of the Dharma (the manifestation of the Dharma-nature as the *self* of the casting off of body-mind) as the "body of emptiness," does it fully and self-consciously encounter this?

The naiveté discussed above that is implied in both views cannot be realized insofar as one is limited to one standpoint or the other. But if the naiveté is realized from either standpoint through a radically internal confrontation on the basis of existential experience with the other standpoint, then even the Dharma maintained until this moment is broken through to its bottomless bottom, and one discovers oneself in the midst of its absolutely bottomless nothingness. This is the standpoint of *absolute nothingness* as the *realization of no-Dharma* which does not recognize the Dharma itself. It is the standpoint of nothingness as the realization of no-practice, no-faith, and no-realization. It is the world that is "nothing but rubbish" as far as one can see. It is, however, of course not a standpoint of mere nothingness. Instead, it is the standpoint of a twofold nothingness which is realized by the breakdown of the Dharma itself that overcame and fulfilled the nothingness realized by the breakdown of human life.

The world of "nothing but rubbish" indicates the world of no-Dharma as realized in the dimension of twofold nothingness in this sense. It is only through the realization of no-Dharma that the *distinction* discussed above between the development of what is truly or inversely corresponding to the Dharma is realized, and in regard to this, a sort of naiveté implied in the standpoint of both Dōgen or Shinran becomes problematic. It is only through the twofold nothingness as the realization of no-Dharma that a genuine perspective on this issue is offered. The realizations of the Dharma in Dōgen and in Shinran stand back to back, so to speak, in terms of the Dharma. The perspective encountered in Dōgen's realization of the Dharma is not necessarily completely encountered in Shinran's realization, and the perspective encountered in Shinran's realization of the Dharma still remains in naiveté in Dōgen's realization. The realization of no-Dharma is nothing but the realization of absolute nothingness that unfolds as the existing Dharma is broken through, when from either standpoint, as discussed above, one side accomplishes a radically internal confrontation on the basis of existential experience with the other side. This occurs especially when modern contemporary rational reason intervenes into the scene.

If the true Dharma exists, then the self's existential realization of it must not only encompass both the truly and inversely corresponding development of the Dharma in its immediate form, but must clearly and self-consciously realize both of these aspects through an authentic existential encounter. The Dharma that really transcends the distinction of true and inverse is not obstructed by the realization, however clear, of the true as true and the inverse as inverse. From such an existential standpoint, the Dharma on the one hand represents independence without reliance or complete emancipation, so that there is no need to use a device to sweep away any "secular dust," as in Dōgen's expression "The Whole Body is far beyond the world's dust."[90] On the other hand, the Dharma must deeply maintain the realization of the unenlightened and defiled person within itself, and through identifying itself with sentient beings of sinful karma without a chance for release, it must transform them from within. This standpoint does not merely freely use pro and con, good and evil, and the coming and going of life-and-death. For liberation from the distinctions of pro and con, good and evil, and the coming and going of life-and-death is already attained in the truly corresponding development of the Dharma, that is, in the manifestation of complete emancipation. The *distinction of true and inverse* discussed here is the distinction between the truly corresponding development of the Dharma in the above meaning and the inversely corresponding development of the Dharma adapted even to one who goes against and falls away from the truly corresponding development of the Dharma by realizing sinful karma extending throughout the *kalpas*. Therefore, the distinction is a more fundamental and radical distinction than the ones between pro and con, good and evil, life and death, and coming and going in regard to the Dharma. This is the distinction that inquires about the Dharma itself, transcending the differences of pro and con, good and evil, life and death, coming and going, etc. It is the distinction directly referring to the self-development of the Dharma. It is the distinction that must be inquired about in order for the *Dharma to realize the Dharma itself.* That is because, for the Dharma to be the truly concrete Dharma, it must encounter and transcend even the more fundamental and radical distinction, that is, the distinction of true and inverse in the self-development of the Dharma, which is realized in a dimension beyond the differences of pro and con, good and evil, life and death, and coming and going. Thus it is the Dharma in which the distinction of true and inverse is clearly and distinctively realized within its existential realization.

What sort of realization in regard to the Dharma is concretely and existentially inquired about when we ask whether or not the distinction of true and inverse is self-consciously realized in an existential experience of the Dharma? It is nothing but this: It is to ask whether the Dharma transcending the differences of pro and con, good and evil, life and death, and coming and going does not truly distinguish between Buddha and Mara;[91] or, whether it is a Dharma prior to the distinction of Buddha and Mara. That is because, from the standpoint of either the Dharma of complete emancipation or the Dharma of the transformative power of the primal vow, the distinction of true and inverse in the self-development of the Dharma may not yet be self-consciously encountered. If the realization stops with this naiveté, such a view of the Dharma can be the Buddha and *at the same time* Mara, due to that naiveté.

For not only Buddha but also Mara is beyond the distinction between pro and con, good and evil, life and death, and coming and going. Accordingly, if the transcendence of that distinction were taken immediately as the standpoint of Buddha or the enlightened one, then that Buddha is not the true Buddha but the Buddha undifferentiated from Mara. Thus, that Buddha must undergo the encounter and confrontation with Mara in order to attain true Buddhahood. This is why, according to legend, the historical Buddha encountered the temptation of Mara, and only after conquering this is he said to have attained perfect enlightenment. This is also why Zen master Lin-chi (J. Rinzai) says:

> [Now] supposing there were a Buddha-Mara, inseparably united in one body, like the mixture of water and milk of which the King of Geese drinks only the milk, the follower of the Way who possesses the true Dharma Eye would handle Mara and Buddha.[92]

Lin-chi also states:

> [Now] he who is a renouncer of home must, acquiring the usual and true insight, distinguish between Buddha and Mara, between the true and the false, the secular and the sacred. If he can do this, then he may be called a true renouncer of home. But if he cannot distinguish Mara from Buddha, then he has only left one home to enter another. He may be dubbed a karma-creating sentient being, but he cannot be called a true renouncer of home.[93]

For Buddha and Mara to be discriminated in regard to the Dharma, the distinction of true and inverse should not be realized merely naively without a serious encounter in the self-realization of the Dharma itself. The Dharma that thoroughly encounters the distinction between true and inverse in the self-development of the Dharma is at once the self of independent nonreliance and complete emancipation and the self that can act in the ways of Mara in the realm of Mara instead of merely remaining as the Dharma prior to distinguishing Buddha and Mara. This must be the self that uses the Buddha and Mara freely without adhering to either Buddha or Mara.

According to chapter 7, on "The Buddha Path," in the *Vimalakirti Sūtra,* "If a bodhisattva treads the wrong ways (*hidō*) he enters the Buddha path."[94] "Treading the wrong ways" is not merely evil practice, breaking the commandments, or the five blunders, but on the deepest level it must include practicing the way of Mara. In the realization of the Dharma itself, if

the developments of what is truly and inversely corresponding
are seen as naively identical without a self-conscious realization
of their distinction, then the Dharma indicates a standpoint
prior to the distinction of Buddha and Mara that unconsciously
lapses into Mara in the name of Buddha and yet believes itself
to be practicing Buddha. In contrast to this, if the distinction of
true and inverse in the self-development of the Dharma is fully
encountered while transcending the distinction within itself,
then at the same time the Dharma prior to the distinction of
Buddha and Mara is discerned. This leads to the realization of
the true Dharma, which is really a nonduality of Buddha and
Mara that uses each freely to save all beings while transcending
the opposition between them from within. Upon attaining the
Dharma that can freely and genuinely use the Buddha and
Mara while self-consciously transcending the difference of true
and inverse in the realization of the Dharma itself, this Dharma
functions as the person who fully embodies the oneness of wisdom and compassion.

But the standpoint of absolute nothingness, or the realization of no-Dharma discussed earlier, is not cognizant of whether
or not the standpoint of such a completely true Dharma exists.
The standpoint of absolute nothingness is nothing but the realization of no-Dharma. This is attained by breaking down the
existing Dharma through the realization of its own naiveté in
the sense that the standpoint of the existing Dharma, or the
Dharma before the twofold nothingness, did not fully and self-
consciously encounter in its own realization the distinction
between the true and the inverse in the self-development of the
Dharma. The realization of its own naiveté in the above sense is
attained through the internal and existential confrontation with
the other standpoint it faces in the opposite direction to itself.
Consequently, the standpoint of emptiness must seek to distinguish Buddha and Mara by clearly realizing that the Dharma in
which the distinction between true and inverse in the self-development of the Dharma is not fully encountered—that is, the
Dharma prior to the distinction of Buddha and Mara—is not the
true Dharma. The true Dharma must be said to exist in breaking
through both Buddha and Mara, as in the expression "Cutting
off the way of a thousand saints and breaking down the realm of
Maras." It is realized with one's whole existence only through
the full penetration of the standpoint of absolute nothingness as
the realization of no-Dharma.[95]

Notes

Editor's Introduction

1. As Heidegger puts it, such works divulge "ways of thinking [that] hold with them that mysterious quality that we can walk them forward and backward, and that indeed only the way back will lead us forward." In Heidegger, *On the Way to Language,* trans. Peter D. Hertz (New York: Harper, 1917), 2.

2. The major work still not translated is *Eihei Koroku.* For review articles covering many of the works cited here, see Thomas Kasulis, "The Zen Philosopher: A Review Article on Dōgen Scholarship in English," *Philosophy East and West* 28 (3), 353–73; and Steven Heine, "Truth and Method in Dōgen Scholarship: A Review of Recent Works," *The Eastern Buddhist* 20 (2), 128–47.

3. See Tamura Yoshirō, *Kamakura shin-bukkyō shisō no kenkyū* (Kyoto: Heirakuji shoten, 1965); and Tamura, "Critique of Original Awakening Thought in Shōshin and Dōgen," *Japanese Journal of Religious Studies* 11(2–3), 243–66.

4. SG "Bendōwa" EB, 144. (The term *realization* has been changed to "attainment.")

5. SG "Gyōbutsuigi," 345.

6. SG "Busshō" (2) EB, 88.

7. William R. LaFleur, "Editor's Introduction," in Masao Abe, *Zen and Western Thought* (London and Basingstoke: Macmillan, 1985), xvii.

Chapter I. The Oneness of Practice and Attainment

1. SG "Butsudō," 378.

2. Tamaki Koshirō, *Dōgenshū, Nihon no Shisō* 2 (Tokyo: Chikuma shobō, 1969), 4.

3. In *Sōtōshū zensho* (Tokyo: Kōmeisha, 1929–38), 16:16 and 17:16a respectively.

4. In *Dōgen* (Tokyo: Yoshikawa Kobunkan, 1962, 61–78) Takeuchi Michio, one of the leading scholars in the history of Japanese Buddhism and a specialist in biographical studies of Dōgen, argues that Dōgen's aspiration to go to China to seek the Buddha Dharma was founded and strengthened at the time of the upheaval of Shōkū (1219–21), a serious power struggle between the imperial court and the Kamakura military regime. During that upheaval Dōgen, while practicing Zen in Kenninji monastery in Kyoto, faced the fact of the persecution of his close relatives who served the imperial court, and thus saw the tragic consequences of human enmity and vengeance. My understanding is that while these experiences surrounding Dōgen certainly *prompted* his aspiration to go to China to seek the Buddhist way of emancipation, this situation in itself does not lessen the importance of Dōgen's doubt concerning the Tendai teaching of original awakening as the foremost motive inspiring his religious quest.

5. Ascribed to Chih-i, in *Tendai Shikyōgi* by Korean monk Taikan in *Taishō* 46: 779a.

6. *Hōkyōki* (1) EB, 117.

7. SG "Bendōwa" EB, 130.

8. SG "Bendōwa" EB, 130.

9. *Hōkyōki* (1) EB, 131.

10. SG "Bendōwa" EB, 129.

11. SG "Bendōwa" EB, 144.

12. SG "Busshō" (2) EB, 88.

13. SG "Gyōji" I, 122.

14. SG "Bendōwa" EB, 144.

15. SG "Busshō" (1) EB, 108.

16. SG "Busshō" (2) EB, 91.

17. SG "Bendōwa" EB, 129.

18. SG "Gyōji" I, 122.

19. SG "Busshō" (1) EB, 88.

20. SG "Bendōwa" EB, 136.

21. SG "Genjōkōan EB, 133.

CHAPTER II. DŌGEN ON BUDDHA-NATURE

1. SG "Busshō" (3) EB, 96. The passage may not actually be from the sūtra but from Zen sayings referring to it; see chapter 3 n. 39.

2. Since the Chinese characters *shitsuu* do not make a distinction between singular and plural, *shitsuu* means both whole-being in its entirety and all beings in their individuality. Dōgen actually uses the term in these two meanings according to context.

3. Strictly speaking, sentient beings other than human beings, such as animals, may not be said to realize their life and death even as "facts," since they do not have self-consciousness.

4. Sanskrit *manusya*, like the English term *man*, is etymologically connected with "mana"—to think. See Nakamura Hajime, *The Ways of Thinking of Eastern Peoples* (Tokyo: Japanese National Commission for UNESCO, 1960), 108–10.

5. Nishitani Keiji, "The Personal and the Impersonal in Religion," in *Religion and Nothingness* (Berkeley: University of California Press, 1982), 49.

6. Nishitani Keiji, "The Personal and the Impersonal in Religion," 58.

7. See Miura Isshū and Ruth Fuller Sasaki, *Zen Dust* (Kyoto: The First Zen Institute of America in Japan, 1966), 253–55.

8. The Senika heresy was a current of heretical thought that appeared during the Buddha's lifetime, emphasizing the concept of a permanent self. It appears in the *Nirvāna Sūtra*, chap. 39. See also SG "Bendōwa" EB, 145–48; SG "Busshō" (1) EB, 100–102.

9. SG "Busshō" (1) EB, 102.

10. SG "Busshō" (1) EB, 99–100.

11. SG "Busshō" (1) EB, 97.

12. SG "Busshō" (1) EB, 97.

13. *Immo* is the Japanese reading of a Chinese term that is a colloquial expression of the Sung dynasty often used in a Zen context. It is (1) an interrogative, meaning "how," "in what way," "in what manner," and (2) a demonstrative, signifying "this," "such," "thus," "thus and so," "that," "like that," etc. Here in Hui-neng's question, *immo* indicates the second meaning, particularly "thus." In *Shōbōgenzō*, Dōgen has a fascicle entitled "Immo," in which he discusses the Zen meaning of the term as he understands it.

14. Spinoza, *Ethics* (part 1, def. 3) trans. R. H. M. Elwes, in *Philosophy of Benedict de Spinoza,* (New York: Tudor, n.d.).

15. R. Kroner, *Speculation and Revelation in Modern Philosophy* (Philadelphia: Westminster Press, n.d.), 126.

16. SG "Busshō" (1) EB, 102.

17. "No Buddha-nature" refers to the ordinary idea of the term, that is, the counterconcept of "Buddha-nature"; "no-Buddha-nature" with a hyphen after "no" indicates Dōgen's idea, that is, the nonobjectifiable Buddha-nature that is freed from "having" or "not having."

18. SG "Busshō" (3) EB, 74.

19. SG "Busshō" (1) EB, 111.

20. SG "Busshō" (3) EB, 74–75.

21. SG "Busshō" (2) EB, 87, 89.

22. SG "Busshō" (3) EB, 87–88.

23. SG "Busshō" (1) EB, 111.

24. SG "Busshō" (3) EB, 88.

25. SG "Busshō" (3) EB, 74–75.

26. In SG "Genjōkōan" EB, 134, Dōgen says, "When buddhas are genuinely buddhas there is no need for them to be conscious that they are buddhas. Yet they are realized buddhas and they continue to realize buddha."

27. SG "Busshō" (1) EB, 97.

28. SG "Busshō" (3) EB, 71–72.

29. Marjorie Grene, "Heidegger, Martin," in *The Encyclopedia of Philosophy*, ed. Paul Edwards (New York: Macmillan and The Free Press, 1967), 3:463.

30. The other two are "Nothing has an ego" and "Nirvāna is tranquil."

31. SG "Busshō" (2) EB, 91.

32. SG "Busshō" (2) EB, 93.

33. SG "Hōsshō," 417.

34. Hegel, *Science of Logic*, trans. W. H. Johnston and L. G. Struthers (London: George Allen and Unwin, 1929), 1:95. Also published as *Wissenschaft der Logik* ed. Georg Lasson (Leipzig: Felix Meiner, 1923) vol. 1, sect. 67.

35. SG "Busshō" (3) EB, 87.

36. "Cosmological" here does not refer to the cosmos created by or distinguished from God, but to the cosmos in its broadest sense, in which even "God" is embraced.

37. SG "Bendōwa" EB, 145-48.

38. SG "Bendōwa" EB, 145.

39. SG "Bendōwa" EB, 136.

40. SG "Sesshin sesshō," 361.

41. "Undefiled" practice in Dōgen's sense does not indicate a mere moral or ethical purity realized through the observance of Buddhist precepts, but rather the practice of "body-mind that has been cast-off" (datsuraku-shinjin), that is, the practice based on the complete negation of ego-centeredness. This does not mean that undefiled practice as understood by Dōgen excludes the importance of observing precepts, even though such observance is not a necessary condition for awakening to one's Buddha-nature.

42. Fukanzazengi EB, 122.

43. SG "Bendōwa" EB, 147.

44. Gakudōyōjinshū DZZ, 2:250.

45. Gakudōyōjinshū DZZ, 2:250.

46. SG "Hotsubodaishin," 646.

47. Dōgen, Hōkyōki, EB (2), 75.

48. SG "Busshō" (1), 101.

49. SG "Busshō" (1), 104.

50. SG "Kūge," 112.

51. SG "Uji" EB, 126.

52. SG "Uji" EB, 116.

53. SG "Uji" EB, 120. (The term passageless-passage is a change from the original.)

54. SG "Genjōkōan" EB, 136.

55. SG "Busshō" (1) EB, 103.

56. SG "Busshō" (1) EB, 104-05.

57. SG "Uji" EB, 120-21.

58. However, in Zur Sache des Denkens (Tubingen: Max Niemayer,

1969), Heidegger discusses "Zeit und Sein" ("Time and Being") emphasizing *"Ereignis"* as a "gift" of "It" (*Es gibt*) in which time and being are inseparable. For a fuller discussion of this issue, see chapter 4 below, "The Problem of Time in Heidegger and Dōgen."

59. Martin Heidegger, *Was ist Metaphysik?* (Frankfurt: Vittorio Klostermann, 1949), 31.

60. SG "Busshō" (3) EB, 84.

CHAPTER III. DŌGEN'S VIEW OF TIME AND SPACE

1. SG "Bendōwa" EB, 151

2. SG "Genjōkōan" EB, 134.

3. SG "Genjōkōan" EB, 134.

4. SG "Busshō" (1) EB, 99.

5. SG "Yuibutsu yobutsu," 781.

6. SG "Busshō" (2) EB, 90.

7. SG "Uji" EB, 118.

8. SG "Bendōwa" EB, 136–37.

9. SG "Busshō" (2) EB, 99.

10. SG "Uji," EB, 116.

11. SG "Uji," EB, 116.

12. SG "Uji," EB, 190.

13. Concerning the nonobstruction of times and times see my essay "Sōzō to Engi" (Creation and Dependent Origination), *Risō*, nos. 531 (1977) and 533 (1977).

14. SG "Uji," 190.

15. SG "Uji," 190.

16. SG "Genjōkōan" EB, 136.

17. SG "Zenki" EB, 204.

18. SG "Zenki" EB, 204.

19. SG "Uji" EB, 120–21.

20. SG "Uji," 190.

21. SG "Uji," 191.

22. SG "Kōmyō," 116.

23. SG "Uji," 190.

24. SG "Sansuikyō," 260.

25. SG "Bukkyō," 311.

26. SG "Uji," 191.

27. SG "Uji," 191.

28. SG "Uji," 191.

29. SG "Shoakumakusa," 278.

30. SG "Busshō" (1) EB, 100.

31. SG "Uji" EB, 118.

32. SG "Kokyō," 185.

33. SG "Muchūsetsumu," 244.

34. SG "Shohōjissō," 371.

35. SG "Yuibutsu yobutsu," 784.

36. SG "Shinjingakudō," 38.

37. SG "Sangai yuishin," 355.

38. SG "Bendōwa," EB, 137.

39. SG "Busshō" (1) EB, 102. This sentence, as it stands, is an actual quote not from the *Nirvāna Sūtra*, but from the *Shūmon Rentōeyō*, a collection of Zen sayings and dialogues published in 1189 and included in *Dainihon Zokuzōkyō*, 2.9b. Dōgen further changes Po-chang's words, which are based on the *Nirvāna Sūtra*.

40. SG "Busshō" (1) EB, 104.

41. SG "Busshō" (1) EB, 104.

42. SG "Busshō" (1) EB, 114.

43. SG "Busshō" (1) EB, 103.

44. SG "Busshō" (1) EB, 104.

45. SG "Kōmyō," 116.

46. SG "Sansuikyō," 258.

47. SG "Bukkyō," 407.

48. SG "Shinjingakudō," 39.

49. SG "Shinjingakudō," 40.

50. SG "Shinjingakudō," 40.

51. DZZ, 2:100.

52. DZZ, 2:100.

53. SG "Den'e," 292.

54. SG "Uji," 192.

55. SG "Uji," 192.

56. SG "Bendōwa" EB, 144.

57. SG "Gabyō," 210.

58. SG "Bendōwa" EB, 144.

59. SG "Busshō" (3) EB, 74–75.

60. SG "Busshō" (3) EB, 75.

61. SG "Busshō" (2) EB, 93.

62. SG "Busshō" (2) EB, 93.

63. SG "Uji," 192.

64. SG "Gyōji" 1, 141.

65. SG "Uji," 190.

66. SG "Keiseisanshoku," 218.

67. SG "Shoakumakusa," 278.

68. SG "Keiseisanshoku," 222.

69. SG "Sokushinzebutsu," 45.

70. SG "Sansuikyō," 258.

71. SG "Uji," 192.

72. Masao Abe, "A Rejoinder," in *The Emptying God: A Buddhist-Jewish-Christian Conversation,* ed. John Cobb and Christopher Ives (Maryknoll, NY: Orbis, 1989), 193.

73. D. T. Suzuki, *Outlines of Mahayana Buddhism* (New York: Schocken, 1963), 198.

74. See Masao Abe, "Will, Sūnyata, and History" in *The Religious Philosophy of Nishitani Keiji*, ed. Taitetsu Unno (Berkeley: Asian Humanities Press, 1990), especially 299–304.

CHAPTER IV. THE PROBLEM OF TIME IN HEIDEGGER AND DŌGEN

The author is grateful to Professor Joan Stambaugh and Mr. Steve Antinoff for their careful review and valuable suggestions, without which the paper would be even more imperfect.

1. Martin Heidegger, *Holzwege* (Frankfurt: Klostermann, 1950), 36.

2. SG "Uji" EB, 114f.

3. Seneca, Marcus Aurelius, Montaigne, Pascal, and Schopenhauer all deal with the problem of death to some extent. In his essay "Death," Robert G. Olson states: "Although most of the great philosophers have touched on the problem of death, few have dealt with it systematically or in detail.... [A]t almost all stages in Western history we are likely to discover more about the topic in the writings of men of letters than in those of technical philosophers." In *The Encyclopedia of Philosophy*, ed. Paul Edwards (New York: Macmillan, 1967), 2:307.

4. Spinoza, *Ethics*, part 4, "Of Human Bondage," proposition 67.

5. Heidegger, *Sein und Zeit* [hereafter SZ], 7th ed. (Tübingen: Niemeyer, 1953), 245. Translated as *Being and Time* [hereafter BT] by John Macquarrie and Edward Robinson (New York and London: Harper and Row, 1962), 289.

6. Heidegger, *Was ist Metaphysik?* [hereafter WM] (6th ed.— Frankfurt: Klostermann, 1951, 35). Translated in *Basic Writings* [hereafter BW] by David Farrell Krell, ed. (New York and London: Harper and Row, 1977), 105.

7. BW, 103.

8. BW, 105.

9. WM, 17.

10. SZ, 145, BT, 186.

11. Heidegger, *Vorträge und Aufsätze* [hereafter VA] (Pfullingen: Neske, 1954), 170–72, 176–77. Translated in *Poetry, Language, Thought* [hereafter PLT], by Albert Hoftstatder, ed. (New York and London: Harper and Row, 1971), 173.

12. VA, 178.

13. VA, 178.

14. VA, 177.

15. PLT, 178, 179.

16. SG "Shoakumakusa," 283.

17. See Ōkubo Dōshū, *Dōgen zenji-den no kenkyū* (Tokyo: Iwanami shoten, 1966), 75–76.

18. Hee-jin Kim, *Dōgen Kigen—Mystical Realist* (Tucson: University of Arizona Press, 1975), 21–22.

19. SG "Shōji" EB, 79.

20. SG "Bendōwa" EB, 147.

21. SG "Shōji" EB, 79 (translation slightly modified).

22. SG "Genjōkōan" EB, 136 (translation slightly modified).

23. Dōgen states in SG "Bendōwa" EB, 133: "From the first time you meet your master and receive his teaching, you have no need for either incense-offerings, homage-paying, *nembutsu*, penance, disciplines, or silent sūtra-readings, only cast off body-mind in sitting meditation."

24. SG "Zenki" EB, 74.

25. SG "Zenki" EB, 76.

26. SG "Bendōwa" EB, 147.

27. SG "Shōji" EB, 78.

28. SG "Shōji" EB, 79.

29. SG "Gyōbutsuigi," 50.

30. SG "Shinjingakudō," 40.

31. SG "Shōji" EB, 79.

32. SG "Uji" EB, 116 (translation slightly modified).

33. SG "Uji" EB, 126.

34. SG "Sansuikyō," 258.

35. SG "Uji" EB, 118.

36. SG "Kōmyō," 119.

37. SZ, 304, BT, 351.

38. SZ, 304, BT, 351.

39. SG "Bendōwa" EB, 147.

40. SZ, 303f; BT, 350f.

41. SZ, 323–25, 331–33; BT, 370–73, 379–82.

42. WM, 35; BW, 105.

43. See n. 32.

44. SG "Uji" EB, 118.

45. SG "Busshō" (3) EB, 99–100.

46. SG "Busshō" (3) EB, 99.

47. SG "Busshō" (3) EB, 100.

48. SG "Busshō" (3) EB, 102.

49. SG "Uji" EB, 122.

50. William J. Richardson, *Heidegger: Through Phenomenology to Thought* [hereafter HPT] (The Hauge: Martinus Nijhoff, 1963), xvi.

51. Richardson, *Heidegger*, xviii.

52. Richardson, *Heidegger*, xii.

53. Heidegger, *Zur Sache des Denkens* [hereafter ZS] (Tübingen: Niemeyer, 1969), 30. Translated as *On Time and Being* [hereafter TB] by Joan Stambaugh (New York and London: Harper and Row, 1972), 28.

54. ZS, 4; TB, 4.

55. ZS, 4; TB, 4.

56. ZS, 20, TB, 19.

57. ZS, 30, TB, 27–28.

58. SG "Genjōkōan" EB, 133–34.

59. SG "Genjōkōan" EB, 134f.

60. SG "Busshō" (1) EB, 97.

61. SG "Kōmyō," 119.

62. SG "Kōmyō," 119.

63. SG "Kōmyō," 119.

64. SG "Yuibutsu yobutsu," 781.

65. HPT, xviii.

66. ZS, 20; TB, 19.

67. ZS, 2; TB, 2.

68. ZS, 2; TB, 2.

69. ZS, 16; TB, 16.

70. ZS, 2; TB, 2.

71. ZS, 3; TB, 3.

72. SZ, 19; BT, 40.

73. ZS, 3; TB, 3.

74. ZS, 4; TB, 4.

75. ZS, 19–20; TB, 19.

76. ZS, 18; TB, 17.

77. ZS, 17; TB, 16.

78. ZS, 17; TB, 16.

79. SG "Uji" EB, 122.

80. SG "Uji" EB, 126.

81. SG "Uji" EB, 122.

82. SG "Uji" EB, 116.

83. SG "Uji" EB, 117.

84. SG "Uji" EB, 122.

85. SG "Genjōkōan" EB, 136; SG "Uji" EB, 126.

86. SG "Shōji" EB, 79.

87. SG "Genjōkōan" EB, 136.

88. SG "Zenki" EB, 76.

89. SG "Kōmyō," 119.

90. SG "Uji" EB, 119.

91. SG "Uji" EB, 120.

92. ZS, 3; TB, 3.

93. ZS, 13; TB, 12–13.

94. ZS, 13; TB, 13.

95. ZS, 14; TB, 13–14.

96. ZS, 14; TB, 14.

97. ZS, 14; TB, 14.

98. ZS, 15; TB, 14–15.

99. SG "Uji" EB, 120–21 (translation slightly modified).

100. ZS, 3; TB, 3.

101. SG "Uji" EB, 120–21.

102. SG "Den'e," 292.

103. ZS, 16; TB, 15.

104. ZS, 16; TB, 16.

105. ZS, 15; TB, 15.

106. ZS, 21; TB, 20.

107. ZS, 19; TB, 18–19.

108. ZS, 23; TB, 22.

109. ZS, 23; TB, 22.

110. ZS, 23; TB, 23.

111. ZS, 23; TB, 23.

112. ZS, 24; TB, 23.

113. ZS, 24; TB, 24.

114. ZS, 25; TB, 24.

115. ZS, 4; TB, 4.

116. ZS, 4; TB, 4.

117. Heidegger, *Identität und Differenz* (Pfullingen: Neske, 1957), 45–48.

118. ZS, 3; TB, 3.

119. ZS, 20; TB, 19.

120. SG "Zazengi," 89.

121. Heidegger, *Gelassenheit* (Pfullingen: Neske, 1960), 32, 63, 73.

122. Heidegger, *Einführung in die Metaphysik* (Tübingen: Niemeyer, 1953), 29–30.

123. Tsujimura Kōichi, *Haideggā ronkō* (A Study of Heidegger) (Tokyo: Sōbunsha, 1971), 45–47.

124. ZS, 23; TB, 22.

125. ZS, 46; TB, 43.

126. SG "Busshō" (2) EB, 91–93.

127. ZS, 23; TB, 23

128. ZS, 24; TB, 24.

129. In *Ching-tê ch'üan-têng lu* (J. *Keitoku dentōroku*), chap. 10 in *Taishō*, vol. 51.

130. *Fukanzazengi* EB, 122.

131. See n. 34.

132. See also Masao Abe, *Zen and Western Thought* (London and Basingstoke: Macmillan, 1985), 65f.

CHAPTER V. THE PROBLEM OF DEATH IN
DOGEN AND SHINRAN, PART I

1. SG "Busshō" (1) EB, 97.

2. Shinran, "Keshindo" in Shin Buddhism Translation Series, *The True Teaching, Practice and Realization of the Pure Land Way: A Translation of Shinran's Kyōgyōshinshō* [hereafter TTPR] (Kyoto: Hongwanji International Center, 1990), 4:536.

3. *Fukanzazengi* EB, 122.

4. *Fukanzazengi* EB, 122.

5. SG "Yuibutsu yobutsu," 781.

6. SG "Jippō," 477.

7. SG "Bukkyō," 407.

8. SG "Keiseisanshoku," 218.

9. In *Tandokumon* (Notes Praising Amida's Virtues), written by Zonkaku (1290–1373), son of the third patriarch of Hongwanji, Kakun-

yo, in *Shinshu shōgyō zenshū*, 3:661–64 (trans. Dennis Hirota). Although this quoted passage has been attributed to Shinran, we do not find it in Shinran's own writings. It is generally considered that Zonkaku expressed Shinran's inner problem as a novice in this passage.

10. Shinran, "Shinjin," in TTPR (1985), 2:213.

11. SG "Shōji" EB, 79.

12. SG "Shōji" EB, 79.

13. SG "Gyōbutsuigi," 48.

14. SG "Zenki" EB, 74–75.

15. SG "Sokushin-zebutsu," 44.

16. SG "Sokushin-zebutsu," 44.

17. SG "Sokushin-zebutsu," 44.

18. From *Kenzeiki*, in *Sōtōshū Zensho* (Tokyo: Kōmeisha, 1929–38), 17:16a.

19. SG "Genjōkōan" EB, 134.

20. *Fukanzazengi* EB, 121.

21. *Fukanzazengi* EB, 121.

22. SG "Bendōwa" EB, 129.

23. SG "Sokushin-zebutsu," 45.

24. Dōgen sought a middle way between two heretical tendencies—the naturalist heresy (*jinen-gedō*), which naively affirms the natural world without spiritual purification, and the Senika heresy (*sennige-dō*), which hypostatizes a substantial, enduring self beyond the natural world; both heresies fail to grasp the impermanence of phenomena and violate the oneness of practice and attainment.

25. SG "Sokushin-zebutsu," 45.

26. SG "Bendōwa" EB, 146.

27. SG "Sokushin-zebutsu," 45.

28. *Fukanzazengi* EB, 122.

29. SG "Dōtoku," 302.

30. SG "Dōtoku," 302.

31. SG "Dōtoku," 302.

32. SG "Immo," 165.

33. SG "Kūge," 108.

34. SG "Jinshininga," 678.

35. SG "Ikka myōju," 62.

36. SG "Jinshininga," 678.

37. SG "Kūge," 108.

38. SG "Gyōbutsuigi," 52.

39. SG "Busshō" (3) EB, 87.

40. SG "Busshō" (3) EB, 76.

41. SG "Zenki" EB, 76.

42. SG "Zenki" EB, 76–77.

43. SG "Shoakumakusa," 280.

44. Shinran, "Shō," in TTPR (1987), 3:357.

45. Shinran, "Jinenhōnishō," in Shin Buddhism Translation Series, *Letters of Shinran (Mattōshō)* (Kyoto: Hongwanji International Center, 1978), 23.

46. Shinran, *Yuishinshō mon'i,* in Shin Buddhism Translation Series, *Notes on "Essentials of Faith Alone"* (Kyoto: Hongwanji International Center, 1979), 33.

47. *Letters of Shinran,* 23.

48. *Letters of Shinran,* 29.

49. Shinran, *Songō shinzō meimon,* in Shin Buddhism Translation Series, *Notes on the Inscriptions on Sacred Scrolls: A Translation of Shinran's Songō shinzō meimon* (Kyoto: Hongwanji International Center, 1981), 38.

50. *Letters of Shinran,* 30.

51. *Letters of Shinran,* 30.

52. SG "Jinzū," 320.

CHAPTER VI. THE UNBORN AND REBIRTH

1. SG "Shōji" EB, 79

2. SG "Shinjingakudō," 41.

3. SG "Shoakumakusa," 283.

4. SG "Shinjingakudō," 41.

5. SG "Shōji" EB, 79 (translation slightly modified).

6. SG "Zenki" EB, 74.

7. SG "Shōji" EB, 79.

8. SG "Bendōwa" EB, 147.

9. SG "Gyōbutsuigi," 49.

10. SG "Busshō," 29 [(3) EB, 76].

11. SG "Bendōwa" EB, 147.

12. SG "Shōji" EB, 79.

13. SG "Shoakumakusa," 284.

14. SG "Shinjingakudō," 40.

15. SG "Yuibutsu yobutsu," 784.

16. SG "Busshō" (1) EB, 99.

17. SG "Busshō" (1) EB, 99.

18. SG "Shinjingakudō," 40.

19. SG "Busshō" (2) EB, 88.

20. Shinran, "Shōzōmatsu Wasan," in Ryukoku University Translation Center, *Shōzōmatsu Wasan: Shinran's Hymns on the Last Age* (Kyoto: Ryukoku University, 1980), 15.

21. SG "Kōmyō," 118.

22. Shinran, "Kōsō wasan," in Ryukoku University Translation Center, *The Kōsō Wasan: The Hymns of the Patriarchs* (Kyoto: Ryukoku University, 1974), 120.

23. Shinran, "Kōsō wasan," 70

24. Shinran, "Keshindo," in Shin Buddhism Translation Series, *The True Teaching, Practice, and Realization of the Pure Land Ways: A Translation of Shinran's Kyōgyōshinshō* [hereafter TTPR] (Kyoto: Hongwanji International Center, 1990), 4:532.

25. SG "Bendōwa" EB, 151.

26. *Tannishō: A Shin Buddhist Classic,* trans. Taitetsu Unno (Buddhist Study Center Press, 1984), 6. *Tannishō* is a collection of Shinran's words with commentaries by Yuien, one of his disciples.

27. Shinran, "Shōzōmatsu Wasan," 96.

28. Shinran, "Shōzōmatsu Wasan," 31.

29. SG "Bendōwa" EB, 144.

30. SG "Bendōwa" EB, 144.

31. SG "Sesshin sesshō," 361.

32. SG "Genjōkōan" EB, 134.

33. SG "Genjōkōan" EB, 134.

34. *Fukanzazengi* EB, 121.

35. SG "Bendōwa" EB, 144.

36. Shinran, "Shinjin," in TTPR (1985), 2:213.

37. *Gakudōyōjinshū* DZZ, 2:260.

38. SG "Bendōwa" EB, 138.

39. *Gakudōyōjinshū,* DZZ, 2:260.

40. SG "Bendōwa" EB, 145.

41. SG "Bendōwa" EB, 145.

42. *Fukanzazengi* DZZ, 2:3.

43. SG "Sokushin-zebutsu," 45.

44. *Fukanzazengi* EB, 121.

45. *Fukanzazengi* EB, 121.

46. Shinran, "Shōzōmatsu Wasan," 94.

47. Shinran, "Shōzōmatsu Wasan," 94.

48. Shinran, *Tannishō: A Primer,* trans. Dennis Hirota (Kyoto: Ryukoku University Press, 1981), 24.

49. Shinran, "Mattōshō," in Shin Buddhism Translation Series, *Letters of Shinran (Mattōshō)* (Kyoto: Hongwanji International Center, 1978), 33.

50. Shinran, "Mattōshō," 33.

51. Shinran, "Gyō," in TTPR (1983), 1:142.

52. Shinran, "Goshōsokushū," in *Shinshū shōgyō zensho* (Kyoto: kōkyō shoin, 1960), 712.

53. Shinran, "Mattōshō," 23.

54. Shinran, "Gyō," 111.

55. SG "Gyōji" 2, 158. (This passage is also found "Bendōwa" and *Hōkyōki;* see chapter 4, n. 23).

56. SG "Bendōwa" EB, 144.

57. *Gakudōyōjinshū* DZZ, 2:255.

58. *Gakudōyōjinshū* DZZ, 2:255.

59. SG "Genjōkōan," 133.

60. See n. 26.

61. *Fukanzazengi* DZZ, 2:3.

62. *Gakudōyōjinshū* DZZ, 2:260.

63. Shinran, "Kōsō Wasan," 107.

64. Shinran, *Yuishinshō mon'i,* in Shin Buddhism Translation Series, *Notes on "Essentials of Faith Alone"* (Kyoto: Hongwanji International Center, 1979), 33.

65. Shinran, "Shō," in TTPR (1987), 3:364.

66. Shinran, *Tannishō: A Shin Buddhist Classic,* 8.

67. Nishida Kitarō, *Nishida Kitarō zenshū* (Tokyo: Iwanami shoten, 1965), 2:396. See also *Last Writings,* trans. David Dilworth (Honolulu: University of Hawaii Press, 1987), 78.

68. Nishida, *Nishida Kitarō zenshū,* 409. See *Last Writings,* 68.

69. Nishida, *Nishida Kitarō zenshū,* 396.

70. The evil deeds: killing, stealing, adultery, lying, immoral language, slandering, equivocating, coveting, anger, and false views. The five cardinal sins: killing one's father, killing one's mother, killing a saint, injuring the body of a buddha, and causing disunity in a community of monks.

71. Shinran, *Tannishō: A Primer,* 23.

72. Shinran, "Keshindo," in TTPR (1990), 4:536.

73. T'an-luan (476–542) was a Chinese Buddhist who organized the Pure Land school of Buddhism in China. San-lun is the "Three Treatise school," a classical school of Buddhism in China that is based on the Indian Madhyamika school of Buddhism.

74. Shinran, *Yuishinshō mon'i,* 35.

75. Shinran, *Yuishinshō mon'i,* 34–35.

76. Shinran, "Shinjin," in TTPR, 2:205.

77. Shinran, "Kōsō Wasan," 107.

78. Shinran, "Shōzōmatsu Wasan," 16.

79. Shinran, *Tannishō: A Primer,* 24.

80. Shinran, "Shōzōmatsu Wasan," 94.

81. SG "Gyōji" 1, 122.

82. The Senika heresy, or non-Buddhist thought that appeared during the Buddha's lifetime, emphasizing the concept of a permanent self. It appears in the *Nirvāna Sūtra,* chap. 39. For Dōgen's critique, see SG "Bendōwa" EB, 146–47.

83. SG "Bendōwa" EB, 129.

84. SG "Bendōwa" EB, 129.

85. SG "Bendōwa" EB, 129.

86. SG "Gyōji" 1, 122.

87. SG "Gyōji" 1, 122.

88. Shinran, "Shinbutsudo," in TTPR, 3:439.

89. SG "Gyōbutsuigi," 47.

90. *Fukanzazengi* EB, 121.

91. Mara (a Sanskrit term) is a murderous demon who takes the lives or hinders the efforts of good people. However, in the text of Lin-chi, the notion of Mara is taken in contrast to the notion of Buddha as a problem of religious realization, that is, as the principle of anti-Buddha.

92. The "King of Geese" seems to be a metaphor for the person who can discern the real from the temporal, the true from the false, etc. In *The Record of Lin-chi,* trans. Ruth F. Sasaki (Kyoto: First Zen Institute, 1975), 73.

93. *The Record of Lin-chi,* 73.

94. *Hidō* indicates that which is contrary to the Buddha Way. Chapter 8, on "The Buddha Path," begins as follows: "Manjusri asked Vimalakirti: 'How does a Bodhisattva enter the Buddha path?' Vimalakirti replied: 'If a Bodhisattva treads the wrong ways (without discrimination) he enters the Buddha Path.'" In *The Vimalakirti Nirdesa Sūtra,* trans. and ed. Charles Luk (Berkeley: Shambala, 1972), 81. The above exchange is followed by the following passages:

"Vimalakirti replied: '(In his work of salvation) if a Bodhisattva is free from imitation and anger while appearing in the fivefold uninterrupted hell; is free from the stain of sins while appearing in (other) hells...appears as if entering nirvāna but without cutting off birth and death; Manjusri, this Bodhisattva can tread heterodox ways because he has access to the Buddha path.'" *The Vimalakirti Nirdesa Sūtra,* 81–83.

95. See Masao Abe, "Kyogi to akuma" ("Falsehood and Devil"), in *Risō* (December 1962), 20–33; and "Hibutsu hima" ("Non-Buddha, Non-Devil"), in *Bukkyō no hikaku shisōronteki kenkyū* (A Study of Buddhism in Comparative Philosophy) (April 1979), 635–710.

Glossary of Sino-Japanese Terms

佛性   *Busshō*—Buddha-nature. (Skt. *buddhatā.*)

朕兆未萌の自己   *Chinchōmibō no jiko*—The Self prior to the universe's sprouting any sign of itself.

脱   *Datsu*—Self-extrication.

脱落身心   *Datsuraku-shinjin*—Body-mind that has been cast off.

同時成道   *Dōji-jōdō*—Simultaneous attainment of the Way.

道得   *Dōtoku*—Expressing the Way.

不傳の傳   *Fuden no den*—Transmission of nontransmission.

不昧因果   *Fumai-inga*—Not obscuring causation.

不落因果   *Furaku-inga*—Not-falling into causation.

不思量   *Fushiryō*—Not-thinking.

不生   *Fushō*—The unborn.

不生不滅   *Fushō-fumetsu*—Unborn and undying; non-production and nonextinction.

願力自然   *Ganriki-jinen*—Naturalness through the power of the vow (in Shinran's thought).

現成 *Genjō*—Presencing (or spontaneous manifestation).

現成公案 *Genjōkōan*—Manifestation of ultimate reality.

現前 *Genzen*—Manifestation.

業道自然 *Gōdo-jinen*—Karmic naturalness.

吾我 *Goga*—Ego-self.

究尽 *Gūjin*—Penetrating exhaustively.

逆対応的 *Gyakutaiōteki*—Inverse correspondence (to the Dharma).

行持 *Gyōji*—Continuous practice.

行持道環 *Gyōji-dōkan*—Unceasing circulation of continuous practice.

徧界不曾蔵 *Henkai-fusōzō*—Nothing concealed in the entire universe.

非道 *Hidō*—Wrong ways.

非思量 *Hishiryō*—Nonthinking.

非思量底の思量 *Hishiryōtei no shiryō*—Thinking of nonthinking.

一時の位 *Hitotoki no kurai*—A situation of (timeless-) time.

法 *Hō*—Dharma.

法位に住す *Hōi ni jūsu*—To dwell in a dharma-stage (or -situation). (See *jū-hōi*.)

本覚 *Hongaku*—Original awakening.

本来の人間 *Honrai no ningen*—Original Person.

法身 *Hosshin*—Dharma-body.

法性   *Hōsshō*—Dharma-nature.

怎麼   *Immo*—Thus.

自受用三昧   *Jijuyū zammai*—Self-fulfilling samadhi.

直指の本證   *Jikishi no honshō*—Direct pointing to original enlightenment.

自然   *Jinen*—Primordial naturalness.

自然成   *Jinenjō*—Natural becoming.

自然の理   *Jinen no kotowari*—Principle of naturalness (in Shinran).

尽十方界   *Jinjippōkai*—The whole universe throughout the ten directions.

尽十方界真実人体   *Jinjippōkai shinjitsunintai*—True Person revealed in and through the whole universe throughout the ten directions.

尽界を以て尽界主界尽する   *Jinkai o motte jinkai o kaijin suru*—Entirely worlding the entire world with the whole world.

時節既至   *Jisetsu kishi*—The time already arrived.

時節若至   *Jisetsu nyakushi*—If the time arrives (interpreted as the time and occasion thus come).

住法位   *Jū-hōi*—Dwelling in a dharma-stage (or -situation).

経過   *Keika*—Passing away.

建撕記   *Kenzeiki*—*The Record of Kenzei* (traditional biography of Dōgen).

起滅   *Kimetsu*—Appearance-disappearance.

帰命   *Kimyō*—Taking refuge (in Shinran).

光明   *Kōmyō*—Light; illumination.

経歴   *Kyōryaku*—Passageless-passage.

末法   *Mappō*—Last (or degenerate) Law.

無碍   *Muge*—Without hindrance.

無為自然   *Mui-jinen*—Effortless naturalness.

無時   *Muji*—Nothingness-time.

無佛性   *Mubusshō*—No-Buddha-nature.

無常佛性   *Mujō-busshō*—Impermanence-Buddha-nature.

無心   *Mushin*—No-mind.

妙修   *Myōshū*—Wondrous practice.

成る 生成する   *Naru-seiseisuru*—Turns into or becomes.

涅槃   *Nehan*—Nirvāna.

念   *Nen*—Thought.(Skt. *smriti*.)

而今   *Nikon*—Immediate now.

如来   *Nyorai*—Tathāgata.

往生   *Ōjō*—Rebirth in the Pure Land (in Shinran).

悟り   *Satori*—Enlightenment or awakening.

生成   *Seisei*—Becoming.

正当応的   *Seitaiōteki*—True correspondence (to the Dharma).

先尼外道   *Sennigedō*—Senika heresy.

始覚   *Shikaku*—Acquired awakening .

祇管打坐   *Shikantaza*—Just sitting .

信心   *Shinjin*—Faith (in Shinran).

身心脱落   *Shinjin-datsuraku*—Casting off of body-mind.

真実人体   *Shinjitsunintai*—The body of the true Person.

真人   *Shinnin*—True Person.

思量   *Shiryō*—Thinking.

死すべきもの   *Shi subeki mono*—Something that must die.

悉有   *Shitsuu*—Whole-being.

悉有佛性   *Shitsuu-busshō*—Whole-being Buddha-nature.

生死   *Shōji*—Life-and-death (or birth-and-death).

生死去来   *Shōjikorai*—Coming and going of birth-and-death.

生死の罪   *Shōji no tsumi*—The sins of birth-and-death.

生死する者   *Shōji suru mono*—Something that undergoes birth-and-death.

正定聚   *Shōjōjū*—Truly settled ones (in Shinran).

證上の修   *Shōjō no shu*—Practice in realization.

生滅性   *Shōmetsusei*—Generation-extinction nature. (Skt. *utpādanirodha*.)

生滅するもの   *Shōmetsu suru mono*—Something that undergoes generation-extinction.

衆生   *Shujō*—Living beings in samsara.

修証一等   *Shushō-ittō*—Oneness of practice and attainment.

即心是佛   *Sokushin-zebutsu*—This very mind itself is buddha.

即得往生   *Sokutokuōjō*—Immediate attainment of rebirth (in Shinran).

轉   *Ten*—Transformation.

度脱   *Tōdatsu*—Emancipation.

當観   *Tōkan*—Just seeing.

等正覺   *Tōshōkaku*—Equal of perfect enlightenment (in Shinran).

有為自然   *Ui-jinen*—Conditioned naturalness.

有時   *Uji*—Being-time.

有無   *Umu*—Being and nonbeing.

有無的限定   *Umuteki gentei*—Limitations of being and nothingness.

移る 生成する   *Utsuru-seiseisuru*—Moves, changes, or generates.

罪悪生死   *Zaiaku shōji*—Sinful birth-and-death.

罪業   *Zaigō*—Sinful karma.

坐禅   *Zazen*—Sitting meditation.

前後際断   *Zengo saidan*—Beyond before and after.

全機   *Zenki*—Total dynamic functioning.

全機現   *Zenkigen*—Manifestation of total dynamism.

絶対無   *Zettai mu*—Absolute nothingness.

Index